When E. M. Forster described Lawrence as the greatest imaginative novelist of his generation, his comment was a challenge to a world where ̶L̶a̶w̶r̶e̶n̶c̶e̶ had nurtured but there was no ag̶̶̶̶̶̶̶̶̶̶̶ standing. Now, ̶ Lawrence's dea̶̶̶̶̶ achievement is s̶̶̶ Although Lawre̶̶̶̶

English writer, h̶̶̶ ̶w̶i̶d̶e̶-ranging vision has aroused passionate interest in many countries beyond his own. It is in these two senses – as a writer in the twentieth century, and as one with international standing – that this book presents Lawrence 'in the modern world'.

He is seen from the viewpoint of the textual editor, the psychologist and the social historian. He is placed in the wide contexts of the puritan imagination, British society drama and the regional novel; there are studies of such stylistic issues as his characteristic narrative voices; and philo-sophical matters are touched on in an exploration of his concept of dualism.

The essays, although the work of Lawrence enthusiasts, are not uniformly reverential in tone. There is a keen appreciation of those areas of Lawrence's work which have always made disturbing reading. All the authors are alive to the fundamentally exploratory nature of Lawrence's imagination, and his consequent failures as well as triumphs in both conception and achievement. Overall, however, the essays bear witness to the continuing power of a writer whose works, whether they delight or anger, seem now as alive and pertinent, as open to engagement, acceptance or disagreement as at any time in the seventy-five years since they first began to appear.

English, University of Kent at Canterbury
Tom Paulin – Lecturer in English, University of Nottingham
Bridget Pugh – Tutor in Literature, Extra-Mural Department, University of Birmingham
Claude Sinzelle – Lecturer in English Language and Literature, Dijon University
John Worthen – Senior Lecturer in English, University College, Swansea

D. H. LAWRENCE IN THE MODERN WORLD

D. H. Lawrence in the Modern World

Edited by

PETER PRESTON

Staff Tutor in Literature
Department of Adult Education
University of Nottingham

and

PETER HOARE

University Librarian
University of Nottingham

Cambridge University Press
Cambridge

New York   New Rochelle   Melbourne   Sydney

First published in 1989

Published in North America by the Press Syndicate of the
UNIVERSITY OF CAMBRIDGE
32 East 57th Street, New York, New York 10022

Typeset by Wessex Typesetters
(Division of The Eastern Press Ltd)
Frome, Somerset

Printed and bound in Great Britain

Library of Congress Cataloging-in-Publication Data
D. H. Lawrence in the modern world.
Includes index.
1. Lawrence, D. H. (David Herbert), 1885–1930—
Criticism and interpretation—Congresses. I. Preston,
Peter, 1944–   . II. Hoare, Peter.
PR6023.A93Z623389   1988   823'.912   88–28544
ISBN 0–521–37169–4

Contents

Preface

The essays gathered in this book were first presented as papers to the Lawrence Symposium, held at the University of Nottingham in September 1985. This Symposium, 'D. H. Lawrence in the Modern World', was among the numerous events organised in Nottingham and elsewhere to mark the centenary of Lawrence's birth. From a very early stage in its deliberations, the Lawrence Centenary Festival Committee believed that these events would be incomplete without a major academic contribution from the University at which, in its earlier form as University College, Nottingham, Lawrence had been a student. A summer school for adult students, a Library exhibition and a special issue of *Renaissance and Modern Studies*, the University's humanities review, were already planned; but it was felt that there should also be an event of a more scholarly nature, celebrating Lawrence's connection with the University and at the same time acknowledging his stature as a writer with a reputation extending far beyond the county of his birth and education.

It was with these considerations in mind that, in 1983, the Festival Committee asked its four University representatives[1] to begin plans for a Symposium which, while not part of the official Festival programme, would take place at the same time as the Festival and offer scholars from all over the world an opportunity to celebrate the centenary. But the way forward proved not to be smooth: initial moves met with difficulties, and it was not until September 1984 that we felt confident enough to think of ourselves as a Symposium planning committee. We had barely twelve months in which to organise a major scholarly conference.

Our primary aims in planning the event are implicit in the title of the Symposium and of this book. When E. M. Forster described Lawrence as the greatest imaginative novelist of his generation, his comment was a challenge to a world where Lawrence had notoriety but there was no agreement as to his literary standing. Although the innovative character of his best work was always generally recognised, its disturbing implications – frequently misunderstood – aroused controversy, condemnation and censorship. Now, nearly sixty years after Lawrence's death, the nature of his achievement is still being debated, and his work has been the subject of a wide variety of critical interpretation, but he is inescapably established as part of the modern literary canon. Furthermore, although Lawrence thought of himself as an English writer, whose 'Englishness is my very vision' (writing to Lady Cynthia Asquith, 21 October 1915), his exploration of the complexities of human relationships, his fresh and open response to the natural world and to new places, his concern with both spiritual and physical experience, and his critiques of modern industrial society have aroused passionate interest in many countries beyond his own. It was in these two senses – as a writer in the twentieth century, and as one with international standing – that we wished to present Lawrence 'in the modern world'.

The extent to which we achieved these aims must, ultimately, be judged by those who attended the Symposium and who read this book. In statistical and geographical terms, though, we seem to have attained some kind of internationalism. Speakers came not only from this country but also from France, Israel, Italy, Korea and the USA. Over half of the seventy or more participants were drawn from an even wider area, including groups or individuals from Australia, Canada, Denmark, Finland, France, India, Italy, Japan, Mexico, Portugal, Spain, Sweden, the USA and West Germany. Until the very last moment, when a minor diplomatic crisis appears to have prevented his arrival, we expected also to be joined by a scholar from the USSR. In terms of the approaches to Lawrence's work we also achieved some variety. He was seen from the point of view of the textual editor, the psychologist and the social historian; he was placed in the wide context of modern literature as well as in the more narrow contexts of the puritan imagination, British society drama and the regional novel; there were studies of such stylistic issues as his characteristic narrative voices; and philosophical matters were touched on in an exploration of his concept of dualism.

Even so, we were not able to represent *all* the possible approaches to his work, and at least one observer[2] accused us of producing a 'safe' event, which effectively insulated Lawrence from the more uncomfortable conclusions which feminist, structuralist or deconstructionist analyses might have produced. In one sense we were open to the charge of 'safeness' in that, for most of our speakers, we turned to names already well known in the field of Lawrence studies – although we were pleased also to extend invitations to some younger and less well-established scholars. The only stipulations we made had to do with the length of the papers, not their content, and we did not set out to ensure that we represented this or that school of criticism. None the less, in the papers by Barbara Hardy, Claude Sinzelle and H. M. Daleski readers will find an awareness of how Lawrence appears in the light of recent ideas in literary criticism. They will also find that the papers, although the work of Lawrence enthusiasts, are not uniformly reverential in tone. There was, during the Symposium, a keen appreciation of those areas of Lawrence's work – notably, phases in his attitudes towards women, democracy and the need for a strong leader – which make, and have always made, disturbing, even distasteful reading. And all the speakers were equally alive to the fundamentally exploratory nature of Lawrence's imagination, and his consequent failures as well as triumphs in both conception and achievement. In the end, though, we were gathered to celebrate Lawrence, and the excellence of the papers and the liveliness of the debates which followed them bore witness to the continuing power of a writer whose works, whether they delight or anger, seem now as alive and pertinent, as open to engagement, acceptance or disagreement as at any time in the seventy-five years since they first began to appear.

In his opening speech to the Symposium, reprinted as the Introduction to this volume, Professor Boulton paid fitting tribute to the contributions to Lawrence studies made by Professors V. de Sola Pinto and J. D. Chambers, both of the University of Nottingham. What he did not mention, with proper and characteristic modesty, was his own remarkable and long-standing contribution. Although Professor Boulton has for many years been known as an outstanding scholar of eighteenth-century literature, his interest in Lawrence goes back at least to 1968 when he published an edition of Lawrence's letters to Louie Burrows, which had recently been purchased by the University Library at Nottingham. This was followed by an exemplary study of an early version of 'Odour of Chrysanthemums', and an edition of *Movements in European History*, as well as some briefer scholarly notes.[3] It was no doubt these evidences of outstanding textual scholarship which led the Cambridge University Press to invite

Professor Boulton to become one of the editors of their planned edition of Lawrence's writings. Lawrence is among the first of the major twentieth-century writers to receive the benefit of thorough-going editorial scholarship, certainly the first whose letters and other works are being issued as part of a single unified edition. As John Worthen's contribution to this book makes clear, the corrupt nature of virtually all the published texts, and the tangled history of their progress from manuscript to print make such work more necessary for Lawrence than is the case with most writers. Professor Boulton's qualities of penetrating literary insight combined with the most meticulous scholarship, expressed in a language which is direct, vigorous and illuminating, were exactly fitted to the task, and are not only to be found in those volumes of the letters for which he has been wholly or partly responsible: they have left their mark on the volumes which he has overseen as General Editor. If the heart of that edition is now located in Birmingham, it is because Professor Boulton is there, and we can at least console ourselves with the fact that the work was begun in Nottingham. When the Organising Committee came to consider a Chairman for the Symposium, Professor Boulton was the obvious choice, and we were delighted when he accepted our invitation. Throughout the period of planning we benefited from his encouragement and advice, and the Symposium itself was enriched by his presence.

In the course of organising such an event and in preparing this book for publication, we have inevitably incurred many debts of gratitude, and it is a pleasure to have a public and formal opportunity to thank the many people who have helped us. First must come the speakers, now the contributors to this volume, who were generous with their time and energy, not only in producing their papers but also in taking part in prolonged and vigorous afterhours discussions.[4] Similarly, the other participants were ready and pertinent with their questions and contributions, and so friendly as to make the actual running of the Symposium a great pleasure. We always enjoyed the full support of our fellow-members on the Lawrence Centenary Festival Committee, whose belief in what we were doing was a great encouragement, particu-larly in difficult times. Within the University, we are grateful for the support of the Vice-Chancellor, Dr B. C. L. Weedon; the cooperation of the Conference Office; and the helpfulness of Deborah Grant and her staff at Rutland Hall. For administrative purposes, the Symposium was a joint enterprise of the Department of Adult Education and the University Library, and we should like to thank the staff of both: in particular, Sue Alvey and Val Munson helped a lot in the preliminary stages of planning, while Jo Dow prepared much of the material for the running of the weekend. During the Symposium itself we all appreciated the courteous willingness of our Administrative Assistants, Caroline Hoare and James Morris. Gerald Pollinger, agent to the Lawrence Estate, helped us considerably in planning both the Symposium and this volume. Finally, although the names of only two of the planning committee appear as editors of this book, we want to emphasise that both the Symposium and this record of its proceedings have been the outcome of a collaboration in which we have shared the work, the responsibility, the anxieties, the disappointments and, not least, the pleasures, involved.

P.P.
University of Nottingham

Notes

1. The representatives were: Alan Cameron, then Acting Keeper of the Manuscripts; Peter Hoare, University Librarian; Peter Preston, Staff Tutor in Literature in the Department of Adult Education; and Allan Rodway, sometime Reader in English Studies.
2. Lorna Sage in *The Times Literary Supplement*, 27 September 1985, p. 1061.
3. See J. T. Boulton: *Lawrence in Love: Letters to Louie Burrows* (Nottingham: University of Nottingham, 1968); 'D. H. Lawrence's *Odour of Chrysanthemums*: an Early Version', *Renaissance and Modern Studies*, XIII (1969) pp. 5–48; D. H. Lawrence, *Movements in European History*, ed. J. T. Boulton (London: Oxford University Press, 1971); 'Jessie Chambers's *The Bankrupt*: an Unpublished Short Story', *Renaissance and Modern Studies*, XV (1971) pp. 5–22; 'D. H. Lawrence: Study of a Free Spirit in Literature: a Note on an Uncollected Article', *Renaissance and Modern Studies*, XVIII (1974) pp. 5–16.
4. By its very nature, one event in the Symposium programme – Professor Marilyn Gibson's slide presentation of Lawrence's travels – could not be included in this book.

Acknowledgements

The editors and publishers wish to thank the Estate of Frieda Lawrence Ravagli and the Literary Executor of the Estate, Laurence Pollinger Ltd, for permission to quote the extracts from Lawrence's works.

List of Abbreviations

The following editions of Lawrence's works are referred to by brief title in the references following each chapter. All other editions are cited explicitly as they occur.

Letters, I	James T. Boulton (ed.), *The Letters of D. H. Lawrence*, vol. I (Cambridge: Cambridge University Press, 1979).
Letters, II	George J. Zytaruk and James T. Boulton (eds), *The Letters of D. H. Lawrence*, vol. II (Cambridge: Cambridge University Press, 1982).
Letters, III	James T. Boulton and Andrew Robertson (eds), *The Letters of D. H. Lawrence*, vol. III (Cambridge: Cambridge University Press, 1984).
Letters, IV	Warren Roberts, James T. Boulton and Elizabeth Mansfield (eds), *The Letters of D. H. Lawrence*, vol. IV (Cambridge: Cambridge University Press, 1987).
Moore	Harry T. Moore (ed.), *The Collected Letters of D. H. Lawrence*, 2 vols (London: Heinemann, 1962).
Complete Poems	Vivian de Sola Pinto and Warren Roberts (eds), *The Complete Poems of D. H. Lawrence*, vols I–II (Harmondsworth, Middx: Penguin, 1964).
Phoenix	Edward D. McDonald (ed.), *Phoenix: The Posthumous Papers of D. H. Lawrence* (London: Heinemann, 1936).
Phoenix II	Warren Roberts and Harry T. Moore (eds), *Phoenix II: Uncollected, Unpublished and other Prose Works by D. H. Lawrence* (London: Heinemann, 1968).

The D. H. Lawrence Review (Fayetteville, 1968–) is cited as *DHL Review*. References to other journals, and to critical or biographical works, are given in full.

Notes on the Contributors

James T. Boulton, Professor of English Studies, University of Birmingham, had edited *Lawrence in Love: Letters from D. H. Lawrence to Louie Burrows* (1968) and *Movements in European History* (1971) before becoming General Editor of the Cambridge Edition of the Letters and Works of D. H. Lawrence, in which he has so far edited or co-edited four volumes of the letters. He has also published extensively on eighteenth-century topics, including *The Language of Politics in the Age of Wilkes and Burke* (1963).

Chong-wha Chung is Professor of English Literature at Korea University in Seoul and the Director of its Anglo-American Studies Institute. In 1981 he edited a special issue of *Phoenix*, the University's arts review, devoted to D. H. Lawrence. He has published a number of essays on English literature as well as critical studies and translations of Korean fiction and poetry. He is the General Editor of Routledge and Kegan Paul's 'Korean Culture' series.

L. D. Clark is Professor of English at the University of Arizona at Tucson. His first book on Lawrence was *Dark Night of the Body* (1964), a study of *The Plumed Serpent*; *The Minoan Distance*, on the symbolism of travel in Lawrence's work, was published in 1980. He has also published novels and short stories and has recently completed the Cambridge Edition of *The Plumed Serpent*.

Ian Clarke lectures in English and Drama at Loughborough University. He has written on nineteenth- and twentieth-century theatre and drama and is currently writing a book on late Victorian and Edwardian drama.

H. M. Daleski, Professor of English at the Hebrew University of Jerusalem, is the author of *The Forked Flame: A Study of D. H. Lawrence* (1965; new edn 1987) and of books on Dickens (1970) and Conrad (1977). His most recent books are *The Divided Heroine* (1984) and *Unities: Studies in the English Novel* (1985).

Simonetta de Filippis is Associate Professor at the Istituto Universitario Orientale, Naples. Her previous publications include essays on English literature and literary journalism. She is at present working on the Cambridge Edition of *Etruscan Places*.

Barbara Hardy is Professor of English at Birkbeck College, University of London. Her books on fiction include *The Appropriate Form* (1964), *Tellers and Listeners: The Narrative Imagination* (1975), *Forms of Feeling in Victorian Fiction* (1985), and *Narrators and Novelists: Collected Essays*, vol. I (1987).

Peter Hoare is University Librarian at Nottingham, where his responsibilities include the major institutional collection of Lawrence manuscripts and books in Britain. He has published widely on the history of libraries, and has lectured on Nottingham's Lawrence collections at the Universities of Texas and Richmond, Virginia.

Mark Kinkead-Weekes is Professor of English at the University of Kent at Canterbury. His *Samuel Richardson: Dramatic Novelist* appeared in 1973 and *William Golding: A Critical Study* (with Ian Gregor), first published in 1967, was issued in an extended edition in 1984. He has edited *The Rainbow* for the Cambridge Edition, and heads a team of three working on a new biography of Lawrence, of which his will be the second volume.

Tom Paulin is Lecturer in English at the University of Nottingham. His study of Hardy's poetry, *Thomas Hardy: The Poetry of Perception*, was first published in 1975 and reissued as a paperback in 1986. A collection of essays, *Ireland and the English Crisis*, was also published in 1986. He is also well known as a poet and his volumes include *A State of Justice* (1977), *Liberty Tree* (1983) and *Fivemiletown* (1987).

Peter Preston is Staff Tutor in Literature, Department of Adult Education, University of Nottingham, and as well as helping to organise the Lawrence Symposium he was Director of Summer Schools on Lawrence in 1980 and 1985. Formerly editor of the *Newsletter* of the Lawrence Society, he has published essays and reviews on Lawrence, Bennett and Dickens as well as on the history and practice of adult education. From 1988 he will be Editor of *The D. H. Lawrence Society Journal*.

Bridget Pugh's local guide to D. H. Lawrence, *The Country of My Heart* (1972), was issued in a second edition in 1984. She contributed a Lawrence gazetteer to *A D. H. Lawrence Handbook* (edited by Keith Sagar, 1975) and a paper on Lawrence and industrial symbolism to the special centenary edition of *Renaissance and Modern Studies* (1985), and is now working on a full-length study of Midland novelists. She is a tutor in Literature for the Extra-Mural Department of Birmingham University.

Claude Sinzelle lectures on English language and literature at Dijon University. He published *The Geographical Background of the Early Works of D. H. Lawrence* in 1964 and is at present working on a study of D. H. Lawrence's imagination.

John Worthen is Senior Lecturer in English at University College, Swansea. His *D. H. Lawrence and the Idea of the Novel* was published in 1979. He is on the Editorial Board of the Cambridge Edition of Lawrence's works and has edited *The Lost Girl*, *The Prussian Officer*, *Love Among the Haystacks* and *Women in Love* (with Lindeth Vasey and David Farmer). He is at work on the first volume of a new three-volume biography of Lawrence.

1

Introduction

JAMES T. BOULTON

It would perhaps be generally regarded as inevitable that a symposium to mark the centenary of D. H. Lawrence's birth should be held in Nottingham. But why should it be thought inevitable? And why in a university? Is the explanation any more than the satisfaction of local pride? After all, though Lawrence attended University College, Nottingham, for two years, the bitterness and resentment harboured in the institution of which Ernest Weekley was a prominent member undoubtedly damaged his local reputation. Is there, in any case, any logical necessity why a university should devote a considerable proportion of its library and academic resources to the promotion of interest and research into the writings of a local writer when he is also of national importance? Nottingham's own answer is clear.

Part of the obvious explanation for it is the indelible link that exists between Lawrence's works and specific localities. A glance at the analysis by Bridget Pugh ('Locations in Lawrence's Fiction and Travel Writings')[1] is enough to show that by far the majority of Lawrence's English (as opposed to 'Australian', 'Mexican' etc.) novels, short stories and plays are located in, and draw directly on intimate knowledge of, the East Midlands. What he described as 'the country of my heart' is used with such personal and emotional intensity and with such care for accurate detail that certain kinds of enquiry were almost inevitably best carried on in the local University. But this explanation is insufficient. It was the presence in the University, at a critical time, of two senior academics that was principally responsible for the quickening of interest in Lawrence.

One was a product of the very same locality as Lawrence himself: Jonathan David Chambers, brother of Jessie, Lawrence's 'Miriam'. He was a distinguished scholar in his own right (eventually Professor of Economic History) – but he was also a discriminating enthusiast for Lawrence. He not only remembered Lawrence

1

personally, vividly described the young man's visits to the Haggs Farm and spoke sympathetically about Lawrence's father and rather less sympathetically about his mother;[2] Chambers was also able authoritatively to relate Lawrence's writings to the development of the region both agriculturally and industrially. Moreover he encouraged and directed the research of others (notably A. R. and C. P. Griffin)[3] which proved significant in the same regard.

Second and, from a Lawrentian viewpoint, the more important, was Vivian de Sola Pinto, Professor of English from 1938. Pinto was an inspiring teacher, a man with an extraordinary range of literary knowledge and an infectious enthusiasm for literature. Furthermore he believed that a university has a special responsibility to explore and interpret the work of a great artist who is associated with the locality. This he declared unambiguously in his well-known public lecture delivered in 1951 (and chaired by Lawrence's old friend, William Hopkin), 'D. H. Lawrence: Prophet of the Midlands'.

Pinto gave a lead in discharging that special responsibility through his own publications, through teaching and the supervision of research. He was the founding editor of the University's learned journal, *Renaissance and Modern Studies*, and it is noticeable that the opening article in the first volume (1957) is Pinto's 'D. H. Lawrence, Letter-Writer and Craftsman in Verse' (illustrated by a facsimile of an early draft of the poem 'Piano'). The journal was established to publish essays by members of the University, but as early as volume IV (1960) Pinto made an exception: to accommodate an article by Helen Corke, 'D. H. Lawrence as I Saw Him'. His own subsequent publications included an essay, 'Poet without a Mask' (*Critical Quarterly*, 1961) attacking R. P. Blackmur's 'Lawrence and Expressive Form' which Pinto compared with Johnson on Milton as 'one of those important wrongheaded pieces of criticism that contain valuable elements of truth'. Pinto's essay was reprinted as the introduction to his major contribution to Lawrence scholarship, the edition of the *Complete Poems* (1964) on which he collaborated with Warren Roberts.

In the public lecture already mentioned, Pinto declared it a matter of public pride that Lawrence was a prescribed author in the Nottingham English School in 1951–2. It was, indeed, by no means universal in British universities at that time to find Lawrence the object of study as serious and sustained as was devoted, say, o Wordsworth or Dickens. Undergraduates (if they chose) wrote dissertations on him; at a more advanced level Pinto directed research on his writings by, among others, Gāmini Salgādo, R. P. Draper and George Panichas.

That Pinto's enthusiasm for Lawrence was reinforced by his friendship with F. R. Leavis is not open to doubt: in virtually every one of his publications dealing with Lawrence, Leavis is overtly or tacitly present.[4] But he rarely if ever indulged the Leavisite idiom about 'the wisdom, the revived and re-educated feeling for health that Lawrence brings'. Pinto's inclination was to view Lawrence as a product of the local dissenting tradition (more recently explored by Donald Davie), to place him in the English prophetic tradition which included Milton and Blake, or – as he does in *Crisis in Modern Poetry* (1951) – to see him as an explorer of the outer and inner worlds, a context derived from C. F. G. Masterman's *Condition of England*.

A further responsibility Pinto laid on his University (in his public lecture) was to build up a Lawrence collection in the Library. In 1951 the collection was small, but it had begun to exist. Lawrence's sister Emily and his wife Frieda Ravagli (as she had become) were both approached and both contributed to it, as did others. But Pinto's main contribution to the establishment of the University as a research centre lay in the exhibition he and others organised just before his own retirement in 1961: 'D. H. Lawrence after Thirty Years, 1930–1960'. It still ranks as one of the most significant exhibitions of Lawrence material; the catalogue includes the first printing of extracts from many hitherto unpublished letters; and of course it served to focus attention on the University and to stimulate further growth in the Library's Lawrence collection. Under successive Librarians (notably R. S. Smith and P. A. Hoare) and Keepers of Manuscripts (especially J. H. Hodson and Mary Welch), the University has bought or acquired by gift an ever-increasing quantity of books and manuscripts.[5] With the promised addition of the largest private collection in the world – the Lawrence library of Mr George Lazarus[6] – it will become not only one of the most substantial but also one of the most distinguished collections in existence. Then Pinto's hope that the University Library would house 'the great D. H. Lawrence collection in this country' will have been realised indeed.

Mention should be made at this point of a former City Librarian, David Gerard. It was opportune that some of Pinto's years in the

University coincided with Gerard's at the City Library; they gav
advice to each other; but Gerard in his own right was responsibl
for building up the City's distinctive holding. In certain respects
the combined collections of the County, City and Universit
Libraries are now unrivalled.[7]

It is appropriate also to recall two notable exhibitions at th
City's Castle Museum. The first, in 1972, entitled 'Young Bert'
was described by *The Times* (8 August 1972) as 'a fascinating
beautifully presented exhibition' which 'deserves a wider public
however the translation to Whitechapel which the *Times* correspon
dent envisaged did not take place. And the second, to coincid
with the centenary, brought together, in a very instructive way
works of art which Lawrence copied or wrote about, as well as hi
own paintings, in order to suggest certain stages in the developmen
of what he himself called his 'visionary awareness'.

Nottingham's peculiar role as an important centre for Lawrentia
research is, therefore, relatively simple to define and explain. Wha
remains is to underline the major contribution of universitie
(principally, for obvious reasons, British and American) to establish
ing Lawrence's claims to be regarded as one of the foremost literar
artists of our century. Thomas Rice's volume, *D. H. Lawrence: A
Guide to Research* (1983), with its listing of 2123 items is one kind c
proof of the assertion: that the home of this critical–scholarl
enterprise is pre-eminently the University. In a serious sense thi
ought to be true – it is partly why universities exist – but it cannc
obscure the fact that Lawrence has another reputation which i
independent of and often runs counter to the enterprise charte
by Thomas Rice. There are, indeed, two traditions of response t
and responsibility for Lawrence (to an extent quite unmatched i
the case of, say, Conrad or Eliot or even Joyce): the popular an
the learned.

The terms and their signification are borrowed from an importan
essay on Samuel Johnson by Bertrand Bronson. Bronson draw
attention to the two different approaches to Johnson – to th
personality on the one hand, and to the author on the other
equating them with the popular and learned respectively. It is nc
an exact distinction; it has nothing necessarily to do with levels c
educational achievement – in the case of Lawrence, Witter Bynner'
Journey with Genius, much of Middleton Murry's *Son of Woman*
even of David Chambers's memoir, are in the popular traditior
but it is a distinction which is important.

Bronson rightly points out that a great writer is defined not only by his writings but also by what posterity cumulatively makes of him:

> What he has meant to the generations between his own and ours is an essential part of what he comes to mean to us. After his death there springs up an eidolon of an author, and it is of this everchanging surrogate, not of the original, that we inevitably form our judgments, and that by so judging we further change.[8]

To this 'surrogate' both the popular and learned traditions contribute.

The contributions of the former are well known and readily identifiable. Popular image-making of Lawrence began before his death and continued after it. As early as 1915 James Douglas wrote of Lawrence's 'eloquent lubricity' and Clement Shorter of his decadent tendencies'; the notorious obituaries in 1930 perpetuated the theme with references to Lawrence's being 'enamoured of the abnormal' (*Glasgow Herald*), 'obsessed by sexual fever and frustration . . . his writing full of the cruelty of a personal hell in which was no pity or understanding' (*Manchester Guardian*); and the tradition is alive and well in 1985. Some features of it showed through in newspaper reviews of the Cambridge Edition of *Mr Noon*; it has been reinvigorated by the centenary celebrations. Recently, for example, a 'quality' newspaper printed statements by a named individual reporting Lawrence's attitudes to Eastwood:

> Lawrence hated the bloody place. When he left with Frieda he literally dusted his boots on the tram. He was an intellectual snob, not a likeable person. He wouldn't take a job in the colliery company.
>
> Jessie Chambers didn't know what he was on about. She didn't mind so much being Miriam; it was the family that minded because he was considered odd.[9]

This remarkable amalgam of half-truths, untruths and fiction helps to confirm, perpetuate or create an image which will stimulate answering responses in the future. The integrity of the individual is not in question; he believed in the accuracy of his account; but it illustrates a species of folk-memory which is disconcertingly stronger than the truth of documentary record. It represents, of

course, only one facet of the same tradition which in large measure
provided the source for the *Composite Biography* by Edward Nehls,
a work without which the scholarly efforts of biographers, editors
and critics would be greatly impoverished.

The two traditions are intimately related. Both have their defects,
both are important. The learned tradition, for reasons too obvious
to specify, is principally associated with universities, but not
exclusively so. An essay written for a Cooperative Society journal
in 1928, by 'a bank-clerk with literary aspirations', made as
significant a contribution to that tradition as many a 'scholarly'
article. William Roberts' essay, a 'Study of a Free Spirit in Literature', relies on evidence which can be seen and deductions from
which can be tested.[10] This is one of the main strengths of the
tradition: its commitment to critical investigations grounded in
objective, verifiable data which, in Lawrence's case, are mainly the
words (established as decisively as scholarship allows) he used to
address his readers. This is the tradition that the papers which
follow both illustrate and enhance.

Notes

1. In Keith Sagar (ed.), *A D. H. Lawrence Handbook* (Manchester: Manchester University Press, 1982) pp. 239–64.
2. 'Memories of D. H. Lawrence' by J. D. Chambers was published in
   Renaissance and Modern Studies, XVI (1972) pp. 5–17.
3. See, for example, their 'Social and Economic History of Eastwood and
   the Nottinghamshire Mining Country', in Sagar, *Lawrence Handbook*,
   pp. 127–63.
4. Leavis delivered a public lecture in the University's Great Hall in 1956;
   his subject was 'The Genius of D. H. Lawrence'. It was not the only
   occasion when he lectured in Nottingham on some aspect of the same
   subject.
5. See University of Nottingham, *D. H. Lawrence Collection: Catalogue*, ed.
   M. A. Welch, vol. I: 1979, vol. II: 1983.
6. For an account of the Lazarus collection see *Renaissance and Modern
   Studies*, XXIX (1985) pp. 101–19.
7. See an early *Finding List*, ed. Lucy Edwards (Nottingham: Nottinghamshire County Council, 1968), which recorded their joint holdings.
8. Bertrand Bronson, 'The Double Tradition of Dr. Johnson', *English
   Literary History*, June 1951, p. 90.
9. *Sunday Telegraph*, 28 July 1985.
10. The essay is reprinted in *Renaissance and Modern Studies*, XVIII (1974)
    pp. 5–16.

2

The Restoration of
Women in Love

JOHN WORTHEN

'The Restoration of *Women in Love*': my title consciously refers to
the process of restoring an old or damaged painting – the layers
of varnish to be removed, that had turned brown almost every
colour in (for example) Uccello's *Battle of San Romano* in the
National Gallery in London. Beautiful, but brown: a fine network.
'Restoration' means the removal of that varnish; and also of any
over-painting, where a later hand touched up what appeared to
be faulty: it means the recovery of the colour and the detail of
what the painter painted. It also means, perhaps, the shock of the
new: the startling blues and pinks of the Uccello, even crude-
seeming to the eye accustomed to those fine shades of brown.
'Restoration' can even bring a sense of loss, as familiar obscurities
and mysterious shadows are turned to clean, well-lighted spaces.
A sense of loss, I hope quickly replaced with a sense of exhilaration:
this, now, is the painting itself. From being effectively obscured
within its obscurities, it is liberated to act directly upon our
imaginations.

And so, with editing. And so, with *Women in Love*, above all
other of Lawrence's novels; where years of rewriting and revision
led to thousands of instances of error in the process of transmission.
Three different typescripts, at different times, transmitted the text
of the novel – and one of those typescripts the author himself
never even saw. *Women in Love*: where his own revision was so
extensive, and often so minute, that the resulting text was frequently easy to misread; where his own wife's assistance turned
out not to be quite what one would have hoped for; where errors
in transmission would, over and over again, provoke Lawrence to
repair his damaged text, or seek to do so, as best he could; where
the American and English first editions both suffered from the hand
of the publisher-as-censor, but the English edition in particular was

subject to interference immediately after authorial proof revision, and again – extensively – between the first and second impressions; and even, it turns out, after that, when still further damage was done.[1] 'Restoration' is perhaps too easy a word, too suggestive that the real picture, the real novel, *is* there, waiting to be rediscovered. There are times when there is no such thing as *the* text of *Women in Love*: the novel's speech is distorted, or interrupted, or even plural.

Three decades of scholars have been looking at the textual history of *Women in Love*, and I must say not a word more before acknowledging the work of the pioneers. Back in 1957, Herbert Davis wrote an article pointing out the considerable differences between a typescript of the novel at the University of Toronto, and the published text; he assumed, as was natural, that the alterations must all have been made by Lawrence in proof.[2] In 1964, Eldon Branda wrote about textual changes in the printed editions, and suggested how they might have come about.[3] In 1968, we enter modern times, with Mark Kinkead-Weekes's account of the writing of the 'Sisters' project, which included a discussion of the writing of *Women in Love* in 1916.[4]

But it was the work of David Farmer and Charles Ross which began to transform the picture, began to suggest how it might be cleaned: Ross's work of the early and middle seventies culminating in his book on the composition of *The Rainbow* and *Women in Love*,[5] and in his edition of the latter novel for Penguin,[6] and David Farmer's work coming to a head in the work he did, single-handedly, on the edition of *Women in Love* he began preparing for Cambridge University Press.[7] Since then, Pierre Vitoux has published on the problems of the text,[8] and Lindeth Vasey has been involved in continuing work on David Farmer's edition – an edition of which I am myself, now, the third joint editor.[9] We all of us owe a great debt to the work of Ross and Farmer, and above all to the recent minute work on the manuscript, typescripts and printed editions done by Lindeth Vasey; but I shall not go over in detail ground already covered in print. Instead, I shall suggest that the transmission of that text can now be understood, in almost all its details; and that the Cambridge Edition of the novel presents an authentic text of the novel, together with a full account of its composition history.

Let me briefly outline the problems that confront an editor of the novel. There are a considerable number of surviving artefacts of composition; there are also a number which do not survive; and in both cases there is a problem in establishing exactly what relation these have to each other. So, for example, Ross was able in 1974 to identify the relation between the ten surviving pencil notebooks,[10] a corrected typescript at Texas,[11] its duplicate at Toronto,[12] and the revised typescript also at Texas;[13] and Farmer was able to describe the relationship between the various states of the first English edition.[14] But neither Ross nor Farmer was able to show how that final typescript (which we call TSII) came to reach print, either in England or in America; they could not identify the setting copy, or explain the alterations in the printed texts. Again, both referred to a surviving proof copy of the English edition, now at Texas,[15] but – as its revisions are not identical with those made in the English first edition as published – what relation did that proof copy bear to Lawrence's own corrections? Again, when it came to the detail of the transmission of revisions between the two typescripts, the one at Texas and the duplicate at Toronto (hereafter, TS1a and TS1b), Ross was not able to show what an editor should do; similarly with the revisions in that later typescript, TSII.[16]

The work Lindeth Vasey and I have done can now answer these questions. The history of the composition and revision of the novel, as we understand it, is recorded in Figure 1 and Figure 2. Lawrence wrote the first version of the novel in 1913: we call it (as he did) 'The Sisters'.[17] After many false starts, he began the second version – we call it 'The Sisters II' – in the autumn of 1913, only to abandon it, around page 380, in January 1914. But the third version – which he called 'The Wedding Ring', and wrote between February and May 1914 – ran its full length, was typed, and accepted by the publisher Methuen; and but for the outbreak of war in August 1914 would (perhaps with some cuts) have been printed. Lawrence wrote it all over again between December 1914 and March 1915, to create the 811-page manuscript and typescript of *The Rainbow*, but this time leaving out the second half of the original material; and this material he re-wrote yet again in the period April–June 1916, first to create a 55-page fragment, and then to create what we call 'The Sisters IV', an 863-page manuscript, the last part of which survives in the form of four heavily revised and repaginated notebooks at Texas.

Lawrence then began to type the novel himself; a typed version, for him, meaning one now ready for a publisher. But how much he managed to type in July 1916 is one of the few things that

Figure 1   The composition of 'Women in Love'

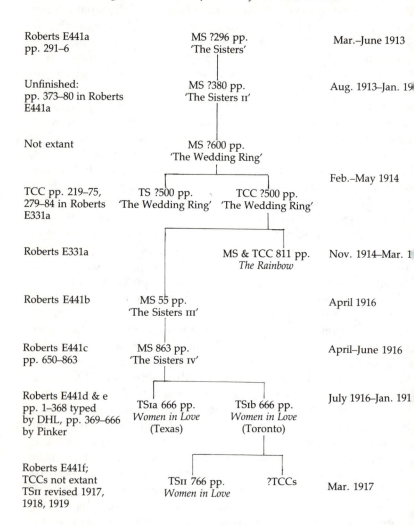

Roberts E441a pp. 291–6		MS ?296 pp. 'The Sisters'	Mar.–June 1913
Unfinished: pp. 373–80 in Roberts E441a		MS ?380 pp. 'The Sisters II'	Aug. 1913–Jan. 19
Not extant		MS ?600 pp. 'The Wedding Ring'	
TCC pp. 219–75, 279–84 in Roberts E331a	TS ?500 pp. 'The Wedding Ring'	TCC ?500 pp. 'The Wedding Ring'	Feb.–May 1914
Roberts E331a		MS & TCC 811 pp. *The Rainbow*	Nov. 1914–Mar. 1
Roberts E441b	MS 55 pp. 'The Sisters III'		April 1916
Roberts E441c pp. 650–863	MS 863 pp. 'The Sisters IV'		April–June 1916
Roberts E441d & e pp. 1–368 typed by DHL, pp. 369–666 by Pinker	TSIa 666 pp. *Women in Love* (Texas)	TSIb 666 pp. *Women in Love* (Toronto)	July 1916–Jan. 191
Roberts E441f; TCCs not extant TSII revised 1917, 1918, 1919	TSII 766 pp. *Women in Love*	?TCCs	Mar. 1917

remain uncertain. He very much needed a new typewriter ribbon, and correspondence with his friend Koteliansky in London (lasting from 4 July to – at least – 25 July, and perhaps 1 August) finally produced, after two wrong ones, the right one.[18] Is it a coincidence that, on page 15 of his new typescript, two thirds of the way down there is a sudden switch to a much blacker impression?[19] That almost certainly signals the arrival of the new ribbon. Against that

Figure 2   The publication of 'Women in Love'

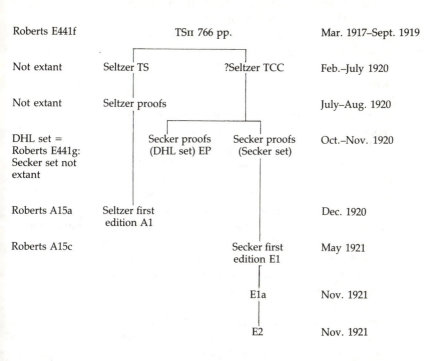

Roberts E441f		TSɪɪ 766 pp.		Mar. 1917–Sept. 1919
Not extant	Seltzer TS		?Seltzer TCC	Feb.–July 1920
Not extant	Seltzer proofs			July–Aug. 1920
DHL set = Roberts E441g: Secker set not extant		Secker proofs (DHL set) EP	Secker proofs (Secker set)	Oct.–Nov. 1920
Roberts A15a	Seltzer first edition A1			Dec. 1920
Roberts A15c			Secker first edition E1	May 1921
			E1a	Nov. 1921
			E2	Nov. 1921

must be set the evidence that, on 21 July, Lawrence had announced to his agent that he had given up typing the novel: 'it got on my nerves and knocked me up' (ɪɪ. 637). Instead, he was 'scribbling out the final draft in pencil'. Had typing 15 pages really done such damage to Lawrence's nerves? Or had he typed a good deal, with the old ribbon, that does not now survive? He did not, anyway, give up typing. He went on, throughout August and September, to produce 368 ribbon and carbon copy pages. If 15 pages in July reduced him to illness and despair, how did he subsequently manage to type so much? There is something of a mystery here, as there is in what exactly he was 'scribbling out'. At the end of this paper I shall hint at a possible answer.

Anyhow, with some pencil revision in mid-July, while waiting for the new ribbon to come (and after deciding to give up typing, before going back to it), Lawrence's typing (which took 'a tremendous time') turned, like the novel, into 'one of the labours of Hercules' (ɪɪ. 665). He finally abandoned it about three-fifths of his way through the novel, around 13 October 1916 (II. 666); and this time he really did get Pinker to finish the job for him, from a newly scribbled-out pencil conclusion (in six new pencil notebooks), and then in those final four from the April–June writing, newly revised and repaginated. He finished this draft of the novel around 31 October (II. 669), and by early November already had the ribbon and carbon copies of the last part of the novel back from Pinker (III. 22, 28–9), to add to those 368 ribbon and carbon pages he had typed himself. Then, a final revision, mostly of the part newly typed by Pinker; and on 20 November 1916 Pinker was sent one of the complete corrected typescripts (TS1a, the one now at the University of Texas) to send around potential English publishers (III. 35).

It was everywhere rejected. But at least one of the publishers commented unfavourably on the heavily corrected state of TS1a[20] (TS1b was, of course, no better); and, anyway, with TS1b destined for American publishers, Lawrence wanted another copy for himself. For these reasons, between late January and late March 1917 Pinker had yet another typescript made, from TS1b (the copy now at Toronto). This created the second typed version of the novel, which we call TS11. In fact, Pinker made at least two and perhaps three copies of this typescript, but only one copy survives today – fortunately the one which Lawrence kept beside him throughout 1917, 1918 and 1919 and to which – especially in 1917 – he made extensive revisions.[21] Ten per cent of the novel was totally re-written in TS11, by 1919, and the other 90 per cent heavily revised.

TS11 finally went to America in September 1919, to the publisher Thomas Seltzer; and from it, Seltzer created the first edition of the novel, which he published in December 1920. But it has not, until now, been understood how Seltzer used TS11. Ross and Farmer both assumed that he actually sent TS11 to his American printers;[22] in spite of the fact that it contains no printers' marks. They also assumed that – as Lawrence had been nagging Seltzer for six months to send TS11 back to Secker, its English publisher – so Seltzer must indeed have sent it back when he had finished with it, and that Secker too used TS11 to send to his English printers. However, it can be proved that TS11 was neither Seltzer's nor Secker's setting copy.

Here is the proof. In chapter 5, Seltzer's American edition shows a desperately wrong reading of TS11; where Lawrence had described

Gerald admiring Birkin's 'versatility', the American printers had come up with the word 'venality'.[23] Now, if Secker had also been working from TSII, it is quite impossible that independently he would have stumbled into the same error. But this is exactly what he did: he also printed 'venality',[24] thus earning Lawrence a sharp little lecture in a review by Rose Macaulay the following year: 'there are many words of which Mr. Lawrence simply does not know the meaning . . . He does not know, for instance, that "venality" means greed for money.'[25] But the same happened to Secker's edition time and again. Where Seltzer had produced the word 'treading' for the coal-trucks rumbling past Gerald and his horse at the level-crossing in chapter 9 (120:5), Secker *also* printed 'treading'. The reading of TSII is 'threading'. Where Seltzer missed out (15:14) the whole four word phrase 'surely he would understand', Secker did exactly the same. And so on.

So, if Seltzer had used TSII as *his* setting copy what could Secker have used? The obvious answer would be 'proofs of Seltzer's American edition': and we have evidence that this might indeed have happened. On 10 August 1920, Lawrence wrote to Secker to say that he had the first batch of Seltzer's proofs to hand, and 'Will let you have them corrected and exact, and you can print from them' (III. 586). So Secker printed the novel from Seltzer's proofs? He cannot have done: that winter, he denied any knowledge that Seltzer had even set the book up in type, in America; something he might have done, if he had had just one batch of corrected proofs from Lawrence, but not if he had been using those proofs during the autumn as setting copy.[26] But, anyway, it is also possible to prove that Secker *cannot* have been using a set of Seltzer's proofs. Where Seltzer had wrongly printed 'frightened' (50:35), Secker somehow managed to restore TSII's 'frightening': where Seltzer had printed 'moments' (102:20), Secker recovered TSII's 'minutes': where Seltzer produced the error 'rim' (362:07), Secker went back to TSII's 'room': where Seltzer printed 'from Eton' (79:16), Secker managed to recover TSII's 'since Eton'. And so on, many many times. We would have to postulate a situation in which Secker had both TSII *and* a set of Seltzer's proofs, and that Secker's printers took a reading now from one, now from the other: sometimes checking TSII, to find that Seltzer was wrong: sometimes not bothering, and letting Seltzer's error stand. No printer I have ever heard of would behave like that.

The solution is much simpler, but much more disturbing.

Between January and July 1920, Seltzer had had the extensively revised TSII re-typed. It cost him 'over $100', he complained to Lawrence's agent Robert Mountsier (III. 673). Seltzer's typist, about whom nothing further is known, must have produced the errors 'venality', 'treaded' and so on. He, or she, also had an aversion to some characteristic English idioms: 'give it you', 'offer it them', 'go and be introduced': in each case modifying the text, to read 'give it to you' (399:06), 'offer it to them' (399:22), 'go to be introduced' (449:15). This happened frequently. Seltzer then sent Secker the new typescript, the 'Seltzer TS' of Figure 2 – or, even more probably, the Seltzer TCC, as he would probably have wanted the ribbon copy typescript for his own typesetting and proof-correction.[27] His printers then produced the errors 'rim', 'frightened', 'moments', 'from Eton', and so on. At least Secker was spared those.

This intervention of yet another typescript, which Lawrence never even saw, made the transmission of the text even more hazardous. Literally hundreds of unauthorised changes gathered in the Seltzer TS, and Lawrence had this time no chance of dealing with them. Nor did he have any chance of correcting Seltzer's proofs; although he had the first batch by 10 August, he did not get a complete set until 18 October (III. 613), much too late to influence the text. He was, however, able to influence the transmission of the text in the English edition. Secker sent him the first batch of English proofs on 14 October (III. 606 n. 2), and Lawrence had gone through the complete set by 22 November (III. 625); he made a number of very significant changes.

But his proof-reading of *Women in Love* unfortunately coincided with the libraries' objections to his most recent novel *The Lost Girl*; and, for that, Secker had asked him to rewrite one page and Secker himself would add unauthorised alterations to three other passages.[28] Secker, feeling 'instinctively that anything to do with D.H. is rather dangerous',[29] now asked Lawrence to alter chapter 7 of *Women in Love* (which you probably know as 'Totem': it is 'Fetish' in the new Cambridge Edition). Then, at the end of December 1920, he further requested 'two or three excisions or paraphrases in the text' (III. 647 n. 1), and sent Lawrence a list of such changes at the end of January (III. 660 n. 1); at some stage, he also cut two paragraphs without telling Lawrence.[30] Lawrence was in general fairly amenable to Secker's requests for modifications, which we must keep quite distinct from his own original proof-correction of October and November. The modifications he now made, at Secker's request, are of course recorded in the textual apparatus, but have not been allowed into the text of the new Cambridge Edition, any more than are the even more extensive changes to the appearance of Halliday and his mistress which Lawrence made under the threat of Philip Heseltine's libel suit the following autumn.[31] His proof-corrections, on the other hand, done before Secker became fearful, *have* been incorporated in the new Cambridge Edition.[32]

But a further problem still, unnoticed by Ross or Farmer, lies in wait. Those surviving page proofs for the English edition, now at Texas, and corrected by Lawrence, do not in all respects correspond with the changes Secker actually made; not only because Secker did not always follow Lawrence's instructions (we know he did not: I shall come to that), but because this is the *duplicate* set of proofs, Lawrence's own set. And, as editors of Lawrence know by now, if ever Lawrence had two copies of any text – be it two typescripts, or two sets of proofs – he invariably entered different alterations in them. The title of chapter 19, for example – 'Moony' in the text you know – appears in the contents list of the duplicate proof set as 'Moonshine'. A suitable title for a chapter in which Birkin's thinking is more than usually alcoholically light-headed? But Secker printed 'Moony', a title he was quite incapable of inventing: just as he printed 'Excurse' as the title for chapter 23, rather than 'Excursion', as the duplicate proof set has it. 'Moony' and 'Excurse' must have appeared on his set ('Moony' does appear as a revision on page 256 of the duplicate set). The new Cambridge Edition has, accordingly, treated the revisions in the duplicate set with great care, in the knowledge that Lawrence may well have corrected Secker's set differently. One important change in the duplicate set which almost certainly appeared in Secker's set, however, and was ignored, was Lawrence's attempt to divide chapter 29 ('Continental') into two, calling its second half 'Snow' (making that chapter 30). Lawrence made this change both on the contents page and at the appropriate place on page 419 of the duplicate proofs. Secker, we believe, flinched from the re-setting of type that such a change would have meant, and ignored it. The new Cambridge Edition has restored it, and thus has 32, not 31, chapters.

I have not yet mentioned, however, in this discussion of the emendations of our base-text, TS$_{II}$, what we shall do about a major problem for the edition which Farmer failed to realise the extent of, and which Ross made light of:[33] contributions made by Frieda Lawrence to the text. Frieda often claimed that she helped Lawrence with his writing. She told Mabel Luhan that she 'wrote pages into' *Sons and Lovers;*[34] she certainly helped copy Lawrence's revisions into the duplicate typescript of *The Wedding Ring*, in the spring of 1914 (some of them still survive, in the carbon copy pages Lawrence re-used in the manuscript of *The Rainbow* in 1915).[35] And she assisted him once again in the summer and autumn of 1916, while he was typing out those first 368 pages of *Women in Love*. She copied his revisions in ribbon or carbon copy into the other copy. On page 248 (see Figure 3, i and ii), for example,[36] she copied Lawrence's revision in TSıa 'I'd done her no hurt' as 'I'd done her no harm'. Two lines lower, Lawrence had inserted a sentence ending 'came up in her I suppose', with no comma; Frieda copied it into TSıb with a comma. Two lines lower, above line nine, Lawrence had ended an insertion – 'the last blow too' – with a full stop. Frieda copied the words accurately enough, but added a dash. And above line thirteen, in TSıb, although she copied Lawrence's insertion 'herself' accurately, she failed to add his ink underlining of the word 'afterwards'.

The bulk of Frieda's copying appears in TSıb; and that was the copy which went to Pinker to be re-typed as TSıı in January 1917; so Frieda's idiosyncrasies of copying (to call them nothing worse) very often got into the final state of the text. A number were then superseded by subsequent revision, but many were not. Our problem is: what status do Frieda's idiosyncrasies of copying have?

We need more information before attempting to answer the question. We can discuss Frieda's contribution to the novel under three main headings. First category: places where she miscopied Lawrence's revisions, such as the 'harm' for 'hurt' just mentioned. This can be complicated by the fact that, in TSıı, Lawrence frequently revised her revision, so that the final state of the text contains elements of what she had done, together with elements of his own. So, for example, he revised TSıa to read 'things past'. She copied that into TSıb as 'things in the past'. He revised that, in TSıı (where it had of course been typed, so that he couldn't see that Frieda was responsible for it), to 'things concluded, in the past' (92:4). Second category: places where Frieda revised Lawrence's French and German. Lawrence had made the elderly professor at the mountain-hut remark, of Loerke's recitation, 'Ja, das war

Figure 3   The text of 'Women in Love'

(i) TS1a

(ii) TS1b

(iii) TS1b

TS11

merkwürdig, das . . .' Frieda revised that, in TS1b, to read 'Das war ausgezeichnet das war famos –' (452:1). She was a native speaker. Does that give her alteration a special authority? Third category: places where Frieda deleted, added or substituted (or failed to add or delete). So, for example, in TS1a Lawrence deleted the sentence 'And I don't care whether you see it or not – that's your affair.', but Frieda allowed it to stand in TS1b, and it got re-typed (103:33). At another point, she herself added a whole phrase: Ursula is talking to Hermione, and says 'Really, something must be left to the Lord' – but Frieda added, in both TS1a and b, 'there always is and always will be' (154:11).

And so on. Frieda altered the substantives of the text in ways that survived subsequent revision on more than 40 occasions. If it had been a typist, or a printer, who had made such changes, we would have had no hesitation in rejecting them, though we would of course have recorded them in our textual apparatus. But is Frieda different, perhaps? Did Lawrence trust her to work with him? Did she assist him in the work of the novel's creation? We simply do not know enough about the terms of any such collaboration. Did she call across the room 'your German is frightful here, Lawrence, you should have said . . .', to provoke the response 'I suppose you know best: stick it down'?

There *are* occasions where we can trace his dissatisfaction with what she had done. He typed 'white cotton crape' as the material of the sisters' dresses at the water-party (169:33). Frieda deleted 'cotton' and substituted 'silky' in both TS1a and b. Lawrence later deleted the word 'silky' in revision of TS11. As he typed it, Hermione's servant–maid twice calls her 'my lady' (94:5, 148:6). Frieda altered both to 'madam': she may have been thinking of (and resenting) Lady Ottoline Morrell, but she may also have felt 'am not I the daughter of a baron? Do I not know how upper classes – even English upper classes – are addressed?' However, in TS11 Lawrence deleted one of her 'madam's.

We have to take a decision: we cannot simply say, as Ross said, 'there is no evidence that Frieda revised'.[37] There *is* such evidence. The policy that Lindeth Vasey and I have adopted is as follows. We have not accorded Frieda special status as collaborator. Where it is possible to evade her contribution, we have done so. Where, for example, she altered Lawrence's text in only one copy of TS1, even if it were TS1b – the copy subsequently retyped as TS11 – then we have gone back to the *other* copy for Lawrence's own words or own punctuation. To his subsequent revision of passages which include *her* revisions, we have adopted the same attitude as we have done to the alterations made by a typist. That is, where subsequent authorial revision moves the text on so far from the unauthorised change as to make it unwise to return to the original text, we have accepted the subsequent revision, unauthorised alteration included. So, for example, in that case I quoted earlier, where 'things past' became 'things in the past' in Frieda's copy, subsequently revised by Lawrence to 'things concluded, in the past' (92:4), we have accepted the final reading on the grounds that it is impossible to return to the original reading. Where, on the other hand, Lawrence's subsequent revision seems to be an attempt to deal with something he did not like but could not, for the moment, see his way around, we have rejected Frieda's contribution and have gone back to the original text.

But where Frieda's contribution, for good or ill, appears in both ['SI]a *and* b, we cannot evade her. She normally leaves us no other text to follow, so we have – in almost every case – to accept *her* text. We have only evaded her, then, if there is evidence – as with Lawrence's later deletion of her word 'silky' – that he actively disapproved of her change, and attempted to get rid of it. In that case, we go back to what he originally wrote: 'white cotton crape'. Elsewhere, it is Frieda whom we must read, not Lawrence – 'there always is and always will be' (154:11): that is Frieda. When Ursula thinks about Birkin and realises that 'her hate was quite abstract' (218:6), that phrase is Frieda's: Lawrence had typed 'she had no reason for hating him'. When Ursula tells Hermione that Birkin wants her 'to give myself up – and I simply don't feel that I *can* do it' (326:20), the 'do it' comes from Frieda: for Lawrence, Ursula simply doesn't feel 'that I *can*'. When you read how Birkin was 'tall and narrow' (300:9), the 'tall and' comes from Frieda: for Lawrence, Birkin was just 'narrow'. Gudrun feels a 'vivid flush' (311:23) go over her, when Winifred presents her bouquet: 'flush' is Frieda: Lawrence typed 'flame'. And so on. Each of these cases receives an explanatory note in the Cambridge Edition, so that the reader at all times knows what it is – and whose it is – that he or she is reading.

Perhaps you will feel that our policy of evading Frieda when possible, elsewhere, is too timid. Are not novels social productions, not the products of a single brain or hand (or typewriter)? Typists, publishers, printers can be seen as collaborators in a communal

enterprise, not as enemies who corrupt the purity of an authorial
text; and if they can be seen as collaborators, how much more
might Frieda deserve that title! Again, the accidental miscopying
of a word or phrase might be seen as equivalent to the random
splash of paint which, for Francis Bacon, can be the stimulus for a
new approach to the painting in hand.[38] Should we judge errors
in copying to be the equivalent of that splash of paint, and see
Lawrence's response to the stimulus as something which excitingly
advances the text of his book?

Against that must be set the fact that Frieda, at times, manifestly
did not improve the novel: and that some of her contributions
certainly interfere rather than assist, or stimulate. So, for example
when Mrs Brangwen says to Birkin 'I have heard speak of you
often enough', which is both clear and colloquial, Frieda inserted
'them' before 'speak': 'I have heard them speak of you often
enough' (173:28). I suspect Frieda of being temporarily thrown by
the English idiom. We must, surely, evade her there. Similarly
when Will Brangwen is shouting at Ursula, and says 'you self
willed bargust'. Lawrence first wrote 'self-willed creature' and then
revised the word to 'bargust', which is Nottinghamshire dialect for
a noisy and unruly child. Frieda obviously didn't know that, and
probably thought her husband off his head: she put 'creature' back
(290:31). But 'bargust' has gone back into the Cambridge Edition
as it clearly must: we *know* Lawrence didn't want 'creature'
'Bargust', consequently, gets into print for the first time, in this
meaning.

That leads me to a topic insufficiently discussed or understood
Lawrence as a deliberate manipulator of the texture of language
something we have been able to restore, like the colours in a
restored painting. 'Bargust' *is* a more richly coloured word than
'creature'. How many readers of the novel have realised what the
chapter title 'Excurse' means? 'Excursion', of course: with perhaps
a hint of 'excursus' – 'a dissertation on a particular matter appended
to a book'. And, I suppose, as Birkin and Ursula move out beyond
their quarrels, they move 'ex-curse'. But the word is really a
Lawrentian invention: obsolete in the *OED*: last used 1587, meaning
'a mad sally or outrush' (335:0). When Birkin and Ursula, at the
end of that chapter, drive into Sherwood Forest, the trees beside
the road are (like Loerke's eyes, later) 'elvin': not 'elfin' (352:35
474:6), as all editions have had it since 1920. The fey overtones of
'elfin' are replaced by the (pre-Tolkien) invention of 'elvin'. Ursula

n the market place buying a chair with Birkin, looks at the young man they meet, and thinks how he would be 'a dreadful, but wonderful lover to a woman, so marvellously contributed' (399:31); that very special colour in the word 'contributed' – given to her, given *up* to her – is Lawrence's own, and will be found in no dictionary.

It is also the case, of course, that precision of language and reference will have been dulled by the passage of time since 1920. This is where an explanatory note may be essential, to restore the meaning. When we see the Pussum (Halliday's mistress) in the Pompadour café, and note that she wears a 'loose, simple jumper' (67:13), most readers will assume that she is dressed with comfortable informality in wool. Not at all: a jumper at that date was 'a loose garment, frequently of knitted cotton, and not tucked into the waist band': here, it is of crêpe-de-chine with a draw string at the neck. When Mrs Crich says to Gerald 'It's quite nuts for you?' (364:10), most modern readers – if they think they know what she means – will be wrong. Not madness: not 'peanuts': but 'a source of pleasure and delight: now *slang*' according to the *OED* (around 1900). Similarly when Ursula calls her sister 'Prune': what kind of address is that? Upper or middle-class slang: 'a slightly disparaging, affectionate endearment for either sex': there's a suggestion of Gudrun's time in Chelsea, there. You may be reminded of P. G. Wodehouse, *The Inimitable Jeeves* (1924): 'my heart warmed to the poor prune' (chapter 4).

This is not to say that every restoration of meaning has been possible. I would, for example, dearly love to know more about the saying 'in and out like a frog in a gallipot' – Will Brangwen's coarse summary of modern young men's attitude to marriage (286:16). I know what gallipots are, and the phrase certainly means 'in and out, just like that': but why, or how, or where frogs got into gallipots, or why they always got out so fast, is a mystery to me. Similarly with the name given to the little Italian Contessa at Breadalby: 'Palestra' (97:11). An ordinary sounding Italian name? It actually *means* 'gymnasium', and is quite impossible as an Italian first name. Our explanatory note on it runs: 'Either an error by Lawrence, or an obscure play on words'. Was there a Contessa at Garsington popularly known as 'Jim', for example?

Turning to the positive restorations of the new Cambridge Edition, however, I am happy to announce that (appropriately) this is the first *Women in Love* with an illustration. Birkin, as school

inspector, instructs Ursula how to teach the children about catkins
'Make a pictorial record of the fact, as a child does when drawing
a face—two eyes, one nose, mouth with teeth—so—'. And
Lawrence drew the face into TS1a, TS1b and again into TS11: we
print the version from TS11 (see Figure 3 iii).

And in so many ways the restored text of the novel is less
obscure: more like the clear, lighted spaces of the cleaned painting
I have been surprised by the number of occasions where the new
restored text has made sense of things which have always puzzled
me. No longer will Birkin consider how 'he knew he did not want
a further sensual experience' (281:8): in our edition, he will know
that he *did* want a further sensual experience: of course he did
Seltzer's typist must have been responsible for the 'not': a puritan
shadow fell across the page, for a moment. Reading aloud the final
dialogue between Gudrun and Loerke, while teaching the novel,
have more than once been caught out by the way Gudrun i
supposed to have 'cried' 'But one needn't go' (523:29). She didn't
she 'said' it, perfectly normally. Her earlier achievement in lifting
her shoulders in a 'low shrug' (51:21) has puzzled me more than
one. How *do* you shrug without lifting your shoulders much?
should have guessed: it should read a 'slow shrug'. Similarly with
Hermione's 'low, odd, singing fashion' (36:14): the typist must
have had a blind spot for the word: for 'low' again read 'slow': a
'slow, odd, singing fashion'. When Birkin criticises his own
response to other people, he will no longer 'sink back at them'
(273:35): what on earth did that mean? He will 'sing back at them'
Those trucks at the level-crossing will no longer go 'treading one
after the other' (120:5): trucks *don't* tread: they will go 'threading
one after the other'. Gudrun will no longer have 'heavy, heavy
black shoes' (262:26): what nameless perversion is suggested by
that? She will have 'rather heavy black shoes'. Hermione will no
longer look at Ursula with 'cool evidence' (324:26): evidence of
what? but with 'cool confidence'. When Birkin gives Ursula the
rings in 'Excurse', she will no longer want to 'try them on her
fingers' (336:39) – presumably to see how they look – but 'try them
on her finger': her ring finger: a very different meaning! Gerald
wandering away at the end of the novel, will no longer 'wander
unconsciously' (528:12): Gerald is never simply aimless, even in
death: he will 'wander on unconsciously', going on seeing it
through.

As I said, the task of restoration is almost complete, the problem nearly all solved; but I referred, very early on, to one that remains with the exact sequence of composition, as suggested by the letter of 21 July 1916, in which Lawrence announces that he cannot face more typing, has given it up, and is now scribbling out 'the fourth and the final draft' in pencil. A crucial letter. Yet we do not know exactly *what* he was scribbling out, at that stage; whatever it was, he could hardly have been '4/5 done now', as he claimed; and why did he announce that he could type no more, when he went on to type over 350 more pages? The letter also suggests that an identical sequence of events occurred twice: once in July, and once again in October: Lawrence, his nerves knocked up by typing, planned to send Pinker the remaining manuscript to type, and scribbled out its last part in pencil. We know he did that in October. Let me offer you one, tantalising fact. The letter in question, dated by Lawrence himself '21 July 1916', is written on a very distinctive 23 line opaque whitish paper. I have checked – or had checked – all 87 surviving letters from Lawrence and Frieda in the period June–December 1916. That paper occurs only fourteen times. Thirteen of those times are in October and November. The fourteenth is the 21 July 1916. Did Lawrence somehow misdate his letter by three whole months – something unprecedented in his correspondence – and thus throw out a generation of scholars in their attempt to establish the exact sequence of writing? There is no way of proving it: logic and good sense both speak against it: yet for me it remains a faint, tantalising possibility.

Notes

1. Re-setting of large parts of the second impression (hereafter referred to as 'E2') took place, including parts unaffected by textual changes: the reason for this is not clear.
2. Herbert Davis, 'Women in Love: a Corrected Typescript', *University of Toronto Quarterly*, xxvii (October 1957) pp. 34–53.
3. Eldon S. Branda, 'Textual Changes in *Women in Love*', *Texas Studies in Literature and Language*, vi (1964) pp. 306–21.
4. Mark Kinkead-Weekes, 'The Marble and the Statue: the Exploratory Imagination of D. H. Lawrence', in *Imagined Worlds: Essays in Honour of John Butt*, ed. Ian Gregor and Maynard Mack (London: Methuen, 1968) pp. 371–418.
5. Charles L. Ross, *The Composition of 'The Rainbow' and 'Women in Love': A History* (Charlottesville: University Press of Virginia, 1979); see too

Charles L. Ross, 'A Problem of Textual Transmission in the Typescripts of *Women in Love*', *The Library*, 5th series, xix (June 1974) pp. 197–205, and 'The Composition of *Women in Love*: a History, 1913–1919', *DHL Review*, viii (Summer 1975) pp. 198–212.

6. D. H. Lawrence, *Women in Love*, ed. Charles L. Ross (Harmondsworth, Middx: Penguin, 1982). This edition, far from being (as Keith Sagar has stated) a departure from all 'the extremely corrupt texts' previously published [*D. H. Lawrence: Life into Art* (Harmondsworth, Middx: Penguin, 1985) p. 149], in fact perpetuates in print literally hundreds of errors. It emends its base-text (the American first edition of Seltzer) only selectively. For one thing, it does not emend any of Seltzer's punctuation errors; for another, extraordinarily in an edition claiming to correct 'all major substantive errors in Seltzer' (p. 47), it emends those substantives both randomly and selectively. I checked eight consecutive pages of Seltzer's text (pp. 274–83), and found exactly 40 occasions where Ross should have emended his text: 28 of them accidentals, 12 of them substantives. Ross altered none of the 28 accidentals, but also altered only 5 of the 12 substantive errors; the emendations required are as follows (*A1* = Seltzer):

276:9	for he asked] *Om. A1*
277:11	so] *Om. A1*
278:36	it] it to *A1*
279:19	a] *Om. A1*
281:8	did] did not *A1*
283:6	accepts] accepted *A1*
283:7	other] others *A1*

I assume that the pattern is repeated throughout Ross's edition: I have found substantive errors in it throughout. He also fails to record, anywhere in his edition, the source from which his emendations are taken. This was the corrected typescript (hereafter TSii) at the Harry Ransom Humanities Research Center, University of Texas. Such a text, on such a basis, produces an unreliable and untrustworthy edition.

7. See too David Farmer, '*Women in Love*: a Textual History and Premise for a Critical Edition', in *Editing British and American Literature, 1880–1920*, ed. Eric Domville (New York: Garland Publishers, 1976) pp. 77–92.

8. Pierre Vitoux, 'The Chapter "Excurse" in *Women in Love*: its Genesis and the Critical Problem', *Texas Studies in Literature and Language*, xvii (1976) pp. 821–36, and '*Women in Love*: from Typescripts into Print', *Texas Studies in Literature and Language*, xxiii (1981) pp. 577–93.

9. I should like to acknowledge the assistance of David Farmer and Lindeth Vasey in my preparation of this paper.

10. Warren Roberts, *A Bibliography of D. H. Lawrence*, 2nd edn (Cambridge: Cambridge University Press, 1982) E441c.

11. Ibid., E441d.

12. Ibid., E441e.

13. Ibid., E441f.
14. Ibid., A15c.
15. Ibid., E441g.
16. Ross, *The Composition*, pp. 153–4, notes Frieda Lawrence influencing the transmission in TS1b, but offers no suggestion of what should be done about her influence, or its effect on DHL's revisions to TS11. His edition takes no account of the pencil notebooks, TS1a or TS1b.
17. Fuller details of the composition history will be found in the Cambridge Edition.
18. See *Letters*, II, pp. 621–2, 628, 636, 638–9. Subsequent references to the Cambridge Edition of the *Letters* will appear in the text, with volume and page number: e.g. (II. 621–2).
19. TS1a, Roberts, *A Bibliography of D. H. Lawrence*, E441d, p. 15. The first chapter, in TS1a, is almost entirely ribbon-copy.
20. Letter from Constable & Co. to J. B. Pinker, 23 January 1917 (Northwestern University).
21. See Ross, *The Composition*, p. 120.
22. Farmer, 'Women in Love': a Textual History', pp. 78–9; Ross, *The Composition*, p. 125.
23. D. H. Lawrence, *Women in Love* (New York, 1920) p. 60, line 34. Subsequent references to Seltzer's edition will appear in the text; e.g. (60:34).
24. D. H. Lawrence, *Women in Love* (London, 1921) p. 60. It might be possible to read DHL's 'rs' as an 'n' (the word appears in a holograph revision), but that would still leave the word as 'venatility'.
25. *Time and Tide*, II (1 July 1921) 629.
26. Letter from Secker to Seltzer, 7 December 1920, University of Illinois.
27. Seltzer also used TS11 in proof-correction at least once: at 428:38–9, he used sentences deleted in TS11 (p. 614) to replace TS11's final readings. He retained possession of TS11 throughout: he still had it in January 1921 (III. 673–4).
28. See D. H. Lawrence, *The Lost Girl*, ed. John Worthen (Cambridge: Cambridge University Press, 1981) p. xxxix.
29. Letter from Secker to Compton Mackenzie, 14 April 1920, University of Texas.
30. See Farmer, 'Women in Love': a Textual History', pp. 89–90.
31. Ibid., pp. 84–7.
32. Ross, in the Penguin edition, attempts to blur the distinction between the two, claiming that the changes to the English edition had all been 'tampering', 'forced labour', 'tinkering . . . at the behest of Secker' (pp. 46–7). He accordingly ignores all the proof-corrections DHL voluntarily made, with the single exception of the chapter titles: themselves an example of work deliberately solicited by Secker: 'I hope you will not mind adding chapter titles . . .' (III. 606 n. 2). Ross also gives, as title for chapter 7, 'Totem' instead of 'Fetish'; 'Totem' was introduced into the novel in its second impression, and represents Secker's response to Philip Heseltine's threats of a libel suit. Elsewhere, Ross describes the second impression of the novel as 'an inconsistent bowdlerization' (p. 46).

33. Ross, *The Composition*, pp. 153–4. Ross's article 'A Problem of Textual Transmission in the Typescripts of *Women in Love*' is a far more serious analysis of the problem, but its findings are ignored by his book. He also ignores, in both article and book, the punctuation changes which Frieda made; his list of problem-cases is incomplete; and his suggested method of editorial procedure (p. 200) is not entirely practical.

34. Mabel Luhan, *Lorenzo in Taos* (New York: Alfred A. Knopf, 1932) p. 50; Frieda did, however, deny the claim later in life.

35. Information from Mark Kinkead-Weekes, whose advice, enthusiasm and scholarship, generously shared over many years, I should here like to acknowledge.

36. Reproduced from Ross, *The Composition*, pp. 159–60.

37. Ross, *The Composition*, p. 154.

38. E.g., 'involuntary marks on the canvas which may suggest much deeper ways by which you can trap the fact you are obsessed by' [David Sylvester, *Interviews with Francis Bacon* (London: Thames and Hudson, 1975) p. 53].

Acknowledgements are due to Cambridge University Press for permission to reproduce material from the Cambridge Edition of *Women in Love*, ed. David Farmer, Lindeth Vasey and John Worthen (Cambridge, 1987); to the Harry Ransom Humanities Research Center, the University of Texas at Austin; to the University of Toronto.

3

D. H. Lawrence's Self-Consciousness

BARBARA HARDY

The self-consciousness of D. H. Lawrence's poems, novels and stories is not obvious or central. To read other writers of the time – T. S. Eliot, Joyce, Virginia Woolf, Beckett – is to encounter head-on books which, through explicit analysis, convolution or analogy, reflect on themselves. These authors look at art, look at the imagination of other artists, and look at themselves. This kind of reflexiveness is not peculiar to the twentieth century (nor did it begin in English and French eighteenth-century literature, and go underground during the nineteenth century). Most art is self-conscious in one way or another, imaginative achievement taking its place congenially amongst imaginative creations. Lawrence is no exception, though his self-consciousness is less conspicuous than that of his contemporaries. Certain kinds of self-consciousness are subjects on which he holds a moral position; they are psychic states of which he disapproves. They are also phases of his imaginative experience through which he needs to pass.

Lawrence rejects self-consciousness – or tries to reject it – for many reasons. He shrinks from it in so far as it tends towards solipsism and away from love. He avoids it because he finds reminiscent and retrospective art repulsive, and tries to write in the present tense. He formulates and makes the strenuous attempt to seize what art finds elusive, the vitality and immediacy of the instant. The analysis of self involves acts of reminiscence and retrospect, and works against the experience of immediacy. That experience lies just beyond the grasp, but his ambition to capture it is one source of the distinctive freshness offered by his art, which contrasts so boldly with the great retrospective fiction of Dickens, George Eliot, T. S. Eliot and Joyce, alike occupied with memorial and retrospect. Lawrence's fiction, poetry and criticism all make a radical effort to inhabit and apprehend the present. The concern with present tense is the authorisation of his particular mode of total and radical revision of words and forms, for which there cannot be many precedents.

One of Lawrence's great unrhyming poems, 'New Heaven and Earth', explores the experience of self-revulsion. He is imagining a self-taste and distaste like that of Gerard Manley Hopkins when he says 'my taste was me . . . Selfyeast of spirit a dull dough sours'.[1]

Eager to be resurrected, Lawrence imagines an old life which has to die. He presents its perverse energy, enclosed in self-knowledge, self-love and self-creation:

> I was so weary of the world,
> I was so sick of it,
> everything was tainted with myself,
> skies, trees, flowers, birds, water,
> people, houses, streets, vehicles, machines,
> nations, armies, war, peace-talking,
> work, recreation, governing, anarchy,
> it was all tainted with myself, I knew it all to start with
> because it was all myself.

> When I gathered flowers, I knew it was myself plucking my
>   own flowering.
> When I went in a train, I knew it was myself travelling by my
>   own invention.
> When I heard the cannon of the war, I listened with my own
>   ears to my own destruction.
> When I saw the torn dead, I knew it was my own torn dead
>   body.
> It was all me, I had done it all in my own flesh.
> I shall never forget the maniacal horror of it all in the end
> when everything was me, I knew it all already, I anticipated it
>   all in my soul
> because I was the author and the result
> I was the God and the creation at once;
> creator, I looked at my creation;
> created, I looked at myself, the creator:
> it was a maniacal horror in the end.

I was a lover, I kissed the woman I loved,
and God of horror, I was kissing also myself.
I was a father and a begetter of children,
and oh, oh horror, I was begetting and conceiving in my own
    body.[2]

The articulation of solipsism reaches a horrified completion and climax in images of fertility; auto-eroticism leads to auto-conception. He loathes selfhood, as Blake did, but out of its monstrous images finds a way to rebirth into relationship, love and procreation.

Lawrence was not only a sensual poet, but also a comic novelist. The rejection of self-consciousness shows itself differently in the language of social comedy. Chapter 5, 'The Beau', of *The Lost Girl* is almost a parody of the scene in *The Rainbow* where Tom Brangwen goes with his bunch of daffodils to do 'a bit of courting'. Albert Witham, a talkative young man from Oxford who 'though he talked in the direction of his interlocutor, . . . did not speak *to* him: merely said his words towards him',[3] has brought a bunch of white stocks for Alvina. Lawrence's presentation of the rituals of donation is an easy-going scene, acutely observant in its social and psychological aspects. He analyses embarrassments of hospitality, present-giving and courtship in a sharply defined environment where dramatised persons, properties, gesture and dialogue play their distinct parts. The interchange of words and feelings carries an amused perception of the collision of grace and awkwardness often involved in ceremonies of giving and receiving. The description of Albert's 'broad, pleased, gleaming smile' and 'shining, pallid eyes', is comically reductive, as is Alvina's banal language of gratitude, 'Are they for me?' and 'Haven't they a lovely scent?'. Albert's attention is caught by the book which James Houghton is reading, J. M. Barrie's *Tommy and Grizel*, and he compounds social embarrassment by awkwardly making conversation:

Albert, rather embarrassed, reached forward, saying:
    'May I see what you're reading?' And he turned over the book. '*Tommy and Grizel*! Oh yes! What do you think of it?'
    'Well,' said James, 'I am only in the beginning.'
    'I think it's interesting, myself,' said Albert, 'as a study of a man who can't get away from himself. You meet a lot of people like that. What I wonder is why they find it such a drawback.'
    'Find what a drawback?' asked James.

'Not being able to get away from themselves. That self-consciousness. It hampers them, and interferes with their power of action. Now I wonder why self-consciousness should hinder a man in his action? Why does it cause misgiving? I think I'm self-conscious, but I don't think I have so many misgivings. I don't see that they're necessary.'[4]

Albert's reliably unreliable question and answer immediately mark him – he is not the man to find or lose the lost girl, who will lose herself, and her self-consciousness, in passion. In poem and novel, Lawrence parades self-consciousness to prepare for negative capability and love. The 'I' of the poem and Albert are joined by their enclosure in knowingness.

Lawrence was able to offer this double experience in many forms. In *Women in Love* he parodies his own distrust of self-consciousness, through the character of Hermione Roddice. In Chapter 3, 'Class-Room', Hermione preaches a crude version of Lawrence's doctrine of spontaneity, instinct, and relaxation of will. Just as he used light social comedy to link Albert's defence of self-consciousness with his distortion by self-consciousness, he uses aggressive irony to dramatise the clash between Hermione's self-consciousness and her doctrine of spontaneity. Her taut, convulsed behaviour of body and voice as she preaches animality dramatises her difficulty of rejecting self, and allows Lawrence to damn her as his conveniently false prophet:

> Then, pulling herself together with a convulsed movement, Hermione resumed, in a sing-song, casual voice.
> 'But leaving me apart, Rupert; do you think the children are better, richer, happier, for all this knowledge; do you really think they are? Or is it better to leave them untouched, spontaneous. Hadn't they better be animals, simple animals, crude, violent, *anything*, rather than this self-consciousness, this incapacity to be spontaneous.'
> They thought she had finished. But with a queer rumbling in her throat she resumed, 'Hadn't they better be anything than grow up crippled, crippled in their souls, crippled in their feelings – so thrown back – so turned back on themselves – incapable——' Hermione clenched her fist like one in a trance – 'of any spontaneous action, always deliberate, always burdened with choice, never carried away.'

Again they thought she had finished. But just as he was going to reply, she resumed her queer rhapsody – 'never carried away, out of themselves, always conscious, always self-conscious, always aware of themselves. Isn't *anything* better than this? Better be animals, mere animals with no mind at all, than this, this *nothingness*——'

'But do you think it is knowledge that makes us unliving and self-conscious?' he asked irritably.

She opened her eyes and looked at him slowly.

'Yes,' she said. She paused, watching him all the while, her eyes vague. Then she wiped her fingers across her brow, with a vague weariness. It irritated him bitterly. 'It is the mind,' she said, 'and that is death.' She raised her eyes slowly to him: 'Isn't the mind——' she said, with the convulsed movement of her body, 'isn't it our death? Doesn't it destroy all our spontaneity, all our instincts? Are not the young people growing up to-day, really dead before they have a chance to live?'

'Not because they have too much mind, but too little,' he said brutally.

'Are you *sure*?' she cried. 'It seems to me the reverse. They are over-conscious, burdened to death with consciousness.'

'Imprisoned within a limited, false set of concepts,' he cried.

But she took no notice of this, only went on with her own rhapsodic interrogation.[5]

Aggression is essential to Lawrence's art, and to his criticism. In his essay 'Surgery for the Novel or a Bomb' his judgement is vituperative, flippant and unfair as he attacks his contemporaries:

> It is self-consciousness picked into such fine bits that the bits are most of them invisible, and you have to go by smell. Through thousands and thousands of pages Mr Joyce and Miss Richardson tear themselves to pieces, strip their smallest emotions to the finest threads, till you feel you are sewed inside a wool mattress that is being slowly shaken up, and you are turning to wool along with the rest of the woolliness.[6]

He insists again and again that 'the serious novel' creates characters obsessed with self:

> And there's the serious novel: senile–precocious. Absorbedly,

childishly concerned with *what I am*. 'I am this, I am that, I am
the other. My reactions are such, and such, and such. And, oh
Lord, if I liked to watch myself closely enough, if I liked to
analyse my feelings minutely, as I unbutton my gloves, instead
of saying crudely I unbuttoned them, then I could go on to a
million pages instead of a thousand. In fact, the more I come to
think of it, it is gross, it is uncivilized bluntly to say: I unbuttoned
my gloves. After all, the absorbing adventure of it! Which button
did I begin with? etc.'[7]

The attack is cheap, as he trivialises the presentation of self
conscious emotion and action by inventing the example of unbut
toning gloves which has no real relevance to Joyce, Dorothy
Richardson or Proust. He is particularly unfair to Joyce, who
certainly develops a more schematic form than Lawrence, but is
less interested in the process of obsessed self-questioning than
with his own version of a quest for relationship and a departure
from self. His embodiment of defects of love and loneliness is
located in a more urban environment than Lawrence's; his quests
and questions are usually metonymised through a small social
community, while Lawrence extends his explorations to the non
human world. But the critical treatment of a paralysing linguistic
abstraction is crucial in both novelists. For example, Joyce questions
and shies away from 'the word known to all men', namely 'love'
in a way Lawrence should have found congenial.

In spite of such attacks on obsessive selfhood, there is one form
of self-consciousness Lawrentian texts cannot escape. Lawrence
opened and eroded conventional forms of art, furiously revising
to touch the here-and-now, but every artist forming and fixing a
language is necessarily aware of art's processes. Lawrence shows
his awareness of the traditions he rejects, adapts and assimilates.
For example, he often looks back to earlier narrative conventions
like the form of direct narrative address. He is not the only modern
novelist to play with this old form: when E. M. Forster in *A Passage
to India* insists on the dark as well as the luminous vision, he
addresses his reader directly, 'wait till you get one, dear reader!';
when Beckett, in *Murphy*, diverts and shames the reader as 'gentle
skimmer',[9] he encourages concentration and makes us amusedly
aware of the novelist's awareness. These two apostrophes are
innovative returns to an older tradition, compounding self-con

sciousness as they address the reader with an ironic air of quotation and a reminder of companionable genre-membership. Instead of being part of a narrative pattern like the Victorian address in Thackeray and George Eliot, these modern pastiches are exceptional, surprising and anachronistic, and in Lawrence's *Mr Noon*, where the device is most sustained, they often try the reader's patience and humour. Address takes the form of a rough and rude treatment of the reader, a form of flouting parody. It is also a rough and rude treatment of the work of art, tearing the fabric of the fiction in a way more violent and thorough-going than in his other novels. In *Mr Noon* authorial address is more sustained and lengthy than in *Vanity Fair* or *The Mill on the Floss*, though it is possible that if Lawrence had revised he might have condensed it. It not only swamps particularised narrative and dialogue, but is indulgently repetitive and jokey:

Since the spoon is one of the essential mysteries of modern love, particularly English modern love, let us clasp our hands before its grail-like effulgence. For although all readers belonging to the upper classes; and what reader *doesn't* belong to the upper classes; will deny any acquaintance with any spoon but the metallic object, we regret to have to implicate the whole of the English race, from princes downwards, in the mystic business.

Dear reader, have we not all left off believing in positive evil? And therefore is it not true that the seducer, invaluable to fiction, is dead? The seducer and the innocent maid are no more. We live in better days.

There are only spooners now, a worldful of spoons. Those wicked young society people, those fast young aristocrats, ah, how soft as butter their souls are really, tender as melted butter their sinfulness, in our improved age. Don't talk of lust, it isn't fair. How can such creamy feelings be lustful! And those Oxfordly young men with their chorus girls – ah God, how wistful their hearts and pure their faces, really! – not to speak of their minds. Then look at young colliers and factory lasses, they fairly reek with proper sentiment.

It doesn't matter what you do – only how you do it. – Isn't that the sincerest of modern maxims? – And don't we all do it nicely and *con molto espressione*? You know we do. So little grossness nowadays, and so much dear reciprocal old-beaniness!

How can there be any real wrong in it? Old wives tales! There i
no wrong in it. We are all so perfectly sweet about it all, and o1
such a sympathetic plane.

Why bother about spades being spades any more? It isn't the
point. Adam no more delves than Eve spins, in our day. Nou
avons changé tout cela. Call a spoon a spoon if you like. Bu
don't drag in garden implements. It's almost as bad as the Greek
with their horrid plough metaphor.

Ah, dear reader, you don't need me to tell you how to sip
love with a spoon, to get the juice out of it. You know wel
enough. But you will be obliged to me, I am sure, if I pull dow1
that weary old scarecrow of a dark designing seducer, and the
alpaca bogey of lust. There is no harm in us any more, is there
now? Our ways are so improved: so spiritualised, really. Wha
harm is there in a bit of a spoon?[10]

– We have risen to great heights, dear reader, and sunk to
great depths. Yet we have hardly fathomed the heights and
depths of the spoon in the Co-op. entry. Don't you wish you
were as good at it as Noon and Emmie? Practise then: and you
too may swing suspended in the heights, or depths, of infinity
like the popular picture we used to see over the railway
bookstalls, winged spooners mid-heaven in the blue ether. Ah
we are all so clean, nowadays: fine clean young men, infinitely
spoony, and clean young spoony maidens to match. Nothing
earthy, not we. All in mid-air, our goings on.[11]

These arch addresses frame a remarkable representation of erotic
sensation, comparable to the finest passages in *The Rainbow*. The
modulation can't be said to be smooth nor is the abrupt shif
functional, but in *Aaron's Rod* the address is reduced and subtly
assimilated. Lawrence's portraits of the artist are usually differen
from the portraits of the artist in Joyce and Virginia Woolf. Stephe1
Dedalus and Lily Briscoe are elaborate and analytic images o
creativity and temperament, in a number of psychic and socia
aspects, whereas Lawrence's portraiture of the artist is scarcely
concerned at all with aesthetic problems and processes. The Aaro1
figure is deliberately differentiated from the novelist: his language
is the language of music. In Chapter 13, rather pretentiously called
'Wie es Ihnen gefällt', Aaron is put through the Lawrentia1

experience of discarding false selves. A sick self-consciousness is wittily dramatised and analysed:

> Thoughts something in this manner ran through Aaron's subconscious mind as he sat still in the strange house. He could not have fired it all off at any listener, as these pages are fired off at any chance reader. Nevertheless there it was, risen to half-consciousness in him. All his life he had *hated* knowing what he felt. He had wilfully, if not consciously, kept a gulf between his passional soul and his open mind. In his mind was pinned up a nice description of himself, and a description of Lottie, sort of authentic passports to be used in the conscious world. These authentic passports, self-describing: nose short, mouth normal, etc.; he had insisted that they should do all the duty of the man himself. This ready-made and very banal idea of himself as a really quite nice individual: eyes blue, nose short, mouth normal, chin normal: this he had insisted was really himself. It was his conscious mask.[12]

Aaron moves from the sense of self, to die a kind of death, in a characteristic image close to those affective definitions in 'New Heaven and Earth'. He feels that he is cracked and expelled from the shell of the preconceived idea, freed from conceptualised restraints:

> Having in some curious manner tumbled from the tree of modern knowledge, and cracked and rolled out from the shell of the preconceived idea of himself like some dark, night-lustrous chestnut from the green ostensibility of the burr, he lay as it were exposed but invisible on the floor, knowing, but making no conceptions: knowing, but having no idea.[13]

The narrative is then opened to a movement of extreme authorial self-consciousness which is completed by a direct recognition of the reader. The narrator makes an imperative request for the reader's participation, at the same time insisting on the difference between the medium of words and music's conscious and subconscious articulation. First comes the expulsion:

> Now that he was finally unmasked and exposed, the accepted

idea of himself cracked and rolled aside like a broken chestnut
burr, the mask split and shattered, he was at last quiet and
free.[14]

This is a rare moment in the novel, and for the novelist. It imagines
the assays of imagination, using the central fictitious character to
assert self-consciously what the novelist himself is doing so well
in words. The reader is addressed cheekily, aggressively and
instructively; the narrator distinguishes between genres:

> The inaudible music of his conscious soul conveyed his meaning
> in him quite as clearly as I convey it in words: probably much
> more clearly. But in his own mode only: and it was in his own
> mode only he realized what I must put into words. These words
> are my own affair. His mind was music.

> Don't grumble at me then, gentle reader, and swear at me that
> this damned fellow wasn't half clever enough to think all these
> smart things, and realize all these fine-drawn-out subtleties. You
> are quite right, he wasn't, yet it all resolved itself in him as I
> say, and it is for you to prove that it didn't.[15]

This assertion of authorial authority and teasing fictionality is smart
and arch but better assimilated to the novel's subject than the
strained non-stop jokiness of *Mr Noon*. A similar assimilation of
authorial address is found in *Kangaroo*, a novel which makes the
large loose baggy monsters of Thackeray's *The Newcomes* and
Tolstoy's *War and Peace* (as Henry James called them) look neat
and trim. *Kangaroo* is a novel which manipulates and juxtaposes
relaxed comedy and serious intensity. For example, in Chapter 14
called 'Bits', the narrator buttonholes us, 'I hope, dear reader, you
like plenty of *conversation* in a novel: it makes it so much lighter and
brisker'.[16] The next chapter, 'Jack slaps back', begins deprecatingly
'Chapter follows chapter, and nothing doing'.[17] T. S. Eliot accused
Lawrence of being no good at thinking, but Lawrence certainly
shows a considerable respect for thinking, and in *Kangaroo* repeatedly insists that the novel is not only 'a mere record of
emotion-adventures', but also 'a thought-adventure', in an explicit
justification of fractured narrative and discursive generalisation:

But man is a thought-adventurer, and his falls into the Charybdi of ointment, and his shipwrecks on the rock of ages, and his kisses across chasms, and his silhouette on a minaret: surely these are as thrilling as most things.[18]

awrence writes flippantly about what he is doing, at the moment f doing it, re-creating Thackeray's comic self-deprecations in a ew-toned style. After the long excursus into Richard Somers' ainful wartime experiences, we are returned to the conventional arrative of character and action. There has been an absence of arrative, a gap in the storyline, and Lawrence uses summary ithorial assertion for summary exposition and reminder:

So what's wrong with Richard's climbing a mental minaret or two in the interim? Of course there isn't any interim. But you *know* that Harriet is brushing her hair in the sun, and Kangaroo looking at huge sums of money on paper, and Jack fishing, and Vicky flirting, and Jaz bargaining, so what more do you want to know?[19]

he language is slapdash and casual:

We can't be at a stretch of tension *all* the time, like the E string on a fiddle. If you don't like the novel, don't read it. If the pudding doesn't please you, leave it. *I* don't mind your saucy plate. I know too well that you can bring an ass to water, etc.[20]

Assimilated self-consciousness helps to make his literary criticism riginal and startlingly alive. He is the most readable of critics ecause he writes his criticism with this dramatised and functional wareness not only of the interlocutor but also of the present oment. One of his apparently casual but intense pieces of critical lf-consciousness occurs in the essay 'Why the Novel Matters'. onsciousness of the physicality of composition creates a rare ent in critical language:

Why should I look at my hand, as it so cleverly writes these words, and decide that it is a mere nothing compared to the mind that directs it? Is there really any huge difference between my hand and my brain? Or my mind?

'hat begins as a rather forced and arch image becomes dynamic.

Language generates a sense of physical motion and moment. We
are brought in touch with touch:

> My hand is alive, it flickers with a life of its own. It meets all the
> strange universe in touch, and learns a vast number of things
> and knows a vast number of things. My hand, as it writes the
> words, slips gaily along, jumps like a grasshopper to dot an i,
> feels the table rather cold, gets a little bored if I write too long,
> has its own rudiments of thought, and is just as much *me* as
> my brain, my mind, or my soul. Why should I imagine that
> there is a *me* which is more *me* than my hand is? Since my hand
> is absolutely alive, me alive.

The critic uses narrative and developmental imagery to look with
increasing intimacy and closeness at the whole act of writing:

> Whereas, of course, as far as I am concerned, my pen isn't alive
> at all. My pen *isn't me* alive. Me alive ends at my finger-tips.

Once more there is that sense of limits, expressed, more intense
and urgently, in the discrimination between novelist and musician
in *Aaron's Rod*. Here it is followed by an amusingly discriminating
image of a bridge and barrier between the organic hand and the
inorganic pen, the finger-nails. The writing mind-and-body is alert
to nuance and scruple, and introduces this image of substance
which is less dead than a pen and less alive than skin:

> Whatever is me alive is me. Every tiny bit of my hands is alive,
> every little freckle and hair and fold of skin. And whatever is
> me alive is me. Only my finger-nails, those ten little weapons
> between me and an inanimate universe, they cross the mysterious
> Rubicon between me alive and things like my pen, which are
> not alive, in my own sense.[21]

In every sense, this brings us to the quick of fiction. The essay
goes on to assert that the novelist's imaginative work depends on
an awareness of bodily liveliness and the distinction between the
self and the other. This apt discourse is characteristic of Lawrence's
eccentrically vivid critical language, an address which puts the
reader in touch with the hand behind the text. It is self-aware in a
way reminiscent of that moment in 'The Fall of Hyperion' when

Keats floods narrative with a personal image of the writing moment, 'When that warm scribe, my hand, is in the grave'.[22] In Keats and Lawrence self-consciousness shocks the reader with the sense of personal physicality and mortality. Both texts have of course been changed by history, a once live self-consciousness transmuted with new poignancy because the artists who wrote these words about their flesh and blood are dead, as Keats though not Lawrence anticipated in his address.

Many of Lawrence's poems discuss and enact the assertion and loss of self-consciousness through the address to a reader. 'The Wild Common'[23] is a fascinating example of Lawrence's revisionary hand and a poem which constructs a departure from self-consciousness. It embodies a human embrace of the non-human phenomenal world, and the intuition of personal wholeness. These twinned imaginative experiences depend on losing the consciousness of self. The poem is a feeling-adventure and a thought-adventure, in Lawrence's language. Its central double conceit is the shadow and reflection which represent the object of which the subject mind is aware, that which we feel we are looking at when we are conscious of self. The experience of self-consciousness is first imaged in the reflection of the man in water:

What is this thing that I look down upon?
White on the water wimples my shadow, strains like a dog
    on a string, to run on.

How it looks back, like a white dog to its master!
I on the bank all substance, my shadow all shadow, looking up
    to me, looking back!
And the water runs, and runs faster, runs faster,
And the white dog dances and quivers, I am holding his
    cord quite slack.

Then it asserts humanist pride in identity:

But how splendid it is to be substance, here!
My shadow is neither here nor there; but I, I am royally
    here!
I am here! I am here! screams the peewit; the may-blobs
    burst out in a laugh as they hear!
Here! flick the rabbits. Here! pants the gorse. Here! say the
    insects far and near.

This image of reflection cannot last. It represents a sense of dualit which must be revised and rejected. Lawrence brilliantly imagine the experience of imprisoned reflection in which the mind is subjec looking at object, then subject looking at subject looking at object in a trap of oscillation and regress. He also imagines the escap from repeated reflection in reflexion. The poem constructs a releas of the subject, a story in which the human figure plunges into th water to join substance with shadow. Dualism is dissolved, wit substance and shadow:

> Over my skin in the sunshine, the warm, clinging air
> Flushed with the songs of seven larks singing at once, goes
>   kissing me glad.
> You are here! You are here! We have found you! Everywhere
> We sought you substantial, you touchstone of caresses, you
>   naked lad!

The poem also images, in a retarded action, the embrace of th human by the non-human phenomenal world. At the end of th action, both senses of division are resolved. The division withi self (duality of subject–object and substance–shadow) and th division in the phenomenal world (duality of human and noi human) is ended. At the end:

> Sun, but in substance, yellow water-blobs!
> Wings and feathers on the crying, mysterious ages, peewits
>   wheeling!
> All that is right, all that is good, all that is God takes
>   substance! A rabbit lobs
> In confirmation, I hear sevenfold lark-songs pealing.

In 'Peach'[24] Lawrence uses authorial impudence more didact cally but still subtly. The poem manages to create the reader of th poem within the poem, making and breaking poem-as-object an reader-as-receptor. It severs the autonomy of the poem an collapses the distance between poem and reader. It begins with wry address:

> Would you like to throw a stone at me?
> Here, take all that's left of my peach.

Then it modulates into its meditation:

> Blood-red, deep;
> Heaven knows how it came to pass.
> Somebody's pound of flesh rendered up.

Its digression is ironically self-conscious, but candidly admits a lack of sentimental feeling for nature first admired and then devoured. Admiring the peach didn't stop him eating it, and eating it doesn't stop him re-animating it in poetry for the purpose of contemplation. The peach is devoured by language in order to be presented in totality. Like Cézanne's apples, as savoured by Lawrence, it is eatable, paradigmatic, past and present:

> I am thinking, of course, of the peach before I ate it.

The poem concludes with another transition from meditation to authorial address:

> Why was not my peach round and finished like a billiard
>   ball?
> It would have been if man had made it.
> Though I've eaten it now.

> But it wasn't round and finished like a billiard ball.
> And because I say so, you would like to throw something at
>   me.

> Here, you can have my peach stone.

The stone is there too, in all its hardness. So is the reader, who is addressed and given an active part, as the 'you' is made identifiable with the reader of the text and with the participant in the implicit dispute and argument. The poem performs the tough feat of dramatising acute consciousness of the self and the other, its action assimilating trope to poem, and internal narration to the story of poet and reader. It is a triumph of openness, another instance of Lawrence's humorous intensity. It is a triumph of total comprehension, of poet, reader, genre, and subject.

Something similar takes place in a different medium, in two poems about tragedy, which are inter-connected as Lawrence's poems often are, generated by each other. One grows out of the other. The first poem, 'Tragedy',[25] is interesting chiefly as the matrix for the second. It dismisses tragic heroes, 'Lear and Macbeth and Hamlet and Timon', for caring too much for themselves, so failing to provoke response from the tragic victims of 'our material-mechanical civilisation', whose defeats are 'shabby' and 'little'. Out of this flat didacticism grows a real poem, 'After All the Tragedies are Over'.[26] In it literary reference is greatly reduced, 'a man can no longer feel heroic about being a Hamlet'. We move from art to life outside art. The withdrawal creates, once more, a space for unselfconsciousness, an acceptance of a natural diminution which looks forward to the passionate absences of his final 'Ship of Death' poems.

> When love is gone, and desire is dead, and tragedy has left
>   the heart
> then grief and pain go too, withdrawing
> from the heart and leaving strange cold stretches of sand.
>
> So a man no longer knows his own heart;
> he might say into the twilight: What is it?
> I am here, yet my heart is bare and utterly empty.
> I have passed from existence, I feel nothing any more.
> I am a nonentity.
>
> Yet, when the time has come to be nothing, how good it is to
>   be nothing!
> a waste expanse of nothing, like wide foreshores where not a
>   ripple is left . . .

In most of Lawrence's novels and poems self-consciousness is asserted in order to be eliminated, as part of a movement towards love, negative capability, apprehension of other existences. But there are some rare occasions when the poetry isolates the latter part, the loss of self and the savouring of otherness. It is possible to think of the stories of development, beginning with assertion and ending in loss, as metonymies or paradigms for Lawrence's work as a whole, which inclines towards an imaginative grasp of the world outside self. There are two kinds of poem where self-consciousness is successfully emptied out of the writing, the poetry which successfully imagines the non-human phenomenal world –

birds, beasts and flowers – and the very late poetry in which the poet is imagining oblivion and death.

Much of Lawrence's nature poetry is anthropomorphic, imagining peaches, pigs and pomegranates as things in themselves, but through images of human experience. I do not mean to suggest that this human projection constitutes artistic failure. It is hard to think of a better poem than 'Snake',[27] and in it Lawrence celebrates the dignity and separateness of the creature through metaphors like 'king' and 'lord' and 'underworld', drawn from political and religious concepts. In 'Bare Almond Trees',[28] the human element is further reduced. Despite technological imagery, as in 'Do you telephone the roar of the waters over the earth?' and 'iron implements', there is a sensuous and precise appraisal of the shape, texture, colours and individuality of the trees. The non-human phenomenon is summoned, through touch, sight, taste and apprehension of form:

> Wet almond-trees, in the rain,
> Like iron sticking grimly out of earth;
> Black almond trunks, in the rain,
> Like iron implements twisted, hideous, out of the earth,
> Out of the deep, soft fledge of Sicilian winter-green,
> Earth-grass uneatable,
> Almond trunks curving blackly, iron-dark, climbing the
> slopes.

Other poems which try to grasp non-human vitality include 'Almond Blossom', 'Sicilian Cyclamens' and 'Fish' which marvellously realise a change of element. 'Fish'[29] is especially vivid as a re-imagining of touch, motion and relationship, transforming its human signifiers to establish difference:

> Slowly to gape through the waters
> Alone with the element;
> To sink, and rise, and go to sleep with the waters;
> To speak endless inaudible wavelets into the wave;
> To breathe from the flood at the gills,
> Fish-blood slowly running next to the flood, extracting fish-
> fire;
> To have the element under one, like a lover;
> And to spring away with a curvetting click in the air,

Provocative.
Dropping back with a slap on the face of the flood.
And merging oneself!

To be a fish!

So utterly without misgiving
To be a fish
In the waters.

That punning pressure on 'misgiving' plays out twinned aspects of self-consciousness: the fish's freedom from self-doubt is fused with its freedom from false offerings and bestowals.

Most originally, Lawrence sheds self-consciousness to imagine the human sense of self 'sponged out, erased, cancelled', and 'made nothing' as he says in the poem 'Phoenix'.[30] His poems of dying are also poems of resurrection, but not of the human rebirth of the love-poems. Resurrection is sensed – if that is the word – as ineffable. In many of the death-poems, repeated images of diminution are touching, slimming down the self, 'the little, slender soul', 'the fragile soul', and 'small frail sail' and 'little ark' with 'little cakes'.[31] There are cadences of lapsing, wonderfully apt for this falling into anonymity: 'We are dying, we are dying, we are all of us dying' ('The Ship of Death').[32] (Lawrence can remake Shakespearean dying falls, perhaps recalling that *Antony and Cleopatra* uses the myth of disintegrated and remembered Osiris, which he used in *The Man Who Died*.) And there is the imagined relaxation, in image, syntax, and rhythmical ebb-and-flow, in 'After All Saints' Day', and 'Shadows'. 'Shadows' uses 'the shadow' without any connotation of dualism, and the companionable sense of the non-human world is made to imagine 'natural' darkening and silence:

And if, as autumn deepens and darkens
I feel the pain of falling leaves, and stems that break in
    storms
and trouble and dissolution and distress
and then the softness of deep shadows folding, folding
around my soul and spirit, around my lips
so sweet, like a swoon, or more like the drowse of a low, sad
    song

singing darker than the nightingale, on, on to the solstice
and the silence of short days, the silence of the year, the
    shadow,
then I shall know that my life is moving still
with the dark earth, and drenched
with the deep oblivion of earth's lapse and renewal.[33]

Such sloughings off are amongst Lawrence's unique apprehensions. They might well have not been embodied without his explorations of self-consciousness.

Notes

1. 'I wake and feel the fell of dark, not day', *The Poems of Gerard Manley Hopkins*, ed. W. H. Gardner and N. H. Mackenzie (London: Oxford University Press, 1967) p. 101.
2. *Complete Poems*, pp. 256–7.
3. D. H. Lawrence, *The Lost Girl* (Harmondsworth, Middx: Penguin, 1978) p. 93.
4. Ibid., pp. 91–2.
5. D. H. Lawrence, *Women in Love* (Harmondsworth, Middx: Penguin, 1965) pp. 44–5.
6. *Phoenix*, p. 518.
7. Ibid.
8. E. M. Forster, *A Passage to India*, ed. Oliver Stallybrass (Harmondsworth, Middx: Penguin, 1979) p. 213.
9. Samuel Beckett, *Murphy* (London: Picador, 1973) p. 51.
10. D. H. Lawrence, *Mr Noon*, ed. Lindeth Vasey (Cambridge: Cambridge University Press, 1984) p. 20.
11. Ibid., p. 23.
12. D. H. Lawrence, *Aaron's Rod* (Harmondsworth, Middx: Penguin, 1977) pp. 197–8.
13. Ibid., p. 198.
14. Ibid.
15. Ibid., p. 199.
16. D. H. Lawrence, *Kangaroo* (Harmondsworth, Middx: Penguin, 1950) p. 311.
17. Ibid., p. 312.
18. Ibid.
19. Ibid., p. 313.
20. Ibid.
21. *Phoenix*, p. 533.
22. 'The Fall of Hyperion', Canto 1, line 18, *The Poems of John Keats*, ed. Miriam Allott (London: Longman, 1970) p. 658.

23. *Complete Poems*, pp. 33–4.
24. Ibid., p. 279.
25. Ibid., p. 508.
26. Ibid., pp. 508–9.
27. Ibid., pp. 349–51.
28. Ibid., pp. 300–1.
29. Ibid., pp. 334–40.
30. Ibid., p. 728.
31. See 'The Ship of Death', ibid., pp. 716–20 and 'After All Saints' Day', ibid., p. 723.
32. Ibid., p. 718.
33. Ibid., p. 726.

4

The Fight for Barbara: Lawrence's Society Drama

IAN CLARKE

Lawrence's plays have often had a bad deal. Frequently they have been held to be of little intrinsic worth apart from any insights they may provide into Lawrence biography, or of little worth except for the extent to which they can be plundered for any thematic implications they have for Lawrence's fiction. The success of the three colliery plays, *A Collier's Friday Night*, *The Daughter-in-Law*, and *The Widowing of Mrs Holroyd*, on the English stage since the late nineteen-sixties has proved that they are not the closet dramas that Eric Bentley and Allardyce Nicoll would have us believe,[1] and that they can exist and work in a specifically theatrical context. In the case of the colliery plays, several scholars, notably Keith Sagar, Sylvia Sklar and Raymond Williams, have asserted the special worth and quality of the plays as plays in their own right.[2] In the case of *The Fight for Barbara*, written in 1912, that has not yet effectively been done. The play continues to labour under supposed severe disadvantages: firstly, that it is no good; secondly, that it is a straightforward and unformed autobiographical account of Lawrence's elopement to Italy with Frieda; and thirdly, that its writing was no more than a relaxation from the really serious business of writing novels, and, moreover, was no more than a sort of therapy for Lawrence. A few examples will suffice to give the temper of the general view:

> The play has the crude immediacy of something transferred too soon from the raw material of life, but as autobiography it is fascinating.

> As a form of relaxation [Lawrence] scribbled down a four-act comedy, *Fight for Barbara*, in the space of three days. The play has no literary value, but it has some interest for the biographer.

> This little comedy has slight value today, except for what biographical information it gives.

> The central situation is clearly that of the Lawrences at the time of writing . . . Lawrence may have found some therapy in writing the play . . . The play is rather slight.[3]

Admittedly these examples are taken from biographies and general surveys of Lawrence's work. But that is not without its own significance, for it is only there, not in the works of literary scholarship which establish the Lawrence canon, that *The Fight for Barbara* appears to deserve mention. It is also true that remarks in Lawrence's letters encourage the general view. In October 1912 he wrote to Edward Garnett: 'I've written the Comedy I send you by this post in the last three days, as a sort of interlude to Paul Morel . . . This comedy will amuse you fearfully – much of it is word for word true – it will interest you. I think it's good'; and Frieda added in the same letter, 'I hope you will like the play, it's all of it really lived, Ernst's very words and me'.[4] The subtext of remarks in the letters of this period and Lawrence's tone, in turn defensive, apologetic and assertive, must be accounted for by the tension between his real belief in the play and his relationship with Edward Garnett who, by virtue of the fact that he had had plays staged, could be considered a more experienced playwright. In a later letter Lawrence made a clear distinction between the quality of *The Fight for Barbara* and two comedies, *The Married Man* and *The Merry-go-Round*, written at roughly the same time – the latter two, unlike *The Fight for Barbara*, are, he admits, 'candidly impromptus' and need reworking.[5] Lawrence's belief in *The Fight for Barbara* never really faltered. Indeed, Lawrence's most forthright and oft-quoted statement of his belief in his own drama, which begins 'I believe that, just as an audience was found in Russia for Tchekhov, so an audience might be found in England for some of my stuff',[6] was occasioned by Garnett's return (and possibly accompanying criticism) of *The Fight for Barbara* and Lawrence's two other comedies.

Even so, the treatment of *The Fight for Barbara* in the small amount of work specifically devoted to Lawrence's drama is at times only a little more encouraging. Keith Sagar, in an early and influential essay on the plays, propounds what remains the general view:

> *The Fight for Barbara* is largely of biographical interest . . . It was
> no doubt of great therapeutic value to Lawrence to present the
> events of this painful period as comedy and amenable to
> resolution.[7]

Two scholars have, however, granted the play serious attention.
Sylvia Sklar, in *The Plays of D. H. Lawrence*, devotes a chapter to
The Fight for Barbara. Given the survey nature of her book, she
provides a perceptive but predominantly descriptive account of
the narrative thrust of the play. Susan Carlson Galenbeck, in her
essay 'A Stormy Apprenticeship: Lawrence's Three Comedies',
examines *The Fight for Barbara* in terms of the tradition of the
comedy of manners extending back to the seventeenth century.[8]
Both writers encounter a difficulty which undervalues the strengths
of their discussion when they deem it necessary to admit what
they perceive to be the quality of the play. Sklar resigns herself to
admitting her opinion of the play, referring to it as 'so slight a
piece as this'; and Galenbeck is in a sense more equivocal. 'No one
contends', she asserts, 'that the comedies are great. Or good.'[9] Is
the conclusion then that they are bad?

The problem is that just as the approach which sees *The Fight for
Barbara* as raw and undiluted autobiography, or as a relaxation, or
as therapy fails to do justice to the true nature and significance
of the play, so does a critical approach which invokes certain
conventional standards of literary value. It is my contention that
the play is best understood by a different approach, by a historically
limited contextualisation within the theatrical opportunities and
the modes of dramatic writing available in the late Victorian and
Edwardian period.[10]

The appropriate late Victorian and Edwardian theatrical and
dramatic context for *The Fight for Barbara* does not reside, as one
might imagine, within the structure of the minority theatre and
the works of Shaw, Galsworthy, Granville-Barker, the regional
drama of the Manchester school and the like. It resides, I believe,
in the commercial theatre, the hegemony of the late Victorian and
Edwardian theatrical organisation, and the body of dramatic writing
known as the society drama which had as its most accomplished
practitioners Henry Arthur Jones and Arthur Wing Pinero. This
was a drama which dealt almost exclusively with upper middle-
class life and which purported to deal seriously and compassion-
ately with the social and moral problems of modern life. For

reasons that will become apparent I wish to examine in detail Pinero's play *The Notorious Mrs Ebbsmith* of 1895. Despite the seventeen year gap between Pinero's play and Lawrence's, *The Notorious Mrs Ebbsmith* is in most of its essential features typical of the society drama, a drama which remained the dominant mode of the serious drama of modern life from the early eighteen-nineties until the outbreak of the First World War. Lawrence's play of 1912 exists securely in this historical context.

Consider Bernard Shaw's analysis of the treatment of relations between the sexes in the society drama:

> A woman has, on some past occasion, been brought into conflict with the law which regulates the relations of the sexes. A man, by falling in love with her, or marrying her, is brought into conflict with the social convention which discountenances the woman. Now the conflicts of individuals with law and convention can be dramatized like all other human conflicts; but they are purely judicial; and the fact that we are much more curious about the suppressed relations between the man and the woman than about the relations between both and our courts of law and private juries of matrons, produces that sensation of evasion, of dissatisfaction, of fundamental irrelevance, of shallowness, of useless disagreeableness, of total failure to edify and partial failure to interest, which is as familiar to you in the theatres as it was to me when I, too, frequented those uncomfortable buildings.[11]

There is a certain amount of Shavian overstatement and oversimplification here and, unfortunately, whilst his account is generally true of many society dramas, the precise details do not exactly fit either *The Notorious Mrs Ebbsmith* or *The Fight for Barbara*. Nevertheless, the general implication of his statement does. That is, that the society drama concerns itself with a situation involving a relationship between a man and a woman which runs counter to the dominant codes of social and moral behaviour, and that the central interest of the play lies not so much in the relationship between the two of them as in their conflict with the embodiment of those social and moral codes in terms of the legal system of divorce courts, and the pressure exerted by family, peers, ministers of religion and busybodies. The emphasis thus is social more than personal.

Consider the outline of the plot of *The Notorious Mrs Ebbsmith*. A man has deserted his wife and is attempting to establish a way of living in a common-law partnership with another woman. Much of the play is concerned with visitations from members of the man's socially highly-placed family who attempt to persuade him to return to his wife, duty and respectability, and the action shows the couple's struggle to stay together in the face of this pressure.

Consider the outline of the plot of *The Fight for Barbara*. A woman has deserted her husband, and is attempting to establish a way of living in a common-law partnership with another man. Much of the play is concerned with visitations from members of the woman's socially highly-placed family who attempt to persuade her to return to her husband, duty and respectability, and the action shows the couple's struggle to stay together in the face of this pressure.

There are several other quite remarkable minor similarities. Both plays are set in Italy.[12] In both plays there are scenes containing comic exchanges between the principals and local servants and tradespeople as they attempt to negotiate the difficulties of speaking in foreign languages. In both plays the woman's wearing of a glamorous and expensive gown is used as an indicator of her allegiances within the sets of relationships. In both plays there is a critique of the hypocritical and dubious sexual behaviour of the aristocracy. And in both plays there is a climactic scene where, in conventional moral terminology, the offended spouse has an interview with either the offending spouse or the sexual and moral interloper. Such similarities are, I am sure, incidental. I have no reason to believe that Lawrence actually knew *The Notorious Mrs Ebbsmith*, but it is beyond doubt the case that the years that Lawrence spent in Croydon gave him opportunity to acquire a familiarity with the standard offerings of the London commercial theatre. The point about any similarities between the two plays, either in terms of basic plot or incidental feature, lies in the very different ways they are treated, mediated and ultimately resolved. My contention will be that, whilst Pinero's play accords very closely to the implications of Shaw's formula, Lawrence's is very much the sort of play Shaw seems to be asking for.

The initial situation of *The Notorious Mrs Ebbsmith* is that, before the play begins, Agnes Ebbsmith, widowed and thus released from an insufferable marriage, has espoused socialist and feminist ideals. After a failed career as street-corner agitator and then as nurse she has set up house with Lucas Cleeve, a rising politician who has run away from an unhappy marriage. At this point the play opens, and they intend to put into practical achievement her feminist ideals by propagating to the world radical theoretical reassessments of relations between the sexes and virulent attacks on the institution of marriage by the writing of works that, we are told, 'bristle with truth',[13] and by organising the way they live their lives together in accordance with such ideals. In this way Pinero immediately sets up a system of definition for the relationship, the emphasis of which effectively deflects concern for the individuals as individuals, for the relationship is defined and mediated in terms of a consciously and overtly formulated ideological position of strands of eighteen-nineties feminist thought, or, perhaps more accurately, Pinero's understanding of that thought. Furthermore, and this is crucial to the way this play resolves itself, like so many other society dramas, the relationship is further defined not just by the assertion of a feminist position but by the late nineteenth-century ideological and social formations which that position challenges – the dominant orthodoxies embodied in the legal system of marriage, divorce and property laws, and as embodied in conventional moral and social expectations, codes of behaviour and prejudice. Indeed, most of the dramatic focus of the first act is centred on the social effects of this morally irregular liaison in terms of social relationships external to the couple themselves, that is in terms of the response of Cleeve's peer group and polite society. The departure from the conventional code of conduct demands their exclusion and ostracism from polite society; their relationship, but more specifically Agnes, represents a dangerous contagion. This is made quite clear when Amos Winterfield, a clergyman, and his sister, Gertrude, who have formed a friendship with Cleeve and Agnes believing them to be married, learn the truth of the situation and immediately feel they have no option but to sever all relations. All four of them are apprised of what is presented as the absolute stricture of society's regulations. This constitutes the climactic incident of the first act and is indicative of where the real dramatic focus lies. The emphasis, and the issue is one of emphasis, is not so much on the couple themselves as on the relationship and attitude of others to them, and, more specifically, on how social response will affect Cleeve's position in society and his career – he is described as *'the* Coming Man' (*NME* 47) in politics. A batch of letters he receives remonstrating against his wayward behaviour indicates where the society drama's central interest in the effects

f this sort of relationship lies; Cleeve supplies both Agnes and
he audience with appropriate extracts:

> Lord Warminster – my godfather: 'My dear boy, for God's
> sake——!' [*Tearing up the letter and reading another.*] Sir Charles
> Littlecote: 'Your brilliant future . . . blasted . . .' [*Another letter.*]
> Lord Froom: 'Promise of a useful political career unfulfilled . . .
> cannot an old friend . . . ?' [*Another letter.*] Edith Heytesbury. I
> didn't notice a woman had honoured me. [*In an undertone.*]
> Edie ——! [*Slipping the letter into his pocket and opening another.*] Jack
> Brophy: 'Your great career——' Major Leete: 'Your career——'
> [*Destroying the rest of the letters without reading them.*] My career!
> my career! That's the chorus, evidently.   (*NME* 46)

osition and career will both be ruined. Society drama *is* predomi-
antly concerned, as Shaw suggests, with social conflict and its
esults.

The inherent sexism of society drama means that Pinero is only
eally interested in the social effect on Cleeve for Agnes only has a
ocial position in relation to him. The double standard of morality,
vhich the society drama does not merely reflect but endorses,
neans that her identity, far more than Cleeve's, is defined by her
noral standing. This definition is ultimately more important than
ny identity arising from her feminism. Furthermore, Pinero's
resentation of Agnes and her feminism is determined not so
nuch by actual late Victorian feminist thinking but by what is in
ssence a literary construct – the figure of the New Woman.
'inero's audiences would almost certainly have been familiar with
is treatment, not so much perhaps by direct contact with the New
Voman fiction of the eighteen-nineties or the recent appearance
f Nora Helmer on the English stage,[14] but from the satire and
ravesty of the figure in the traditionalist and popular press. No
natter how fair Pinero believes he is being to Agnes and her views,
he must be nervous, somewhat mannish, doctrinaire, humourless,
he must ultimately fail in her ideals, and, above all, she must be
s Pinero describes her in the stage directions: '*Her dress is plain to
te verge of coarseness; her face, which has little colour, is at the first
lance almost wholly unattractive*' (*NME* 14).

When these three features coincide – the ideological overlay
nposed upon the relationship, the concern with the social response
) and social effect of the relationship, and, lastly, the satirical

insinuations of the traditionalist typology of the New Woman :
the result is the pattern of society drama that Shaw noted. N<
matter how much Pinero centres attention on the emotional an<
psychological mismatch of Agnes and Cleeve as the cause of th<
failure of the relationship, that is subsidiary to and even a functio:
of the examination of the failure of the relationship in terms c
questions of social and ideological implication. Questions like
'Can the laws which govern marriage and the regulations whic.
govern sexual relationships effectively be set at nought?'; or, 'Ca.
Mrs Ebbsmith's feminist ideals really work in practice?' Th<
resolution of the play indicates with some approval that the answe
to both these questions is 'No'. And thus the play as a whole i
instrumental in endorsing the dominant ideology which gives th<
same answer to those questions. The review in *The Times* recognise
and implicitly applauded Pinero's overall strategy:

> *The Notorious Mrs Ebbsmith* is a painful but, on the whole,
> deeply absorbing play, which, under an unpromising exterio:
> inculcates the highest morality.[15]

The Fight for Barbara starts from a similar basic situation: Barba:
has left her husband and is trying to establish a relationship wit
Jimmy Wesson; in its course the play raises issues of unequivoc<
feminist implication. Barbara, like Agnes, is deeply distrustful <
the binding state of marriage, yet the way the issues are mediate
and the experience that is created are vastly different. Consid<
some statements of Barbara:

> *I* want there to be *no* upper hand. I only want both of us to t
> free to be ourselves – and you seem as if you *can't* have it – yo
> want to bully me, you want to bully me inside.

> Your idea of marriage is like the old savages: hit a woman c
> the head and run off with her.

> All men are alike. They don't care what a woman wants. The
> try to get hold of what they want themselves, as if it were
> pipe. As for the woman, she's not considered – and so – that
> where you make your mistake, gentlemen.[16]

Issues such as assertiveness, power, control, dominance, submi

sion, dependence, independence, ownership, freedom are continually brought up throughout the play and discussed between Barbara
and Wesson. But, unlike *The Notorious Mrs Ebbsmith*, they do not
have the initial overlay of a consciously formulated feminist
ideology, nor do they, in the way that they are presented, despite
their implications, constitute a self-conscious ideological position.
The point is that such issues are mediated as constituting the
emotional and psychological needs of these particular individuals
trying to establish a pattern for living together, trying to establish
identities for themselves in relation to each other in a relatively
new situation where the guidelines are ill-defined.

In the instance of Barbara's attacks on Jimmy, the son of a
coalminer, for his cringing and lack of assertiveness before her
mother and father, members of the minor aristocracy, the dramatic
definition does not reside, as it would in the work of a dramatist
like Galsworthy, in a perception of the vertical class stratification
of Edwardian Britain. Despite Lawrence's extremely acute and
creative use of class-consciousness in his fiction and colliery plays,
the class issue here, although present, is secondary. What is really
at issue is what Barbara needs from this man in their relationship.
In this way the emphasis and central dramatic focus is considerably
different from society drama. Lawrence avoids the deflections
inherent in ordering the material in terms of ideological positions
or literary typology as found in *The Notorious Mrs Ebbsmith*. The
nexus of social effect and social response to an irregular relationship
which is primary in society drama becomes secondary in *The Fight
for Barbara*.

Lawrence is far from being unconcerned with the social ramifications of the relationship between Wesson and Barbara. In those
scenes where they confront the minor characters, her parents and
husband, this is precisely what the major concern becomes, and it
is in the definition of these characters that Lawrence comes closest
to the primary system of definition of the society drama. Modern
critics have found these characters the most difficult with which
to come to terms, and have had recourse to literary criticism's
vocabulary of deprecation, viewing them, especially Barbara's
father, Sir William, and husband, Frederic, as melodramatic,
caricatured, buffoonish or clichéd. Their presentation is explained
by suggesting that Lawrence is attempting parody or satire. This,
I believe, is wrong, and arises from a misunderstanding of the
ways in which Lawrence is drawing positively from a set of

conventions which, from the eighteen-nineties to the outbreak of the First World War, were for contemporary audiences a valid formulation of how they wanted to perceive their society and how it could be constructed in dramatic form. What might have perhaps intrigued, or possibly bemused, an Edwardian audience is Lawrence's adaptation of familiar conventions.

The overt aim of these characters in *The Fight for Barbara* is to restore Barbara to her husband and social respectability; but significant shifts away from the notion of obligation to social codes which lies at the heart of society drama, towards a more privatised sense of familial and marital ties are made in the specific sorts of emotional pressure brought to bear by the tactics of both Frederic and Barbara's mother. A marked difference of emphasis can be detected in the comparable scenes of the interviews between Sybil Cleeve and Agnes Ebbsmith and Frederic and Barbara. Sybil's response to the liaison between Agnes and her husband demonstrates little emotional involvement; there are, befitting a notion of upper middle-class decorum, to be no potentially embarrassing emotional outbursts or effusions, and she is able to discuss the matter largely in terms of social effect and response, reputation and appearance; above all she is concerned predominantly, as in the play as a whole, with Cleeve's career. If Frederic, in comparison, appears embarrassing and ridiculous it is because he is incapable of maintaining a similar emotional detachment, and finds himself in the humiliating and ignoble position of begging his wife to return to him. His petulance, anger, wounded pride, his sense of Barbara's ingratitude, the jealousy he exhibits, even the threat of suicide he makes, are evidence of a response to the situation of a person who is deeply hurt on a level of personal emotion. Significantly, it is on that level that he strikes a respondent note in Barbara herself, who still feels a powerful emotional commitment, affiliation and attachment to him. This most serious threat to the relationship of the two lovers arises from very different sources from the threats in *The Notorious Mrs Ebbsmith*.

Lawrence is at his closest, and yet most clearly demonstrates his aversion, to central features of society drama in his treatment of Sir William, who makes the most baldly explicit statement of the purely social implications of the relationship between Wesson and Barbara:

SIR WILLIAM: It destroys the whole family system, and strikes at the whole of society. A man who does it is as much a criminal as a thief, a burglar, or even a murderer. You see my point?

WESSON: Your point of view.

SIR WILLIAM: You see so much. Then you see what you are doing: a criminal act against the State, against the rights of man altogether, against Dr Tressider, and against my daughter.

(*FFB* 299)

His tone of hard-line moralising is exclusively supportive, not of religious or moral positions, but of those social and civic codes which the relationship challenges. His bullish, authoritarian bullying makes him an unattractive character, but it is only in this that he differs from many a *raisonneur* figure in the society drama and the message that is implicitly embodied by their arguments. The analogous figure in *The Notorious Mrs Ebbsmith* is Cleeve's uncle, the Duke of St Olpherts. Both have somewhat dubious sexual pasts but, whereas Sir William's validity as a critic of the relationship between Wesson and Barbara is severely undercut by this, the Duke is presented as a rather attractive and likeable old roué. The aim and point of view of the two men is the same – the desirability of the restoration of the various parties to a pattern that conforms to the conventional guidelines which regulate marital relationships even down to the acceptability, if not advocacy, of affairs between married men and *unmarried* women within that pattern. But, whilst the brusque hectoring of Sir William coupled with his sexual misdemeanours reveals a fundamental hollowness in his position, it is precisely because of the Duke's sexual past that a certain tone is created which makes him such an effective character. What Sir William lacks is St Olpherts' urbanity, sophistication and occasional sub-Wildean wit. The latter's tone is one of unruffled, detached insouciance; his attitudes purport to be experientially rather than overtly ideologically based, and are pragmatic, slightly cynical and worldly-wise. This gives St Olpherts an incalculable advantage over Sir William as it means that he can support conventional codes of behaviour without the slightest hint of appearing to be uncomfortably and unattractively idealistic or moralistic. The style, essential to the success of society drama, is possibly at its most finely honed in the counsel given to the married Lady Jessica Nepean and Ned Falkner, who are considering decamping together, by Sir Christopher Deering in Jones's *The Liars* of 1897:

> Now! I've nothing to say in the abstract against running away with another man's wife! There may be planets where it is not only the highest ideal morality, but where it has the further advantage of being a practical way of carrying on society. But it has this one fatal defect in our country today – it won't work! You know what we English are, Ned. We're not a bit better than our neighbours, but, thank God! we do pretend we are, and we do make it hot for anybody who disturbs that holy pretence. And take my word for it, my dear Lady Jessica, my dear Ned, it won't work. You know it's not an original experiment you're making. It has been tried before. Have you ever known it to be successful?[17]

The indulgence of both Deering and St Olpherts in an apparently cynical defence of the hypocrisy of society's facades which launder the truth of its dirty linen is sufficient just to mildly shock, not to seriously undermine, the audience's view of the cherished orthodoxies of late Victorian England. But what is even more important for the ideological structuring of the drama is the way in which the view of how people and society work held by characters like Deering and St Olpherts is ultimately proved right by the action of the plays. St Olpherts refuses to take Agnes Ebbsmith's socialist and feminist ideals seriously; his amused tolerance, typical in itself of a traditionalist strategy of disarming late Victorian feminism, not only denies the validity or practical viability of her views but removes any threat they may represent to dominant ideological or cultural codes. His knowledge that her beliefs cannot work is proved right by the action of the play as is his perception of Cleeve's character which renders him psychologically incapable of living a life of feminist idealism. Furthermore, roué that he is, the Duke insists on seeing Agnes, not as feminist, but as sex object and that is precisely how *she* sees herself well before the end of the play. St Olpherts can afford to be assured and nonchalant for, with Pinero on his side, his views are never seriously in doubt; nor is the eventual outcome which will endorse those views. The drama is structured to that end. Such roles within the hierarchical structuring of the Victorian and Edwardian theatre were ideally suited to the actor-manager. For in such parts –

Charles Wyndham as Deering, John Hare as St Olpherts – he could, in the figures he represented on stage, be instrumental in endorsing dominant ideological codes, which befitted his position in the theatrical organisation, and at the same time retain the attractiveness to his audiences demanded by his star status. Some idea of the congruity between the style and tone created by certain actor-managers and the opportunities afforded by such parts is indicated by the fact that in two extremely hostile notices of *The Notorious Mrs Ebbsmith* written by Shaw for the *Saturday Review* just about the only thing he could find to praise was the excellence of John Hare as St Olpherts.

Because of, rather than despite, an essential similarity between Sir William and such figures in the society drama, Lawrence's treatment of Sir William constitutes a radical reversion of expected convention. His lack of success in reuniting the estranged marital partners subverts the expected ideological structure of society drama, and his unattractive presentation contravenes established expectations of the actor-manager's image within the theatre as a whole. Lawrence further subverts expectations of the hierarchical structure of the commercial theatre by the extremely limited amount of space he allows Sir William. Even given the verbosity of much Edwardian dramatic fare, an immoderate amount of time is given to figures like Deering and St Olpherts. Deering, for instance, after the passage quoted above continues almost uninterrupted for a further two pages enumerating the sorry fates of those who have tried the unoriginal experiment Falkner and Lady Jessica are contemplating. In the writing of such parts dramatists could highlight both the ideological position and the special talent which the actor-managers were so keen in presenting to their public. Lawrence simply does not provide an appropriate part for the actor-manager; his allowance to Sir William (a single scene of barely two pages in the whole of *The Fight for Barbara*) calls into question the validity of crucial features of society drama and the organisation of the commercial theatre which promoted it.

Lawrence's reworking of the emphases of the relationship between private and social experience is most profoundly manifested in the handling, in the two plays, of the issue of sex and sexuality. In society drama and *The Notorious Mrs Ebbsmith*, any real treatment of the issue is evaded. The gentlemanly and genteel tone and temper of the commercial theatre under the rule of the actor-managers precludes anything approaching frankness. Sex and relations between the sexes are presented in such a way as to render the subject deodorised and sanitised. The bedroom in *The Notorious Mrs Ebbsmith* is essentially a dressing-room, a room where the characters change their clothes in order to conform to the expectations of public social behaviour, and is therefore concomitant with the social definition which orders so much of the play. The bedroom in *The Fight for Barbara* is also, of course, a room where the characters change their clothes, but, more importantly, it is the room where they sleep, where they go to bed together. An emphasis on the central importance of physicality and sexuality in a relationship, which becomes a crucial issue in the play both in Barbara's marriage to her estranged husband and her relationship with Wesson, is stressed from the very opening in the initial visual images of Wesson and Barbara: '*Enter* WESSON, *in dressing-gown and pyjamas: a young man of about twenty-six, with thick hair ruffled from sleep*'; and Barbara – '*rather a fine young woman, holding her blue silk dressing-gown about her*' (FFB 273 and 274). Here is not the public side but the private and intimate side of their lives together, and it would, I fear, have been just a shade too indecorous and suggestive for the niceties and good taste of the commercial theatre and society drama.

The discussion of sexuality in *The Notorious Mrs Ebbsmith* is mediated initially in terms of Pinero's concept of Mrs Ebbsmith's feminism. There has been and still is, at the beginning of the play, a sexual relationship between Cleeve and Agnes. But it is part of her feminist idealism that she believes they would work much better for the cause if their relationship were, as she puts it, 'devoid of passion' (NME 51). This issue is mediated entirely through the rhetoric of her feminist principles and high idealism, and discussion of it therefore is subject to the formality of that ideological and intellectual ordering. In contrast, there is a much more genuine sense of Lawrence's lovers as lovers in all the senses of that word. The word games they indulge in, the playfulness, physical as well as verbal, the silliness, the pet names they use, all contribute to this effect. There is a sense of genuine delight and joy in their being together in this relationship which finds overt iteration at the end of the play:

BARBARA: Say I am a joy to you.

WESSON: You are a living joy to me, you are – especially this
       evening.

                                                    (FFB 319)

Some commentators seem to find the playfulness in the dialogue embarrassing. But, over and above whatever quality it has as dialogue, it serves a crucial function in the way Lawrence structures and orders his material. There is a huge gap between the register they employ in their love talk when they are on their own and the much more formal register used when they engage with their visitors, Barbara's parents and husband. The linguistic markers reinforce an essential aspect of the play – the disjunction between the world of the lovers as lovers and the social roles they are forced to negotiate in the face of the sorts of social and moral pressures brought to bear by Barbara's family. What is being asserted, partly through these linguistic features, is the possibility of some separateness in a sexual relationship, perhaps just for short moments, of the private and the social. The structure and ordering of society drama does not allow this, and ultimately cannot countenance it. There are, of course, shifts of register in *The Notorious Mrs Ebbsmith*, but the pervading style and tone of the play is that of the formality of varieties of middle-class social and ideological discourse. It is partly for this reason not easy – and that has a greater significance – to imagine Lucas Cleeve and Agnes Ebbsmith in bed together.

Pinero's depiction of Mrs Ebbsmith's ideals conveniently, as it turns out, avoids one important area of late Victorian feminist thought – the assertion of sexual freedom and fulfilment for women. When Agnes realises that Cleeve is not really the fellow-worker she thought he was but a weak-willed, egotistical sensualist, her only hope of keeping him is to enter into a conventional sexual relationship with him. This is represented, not as an assertion of a strand of feminist thought, but as a dismal failure of her ideals. It is presented as the re-assertion of her natural femininity, that she will love him, as she puts it, 'in the helpless, common way of women' (*NME* 75). Just as, in a sense, we always knew that she would, just as we knew her feminism could not really work. Pinero, in keeping with the insinuations of the traditionalist typology, very carefully infiltrates almost from the start of the play those cracks in both Cleeve and Agnes which prepare for the inevitability of failure. One typology is instantaneously exchanged for another literary typology. The image of the New Woman is replaced by the far more prevalent one of the fallen woman. This is why Pinero found it necessary to avoid the question of positive sexual fulfilment as a part of Agnes's feminist thinking; in this way she is, in the earlier part of the play at least, high-minded if extremely misguided, and therefore a certain sort of respect for her is retained. The final battle of the last act is not whether Agnes can keep Cleeve, nor whether their liaison can withstand social attacks, nor whether their feminist belief can be a practical way of living together; it becomes quite overtly the battle for the soul – that is the word that is used – of a fallen woman. The clergyman, Amos Winterfield, who, along with his sister, saves Agnes by the exercise of Christian charity, may bristle at the implicit insult when he is asked if he is the director of a home for penitent whores, but, in terms of the typological definition at the end of the play, that is exactly what his role is. A fitting conclusion is deemed to have been reached when Mrs Ebbsmith no longer believes that she is spearheading a movement of women's liberation, but accepts that she is a wanton seductress and espouses the Victorian female ethic of noble self-sacrifice by giving up Cleeve. And, at the end of the play, she intends to retire to live the life of religious contemplation and prayer in 'some dull hole in the North of England' (*NME* 11), suitably distant from any place where she might further contaminate any susceptible young man from the upper middle classes. In accordance with the double standard of morality, Lucas Cleeve can return to career, social position, and even, it is strongly hinted, not just the façade of marriage but a genuine reconciliation with his wife. The operative ethic that resolves the problem may be religious, that is Christian charity but the resolution is, in the exile of Agnes and the reinstatement of Cleeve, conveniently supportive of the dominant secular and social code. And that has been the ultimate purpose of the play. Any sympathy aroused by the plight of Mrs Ebbsmith is, like the double standard of morality itself, a hypocrisy. The play ends on an implicit note of relief at the certainty that this threat to the social fabric of the dominant class has been removed.

Through his own experience of theatre Lawrence perceived this very hypocrisy and attributed it to a distortion arising from the male hegemony of the structure of both the theatre as an institution and of the fiction of the plays themselves:

Why are the women so bad at playing this part in real life, this Ophelia–Gretchen role? Why are they so unwilling to go mad and die for our sakes? They do it regularly on the stage.

But perhaps, after all, we write the plays. What a villain I am what a black-browed, passionate, ruthless, masculine villain I am to the leading lady on the stage; and, on the other hand, dear heart, what a hero, what a fount of chivalrous generosity and faith! . . .

Dear heaven, how Adelaida [the leading lady at the theatre in Gargagno] wept, her voice plashing like violin music, at my ruthless, masculine cruelty. Dear heart, how she sighed to rest on my sheltering bosom! And how I enjoyed my dual nature! How I admired myself![18]

Lawrence's analysis of the ambivalence of the responses of condemnation and sympathy towards characters such as Agnes Ebbsmith is consonant with the strategy of society dramatists such as Pinero.

Given the patterning of society drama – that it is so organised, not to be merely reflective or expressive of, but actively instrumental in endorsing the dominant ideology – irregular sexual liaisons proved to be a fruitful area for dramatists such as Pinero and Jones. Such liaisons could be presented and eventually explained away as isolated romantic infatuations or sentimental aberrations; and it could further be asserted that the codes which regulate relations between the sexes are after all, like other aspects of the dominant ideology, the best way of organising society. Commentary within the course of the plays and their eventual resolutions prove this. Moreover, the feature noted by Shaw, that the relationship between the man and the woman is suppressed in favour of social and judicial conflicts, is surely an essential function of the patterning of society drama. For, if the relationship itself were investigated more deeply, it could well suggest that it has a seriousness, a validity, a power which could easily threaten or call into question the ideological formations the society dramatists were so adamant in endorsing.

The endorsement of the dominant social code lays the society drama as a whole open to Lawrence's criticism of 'the weakness of modern tragedy, where transgression against the social code is made to bring destruction, as though the social code worked our irrevocable fate'. What he saw as the implicit message of Hardy's novels – 'This is the theme of novel after novel, remain quite within the convention, and you are good, safe, and happy in the long run' – could, with more justification, have been made of the society drama. The emphasis of The Fight for Barbara refuses to make primary 'the greater idea of self-preservation, which is formulated

in the State, in the whole modelling of the Community' or th
idea, actively and positively endorsed by the society drama as
good thing, that 'in the long run, the State, the Community
the established form of life remained, intact and impregnable'.
Lawrence's linking of the concept of the 'State', the same link tha
is overtly articulated by Sir William, with the dominant code c
acceptable social and moral behaviour makes explicit the threat t
political formations which remains unstated in the advice not t
upset the apple cart of sexual relations given by such figures a
Sir Christopher Deering. Lawrence's critique of Thomas Hardy
begun some two years after the writing of *The Fight for Barbar*
demonstrates in many of its contentions a fundamental theoretic
aversion on Lawrence's part to structural, thematic and ideologic
features of the society drama. Lawrence, in his treatment of th
central characters of *The Fight for Barbara*, avoids invoking litera
typologies, moral posturing and the ideological implications c
the resolution of *The Notorious Mrs Ebbsmith*. Lawrence was n
concerned, needless to say, to endorse dominant social and mor
codes; the social ramifications are secondary not primary; th
private details of the relationship between Wesson and Barba
constitute the central dramatic issue and focus.

The formal structure of *The Notorious Mrs Ebbsmith* fully suppor
its ideological structure. Whilst Pinero does not employ some c
the more obvious tricks and turns of chance and coincidence, thos
contrivances of plot deriving from nineteenth-century Frenc
models of the well-made play, to engineer a satisfactory conclusic
such as can be found in his *The Second Mrs Tanqueray* or *His Hou*
in Order or Jones's *The Liars* or *Mrs Dane's Defence*, the effects I
strives for are nevertheless markedly and deliberately sensationa
At the end of Act Three, Winterfield offers Agnes a Bible as a wa
out of her troubles; the sensation of the ensuing action is mo
than adequately described by the *Times* reviewer:

> Mrs Ebbsmith, in a bitterly cynical speech which thrills th
> audience to their marrow, flouts the book in which she ha
> already sought comfort without finding it, and throws it into th
> fire. Instantly, however, she repents of her action, and, plungin
> her bare arm into the depths of the Italian stove, recovers th
> sacred volume and clasps it to her bosom as the act-dro
> descends. The effect upon the house can only be described a
> electrical.[20]

William Archer may have been right when he suggested that Pinero 'could not conceive a woman who had never dreamt of attributing to the Hebrew Scriptures any magical virtue',[21] but what the incident marks is the last stage in the strategy of the typological definitions – a move from brazen fallen woman to penitent fallen woman – which is essential to Pinero's resolution of the problem in the final act. The theatrical effectiveness resides entirely in the sensation, the 'electrical' effect of the potentially horrific thrill afforded the audience by this act of sacrilege in whose end Pinero does no more than exploit the technique of the pictorial tableau which had pointed those moments of high emotion and tension at the act-drops of melodrama for the previous seventy years.

Similarly, when Agnes finds Cleeve slipping away from her, she employs her feminine allurements to win him back and makes a stunning entrance having changed her dowdy, plain dress for a glamorous gown Cleeve has bought for her. Shaw was particularly unimpressed by:

> the great stage effect at the end of the second act, where Mrs Patrick Campbell enters with her plain and very becoming dress changed for a horrifying confection apparently made of Japanese bronze wall-paper with a bold pattern of stamped gold. . . . It was cut rather lower in the pectoral region than I expected; and it was, to my taste, appallingly ugly.[22]

In terms of the typological definition imposed upon Mrs Ebbsmith, the donning of the dress is a visual signifier of her move from New Woman to fallen woman and the audience is provided with the titillation and excitement of the spectacle of what amounts to a rather formalised sensuality. Elsewhere Shaw remarked of the late Victorian play that 'nice dresses' are 'indispensable'; and Granville-Barker satirically noted 'In the popular play . . . pretty ladies must parade in smart frocks, half a dozen at least, and as many more as the playwright could provide for and the management afford.'[23] Pinero caters for this predilection of late Victorian and Edwardian audiences, of which Lawrence, too, was fully aware. When he and Jessie Chambers saw *Making a Gentleman* by the second-wave society dramatist Alfred Sutro, he explained to Jessie that 'the theatre existed mainly in the interests of fashion, and that the leaders of Society came not for the play . . . but to observe the varied and beautiful dresses worn by the leading ladies'.[24] The implication of Barbara's wearing of an expensive dress in *The Fight for Barbara* avoids the titillation or the typological definition of the similar incident in *The Notorious Mrs Ebbsmith*, and is superficially far simpler and more pertinent: to which of these two men, Wesson or Frederic, does Barbara belong? Lawrence is quite clearly rejecting certain expectations and functions of sartorial elegance which were part of the standard fare of the commercial theatre.

In contrast, the act-endings of *The Fight for Barbara* are muted and deliberately avoid sensation. Moreover, the formal structure of the whole of Lawrence's play is so organised as to throw emphasis away from the social concern on to the couple themselves and their relationship. Unlike *The Notorious Mrs Ebbsmith*, where the act-endings are sensational and mark the successes or setbacks in the attempts from external sources to split up Agnes and Cleeve, in *The Fight for Barbara* the attacks from Barbara's relations occur and are dispensed with in the middle of the acts and the curtain lines throughout indicate Barbara and Wesson groping forward, tentatively and uncertainly, to work out their relationship with each other and the nature of their love for each other. The stage picture at the end of the play is not one of the success of Barbara's family in reuniting her and her husband but of the two lovers alone with no certainty but at least the possibility of making something of a relationship which social and moral codes condemn. Although decidedly meek in comparison to the sensational style of *The Notorious Mrs Ebbsmith*, the assertion of the validity of their relationship at the end of the play constitutes a real and radical revision and questioning of fundamental premises which lie at the heart of the dominant mode of late Victorian and Edwardian dramatic writing, and it is within the terms of that context that the true nature and significance of Lawrence's play can be best appreciated and understood.

Notes

1. See Eric Bentley, *The Playwright as Thinker*, rev. edn (New York: Meridian Books, 1955) p. 76; and Allardyce Nicoll, *English Drama, 1900–1930* (Cambridge: Cambridge University Press, 1973) p. 383.
2. Keith Sagar, 'D. H. Lawrence: Dramatist', *DHL Review*, IV (1971) pp. 154–82; Sylvia Sklar, *The Plays of D. H. Lawrence* (New York: Barnes and Noble, 1975); D. H. Lawrence, *Three Plays*, with an Introduction by Raymond Williams (Harmondsworth, Middx: Penguin, 1969).
3. Philip Callow, *Son and Lover* (London: Bodley Head, 1975) p. 212; Robert Lucas, *Frieda Lawrence* (London: Secker and Warburg, 1973) p. 93; Harry T. Moore, *The Priest of Love*, rev. edn (Harmondsworth, Middx: Penguin, 1976) p. 215; F. B. Pinion, *A D. H. Lawrence Companion* (London: Macmillan, 1978) p. 271.
4. 30 October 1912, *Letters*, I, pp. 466–7.
5. 19 November 1912, *Letters*, I, p. 477.
6. 1 February 1913, *Letters*, I, p. 509.
7. Sagar, 'D. H. Lawrence: Dramatist', p. 172.
8. Susan Carlson Galenbeck, 'A Stormy Apprenticeship: Lawrence's Three Comedies', *DHL Review*, XIV (1981) pp. 191–211.
9. Sklar, *Plays of DHL*, p. 176; Galenbeck, 'A Stormy Apprenticeship', p. 209.
10. Both Sklar and Galenbeck indicate in passing that *The Fight for Barbara* might fit into the sort of context I wish to examine, but neither follows through its implications.
11. George Bernard Shaw, 'Epistle Dedicatory' to *Man and Superman* in *The Bodley Head Bernard Shaw: Collected Plays with their Prefaces*, II (London: Bodley Head, 1971) pp. 496–7.
12. Although the setting of *The Fight for Barbara* might primarily be determined by autobiographical factors, it is a firmly established convention of society drama that such irregular liaisons must be conducted abroad. The setting of *The Fight for Barbara* would, I am sure, have been understood by an Edwardian audience in terms of that convention.
13. Arthur Wing Pinero, *The Notorious Mrs Ebbsmith* (London: William Heinemann, 1895) p. 64. Hereafter references to this edition will appear in the body of the text with the abbreviation *NME*.
14. *A Doll's House* was staged at the Novelty Theatre, London in 1889.
15. *The Times*, 14 March 1895, p. 10.
16. *The Complete Plays of DHL* (London: Heinemann, 1965) pp. 280, 281 and 314–15. Hereafter references to this edition will appear in the body of the text with the abbreviation *FFB*.
17. *The Liars*, Act IV in *Plays of Henry Arthur Jones*, ed. Russell Jackson (Cambridge: Cambridge University Press, 1982) p. 215.
18. D. H. Lawrence, *Twilight in Italy* (Harmondsworth, Middx: Penguin, 1960) p. 72. In the earlier version of the essays, published as 'Italian Studies', *English Review*, XV (1913) pp. 202–34, Lawrence's observations are directly related to his experience of the Edwardian commercial stage.

19. D. H. Lawrence, 'Study of Thomas Hardy', in *Study of Thomas Hard* *and other Essays*, ed. Bruce Steele (Cambridge: Cambridge Universi Press, 1985) p. 21.
20. *The Times*, 14 March 1895, p. 10.
21. William Archer, *The Old Drama and the New* (London: William Hein mann, 1923) p. 314.
22. George Bernard Shaw, 'Mr. Pinero's New Play', in *Dramatic Opinio* *and Essays with an Apology* (New York: Brentano's, 1922) I, pp. 45–6.
23. 'Preface' to *Three Plays for Puritans*, in *The Bodley Head Bernard Sha* II, p. 21; Harley Granville-Barker, 'The Coming of Ibsen', in *T Eighteen-Eighties*, ed. Walter de la Mare (Cambridge: Cambridge Ur versity Press, 1930) p. 166.
24. Jessie Chambers, *D. H. Lawrence: A Personal Record*, ed. J. D. Chamber 2nd edn (London: Cass, 1965) pp. 165–6.

5

In Search of the Dark God: Lawrence's Dualism

CHONG-WHA CHUNG

I

Lawrence was perhaps one of the most travelled writers of his time and possibly of all time. Not only did he move round in England; he made restless trips to Italy, Germany, Ceylon, Australia, New Mexico, Mexico, and then back to Europe. Even after his death he took a long journey (from France to New Mexico). However, he was not just an ordinary tourist. He was a pilgrim in search of 'the Truth', and what he sought and found he recorded in his poems, essays, novels, short stories and even in paintings. Lawrence in this sense is best understood in terms of his short and long journeys from country to country, from continent to continent.

What did he search for? What did he find in the process of his tireless travels? Did he ever succeed in unearthing 'the Truth' in 'the spirit of place'? In each different place he used different key words for the vision of his truth: the rainbow, the phoenix, the crown, the Holy Ghost, the Great Peace, the poppy, the dark god, the morning star, the forked flame, and many others like the Absolute, the infinite, or the Ultimate Whole. After Lawrence left his home town of Eastwood for Germany with his future wife in 1912, he was on the road, so to speak, always on the look out for the relevation of these symbols. Sometimes he saw the vision in England in the form of Rananim[1] or the crown, sometimes he saw the rainbow of new hope across the vast oceans, sometimes he saw the dark god in the Australian bush, and sometimes he saw the morning star in the Mexican skies; other times he felt the Holy Ghost, the forked flame, the Absolute or the infinite coiled inside the depths of the unconscious.

I assume that all these diverse appellations and multifarious forms of 'the Truth' reflect Lawrence's arduous task of grasping his protean object of pursuit. No sooner did he have a momentary vision of his rainbow than its colour faded. But Lawrence did not give up; he pursued the revelations of his 'Truth' all over the world. In this paper I am going to focus on the nature of his visions and on how all his revelations are related to one another. I think Lawrence and his 'Truth' are best understood in the unfolding of some of his symbols. I am therefore going to start with an examination of his philosophy of dualism in human relationships and in the individual.

II

In 'Study of Thomas Hardy' Lawrence explains his dualism; 'Man and woman are, roughly, the embodiment of Love and the Law; they are the two complementary parts.'[2] According to him, 'what we want is always the perfect union of the two,' which is 'the Law of the Holy Spirit, the Law of Consummate Marriage.'[3]

Love is the embodiment of positive nature and mobility, and the Law passive nature and stability; in the perfect union of the two forces is the happiness of love, making man and woman a hermaphrodite, which had at one stage, according to Plato, four hands and four legs in one body. Separate, man and woman are incomplete and only in union do they become whole and perfect. Lawrence explicates this in the same essay:

> He must know that he is half, and the woman is the other half, that they are two, but that they are two-in-one.
> He must with reverence submit to the law of himself, and he must with suffering and joy know and submit to the law of the woman: and he must know that they two together are one within the Great Law, reconciled within the Great Peace.[4]

The 'Great Law' and 'the Great Peace' are symbolic terms for what Lawrence calls the fulfilment of love, the happiness of which fills the whole of *Look! We Have Come Through!*

> But now I am full and strong and certain
> With you there firm at the core of me
> Keeping me.

How sure I feel, how warm and strong and happy
For the future! How sure the future is with me
I am like a seed with a perfect flower enclosed.[5]

This is a good example of 'Consummate Marriage' of Love and the
Law united in the 'Holy Spirit' of an androgynous body of man
and woman, which A. J. L. Busst calls 'the divine body'. Busst
quotes from *L'Eve Nouvelle*:

mais une véritable troisième personne formée des deux que nous
voyons, un être supérieur complet qui existe au dessous d'eux,
d'une vie divine.[6]

Lawrence also makes the consummate state of his hermaphrodite
a 'divine body', which he speaks of in his 'Study of Thomas Hardy':

David, when he lay with a woman, lay also with God; Solomon,
when he lay with a woman, knew God and possessed Him and
was possessed by Him. For in Solomon and in the Woman, the
male clasped hands with the female.[7]

These highest moments in the union of man and woman are what
Lawrence calls in 'The Crown' 'the timeless, absolute and perfect'
states of 'the utter relation between two eternities' in which
God manifests.[8] God for Lawrence is a symbolic name for the
culmination in the fusion of two bodies in love. The man and
woman relationship is based on the polarisation of the two
individualities balancing each other in the state of star-equilibrium.
In sex the two partners are most intimately united, but they must
retreat like 'the systole and diastole movement of the heart' or like
the ideal movement of the sea, which Anna and Will in *The Rainbow*
battle through. The Great Peace is possible when each partner
respects the other's integrity. Hence Lawrence in 'The Crown'
refers to God as 'the flowing together and the flowing apart'.[9]

Lawrence uses various metaphors for the mobile nature of love
and the separateness of the individual in fulfilment. He calls man
and woman twin rivers which run parallel and mingle from time
to time, an image with which he seems to have intended to
repudiate the fixity of the relationship. But the river image fails to
explain the true nature of mobility and flexibility. Though the two
rivers of the individuals flow constantly within the bond of

relationship and once the flow stops the strength of the partnership dries up, there cannot be such twin rivers that run along side by side and conjoin from time to time only to take their separate courses again later. Lawrence suggests the Blue and White Nile flowing into Niles Flux, but once the two rivers come together in the Great Nile they are joined forever. The river metaphor holds water, as it were, only to the point where the two of them meet in the main stream.

With the tidal and systolic movements Lawrence clarifies better the characteristics of a perfect union, but whether the meeting and goings of a man and a woman can be as regular as the pounding of the heart or the breaking of the waves is highly questionable.

The hermaphrodite theory is a poetic interpretation which puts a great emphasis on the union of two longing lovers, but it does not work out to denote the separateness of two bodies. On the other hand, the star-equilibrium excludes the happy movement of intimacy, as the stars are forever fixed in polarisation. It is the same with the metaphor of the crown. The lion and unicorn are fighting eternally without any chance of uniting together, 'If they made friends and lay down side by side, the crown would fall on them both and kill them'.[10]

Although the wholeness in the union of hermaphrodite halves is equally important, the complementary nature of two partners with separate identities seems to entail the contention of both sides like Blake's 'true friendship in opposition', which the marriages of Birkin and Ursula and of Somers and Harriet illustrate most vividly. 'Remove the opposition and there is collapse' says Lawrence,[11] for whom the eternal opposition and strife is by itself absolute, and wherein he finds peace and harmony. The eternal opposition and strife of the lion and the unicorn provides a good case:

> The crown is upon the perfect balance of the fight, it is not the fruit of either victory. The crown is not the prize of either combatant. It is the *raison d'être* of both. It is absolute within the fight.[12]

The fight here appears to be very close to Heraclitus's concept of dualism. In the 'fragments' of his thoughts, the Greek philosopher describes the dualism of 'day and night, winter and summer, war and peace, satiety and hunger'[13] as two sides of the same process.

neither being possible without the other, and it is the 'opposite tension' that keeps things and maintains them in equilibrium. In the light of Lawrence's indebtedness to John Burnet's book *Early Greek Philosophy*, his theory of dualism must be based on Heraclitus.[14] When writing 'The Crown' Lawrence seems to have been inspired by Heraclitus, who thought that 'justice is strife, and that all things come into being and pass away through strife' (Fragment 62) and who considered that:

> Homer was wrong in saying: 'Would that strife might perish from among gods and men!' He did not see that he was praying for the destruction of the universe; for if his prayer were heard, all things would pass away.   (Fragment 43)[15]

Similarly, for Lawrence nothing can be created when the lion and unicorn no longer fight.[16] It is only from the constant fight between the two parties that harmony and peace arise and keep them in polarisation, which is symbolised in the crown and the rainbow: 'the rainbow, the iridescence which is darkness at once and light, the two-in-one; the crown that binds them both'.[17] It is also the state of star-equilibrium, in which 'man had being and woman had being, two pure beings, each constituting the freedom of the other, balancing each other like two poles of one force.'[18]

Yet Lawrence's opposition of the two forces does not exclude the androgynous union of lovers in the movements of intimacy. To present the whole picture of the relationship, Lawrence adopts the symbol of the phoenix – a legendary bird of both sexes, which goes through the cycle of death and rebirth in the flame of consummation. In 'The Crown' Lawrence explains the bird of his personal ensign:

> the phoenix in her maturity becomes immortal in flame. That is not her perishing: it is her becoming absolute: a blossom of fire. If she did not pass into flame, *she* would never really exist. It is by her translation into fire that she is the phoenix.[19]

Flame here is the core of the mingling together and the zenith of the coital act. The phoenix in flame, in other words, symbolises the consummation of dual forces and the perfect moments in which the birds becomes 'one with the fiery Origin', the God.[20] I think

among the Lawrence key-symbols the phoenix expresses mos
comprehensibly the truth of his dualism.

III

Like Goethe, George Eliot or Virginia Woolf, Lawrence acknowl
edges dualism in the individual. In the vein of Goethe whose Faus
confesses, 'Two souls, alas, are housed within my breast, / Anc
each will wrestle for the mastery there',[21] or of Woolf who write
in *A Room of One's Own* that 'in each of us two powers preside
one male, one female',[22] Lawrence argues that an individual i
'compound of two waves' and is 'framed in the struggle anc
embrace of the two opposite waves of darkness and of light'.

> There is the wave of light in me which seeks the darkness
> which has for its goal the Source and the Beginning, for its Goc
> the Almighty Creator to Whom is all power and glory. Thithe
> the light of the seed of man struggles and aspires into the infinit
> darkness, the womb of all creation.[23]

And Lawrence goes on to suggest that both sides should mix anc
achieve a 'perfect consummation' in the individual. Virginia Wool
wonders about this nature in *A Room of One's Own*: 'whether ther
are two sexes in the mind corresponding to the two sexes in the
body, and whether they also require to be united in order to ge
complete satisfaction and happiness'.[24] Lawrence is more positive
about this. When man is well balanced between the male anc
female in him he is 'happy, easy to mate, easy to satisfy, anc
content to exist'.[25] Woolf again in *A Room of One's Own* thinks along
the same lines: 'in the man's brain the man predominates over the
woman, and in the woman's brain the woman predominates ove
the man', and therefore the 'normal and comfortable state of being
is that when two live in harmony together'.[26] But the balance i
rare: 'every man comprises male and female in his being, the male
always struggling for predominance. A woman likewise consist
in male and female, with female predominant.'[27]

Lawrence's whole life was a constant search for this impossible
state of the perfect union of dual forces in the body and in the
relationship of man and woman: 'there is never to be found a
perfect balance or accord of the two Wills, but always one triumph

over the other, in life, according to our knowledge'.[28] The two elements of the dual Will, the 'Will-to-motion' and the 'Will-to-inertia' remain separate. There is neither a harmonious reconciliation of the two principles in the body, nor a balanced state of two sides in human relationships. If the male spirit wants action and change, the female spirit of stability becomes passive. The centrifugal and centripetal forces do not gain balance in the body, and the individual usually becomes a one-sided and unbalanced person. There is peace and harmony in man only when the two opposing forces complement each other. It seems that Lawrence fiercely guarded against the fusion of the two sides in the event of the man–woman relationship, emphasising their separateness from the symbols of the lion and the unicorn or the metaphor of star-equilibrium, but in the case of the individual he stressed the fusion of male and female spirits in a hermaphrodite, grieving over the divorce of the dual elements in the body.

Lawrence called what he missed 'the religious effort of man'. Man must strive for the perfect reconciliation of dual force: 'so must the human effort be always to recover balance, to symbolize and so to possess that which is missing'.

> The religious effort is to conceive, to symbolize that which the human soul, or the soul of the race, lacks, that which it is not, and which it requires, yearns for. It is the portrayal of that complement to the race-life which is known only as a desire: it is the symbolizing of a great desire, the statement of the desire in terms which have no meaning apart from the desire.[29]

Lawrence, however, does not give up his search and just leave 'the religious effort' as 'a great desire' which is never to be fulfilled. Occasionally the perfect balance is gained, which Lawrence saw in the Greek artists – Phidias, Sophocles, Alcibiades and Horace:

> There is sufficient of the female in the body of such a man as to leave him fairly free. He does not suffer the torture of desire of a more male being. It is obvious even from the physique of such a man that in him there is a proper proportion between male and female, so that he can be easy, balanced, and without excess.[30]

Naturally if a work of art is a full reflection of a writer's whole personality without a tint of bias, the work produced in this state registers the artist's mellow and rounded artefact. Male and female have an artistic fusion, to use a Lawrentian expression, in the flame of the phoenix in the androgynous body and produce the rainbow of 'the Truth', 'that momentary state when in living the union between male and female is consummated'.[31]

Lawrence does not seem to explain well the greatest moment of balance and reconciliation. By 'the Truth' he seems to mean the highest achievement of any great artist, the level which in Lawrence's view even the greatest painters like Botticelli and Raphael, or the greatest writers like Tolstoy, Dostoevsky, Hardy or Flaubert failed to reach. It is the sincerest expression of the soul a great artist can articulate. It is the perfect moment of 'the Great Peace', 'the Rainbow', 'the Crown' or 'phoenix', and 'the utter relation between two eternities, in which God manifests'.

Perhaps Paul Tillich explains it better by calling 'the deepest ground of our being and of all being, the depth of life itself'.[32] Lawrence calls it 'Life' though rather loosely: 'When the two are acting together, then Life is produced, the Life, or Utterance, Something, is *created.*'[33] Tillich again defines this 'depth of life' as a state of godhead:

> The name of this infinite and inexhaustible depth and ground of all being is *God*. That depth is what the word *God* means. And if that word has not much meaning for you, translate it, and speak of the depths of your life, of the source of your being, of your ultimate concern, of what you take seriously without any reservation. Perhaps, in order to do so, you must forget everything traditional that you have learned about God, perhaps even that word itself. For if you know that God means depth, you know much about Him.[34]

One can think of some notable examples of this godly state. In *The Rainbow*, Will experiences an intensely religious moment almost comparable to a sexual ecstasy when he goes to Lincoln Cathedral. It is the moment of revelation when he becomes one with God, reaching the 'infinite and inexhaustible depth and ground' of his whole being. It is a moment of epiphany, to use the Joycean term. Like Gabriel Conroy and Stephen Dedalus, Ursula also comes to know a great moment of truth when she has the vision of the rainbow. Hardy in *Tess of the D'Urbervilles* presents, in spite of

Lawrence's conclusion that he failed in his 'religious effort', a most illuminating example of the revelatory case, when Tess at the height of her motherly anxiety performs the ceremony of baptism for her bastard son. This desperate gesture to save her 'Sorrow' from falling into the nethermost corner of hell is the most sincere expression of human being that comes from Tillich's 'the deepest ground of our being'. And Tess becomes synonymous with God. Hardy describes Tess's godly state:

> The ecstasy of faith almost apotheosized her; it set upon her face a glowing irradiation, and brought a red spot into the middle of each cheek; while the miniature candle-flame inverted in her eye-pupils shone like a diamond. The children gazed up at her with more and more reverence, and no longer had a will for questioning. She did not look like Sissy to them now, but as a being large, towering, and awful – a divine personage with whom they had nothing in common.[35]

Hardy's picture of a divine Tess is intentional, drawing her in the image of the immaculate Virgin Mother, using adjectives like 'large', 'towering' and 'awful', which are the attributes of Tillich's God.

Lawrence has another name for this God, 'the Holy Ghost', which he explains in 'Study of Thomas Hardy':

> Now the aim of man remains to recognize and seek out the Holy Spirit, the Reconciler, the Originator, He who derives the twin principles of Law and of Love across the ages.
> Now it remains for us to know the Law and to know the Love, and further to seek out the Reconciliation. It is time for us to build our temples to the Holy Spirit, and to raise our altars to the Holy Ghost, the Supreme, who is beyond us but is with us.[36]

A work of art which is 'the Reconciliation' of the Law and Love with the Holy Spirit is, to use a Lawrentian term, a 'supreme art' that any great artist should aim at as his final goal of achievement. In reality, however, it rarely happens. It is 'that momentary state' of 'the Truth'. The 'Holy Ghost' is only one other symbol for the impossible, eternal union of irreconcilable components which he despairingly calls 'the religious effort'.

On the other hand he coins another term for a more realistic mode of writing, which he calls 'the artistic effort':

> the artistic effort is the effort of utterance, the supreme effort of expressing knowledge . . . where the two wills met and intersected and left their result, complete for the moment. The artistic effort is the portraying of a moment of union between the two wills, according to knowledge.[37]

Obviously Lawrence knows what is possible and what is not, and compromises on a practical level. I think he knew that the rainbow was only a temporary vision and the Holy Ghost just a mere ghost most of the time. Yet bravely Lawrence went on in search of his symbols of eternal ideal – the rainbow, the crown, the Holy Ghost, the dark god, the morning star, the forked flame – just for a momentary reconciliation and a temporary state of the Great Peace. In this sense he was a pilgrim.

All his life Lawrence went through a series of battles between the two spirits, and in each book a process of the fight of the two for supremacy is vividly recorded. *Sons and Lovers* is a good example of the oscillation between a dark, sensual force and a streak of puritanical spirituality. Even in *The Rainbow* the Law overcomes Love, or Love submerges the Law in turn. Though there were times when the two sides were in accord with each other and left the supreme result of the artistic effort, Lawrence was, on the whole, subject to the predominance of one side or the other. His writing became increasingly unbalanced during his leadership period or even before. In *Women in Love*, for instance, Lawrence lets the dark, negative force get the upper hand, and he prays for the destruction of the world and humanity: 'Let mankind pass away – time it did. . . . Let humanity disappear as quick as possible.'[38] This was the time when the war machinery of the government disturbed his peace of mind and drove him into an extremely angry mood. During this period the tender beauty and gentle passion of the man–woman relationship was gone, and a dark aggressive aspect has control over the other warm, poetic side. He became almost completely bloody. All four leadership novels (including *The Boy in the Bush*) suffer from lack of warmth and tenderness. The man and woman relationship is either lust-slaking or violently antagonistic. No rainbow of reconciliation seems to stand in the sky, nor does any great moment of epiphany occur, and the phoenix remain a legendary bird in the ashes of great desire.

Birkin in *Women in Love* explains Lawrence's stance eloquently in his famous Pompadour letter: 'the desire for destruction overcomes every other desire . . . seeking to *lose* ourselves in some ultimate black sensation, mindless and infinite – burning only with destructive fires'.[39] Lawrence here reveals that he has undoubtedly become a victim of a dark, violent passion, which is seen in *Kangaroo* when Jack Callcott declares that 'Killing's natural to a man. . . . It is just as natural as lying with a woman.'[40] Certainly Lawrence presents a case in which the Law is eclipsed and a destructive passion has broken the balance of the crown.

IV

The destructive passion, however, is not the sole expression of Lawrentian love. 'In every creature, the mobility, the law of change is found exemplified in the male; the stability, the conservatism is found in the female.' While the 'woman grows downwards', the 'man grows upwards, like the stalk, towards discovery and light and utterance'.[41] This mobility principle takes Lawrence to an imaginary world of social and political activities away from his previous world of man and woman. 'Let the men scout ahead', writes Lawrence in 'Education of the People', an essay he finished on the eve of his leadership period, 'ahead, scouting, fighting, gathering provision, running on the brink of death and at the tip of the life advance.'[42] This is the very basic principle of his social vision which later expands into a mixture of aristocracy, democracy and dictatorship.

At the same time Lawrence proposes a 'deathless friendship between man and man'. 'In the great move ahead, in the wild hope which rides on the brink of death, men go side by side', 'at the extreme bond of deathless friendship',[43] which Lawrence believes is the 'great creative or religious or constructive activity'.[44]

But in the end Lawrence loses faith in all these leadership principles. So Somers comes back from the city, after a bout of planning and attempting 'to change the world', to his wife, who laughs at him: 'I'm hanged if it wouldn't be more fun than this business of seeing you come back once more fooled from your attempts with men – the world of men, as you call it.'[45]

This echoes the failure of another leader: in *The Plumed Serpent* Kate tells Cipriano about Joachim's death-bed confession of his social mistake.

> And when he was dying, he said to me: *Kate, perhaps I've let you down. Perhaps I haven't really helped Ireland. But I couldn't help myself. I feel as if I'd brought you to the doors of life, and was leaving you there. Kate, don't be disappointed in life because of me. I didn't really get anywhere. I haven't really got anywhere. I feel as if I'd made a mistake.*[46]

Lawrence's italics indicate the emphasis he puts on Joachim's failure as a political leader and on his inability to provide the fulfilment of life to his wife and his people. When Kate arrives in Mexico at the beginning of the book, she is suffering from inertia and the emptiness of her life. What she needs is for her life to be fulfilled. She is tired and disappointed, and weary of human society. So is Somers in *Kangaroo*, who realises that his salvation is 'to be alone' from all social activities. Somers confesses his doubts about his concern for social reform and at the same time his weariness of people.

> Sometimes I feel I'd give anything, soul and body, for a smash up in this social–industrial world we're in. And I would. And then when I realise people – just people – the same people after it as before – why, Jaz, then I don't care any more, and feel it's time to turn to the gods.[47]

So he decides to 'cut himself finally clear from' social plans and humanity and to 'turn to the old dark gods, who had waited so long in the outer dark'.[48]

But why does he turn to the dark gods in the outer dark? What is the dark god? Why did he wait for Somers so long? Where is the outer dark? Lawrence doesn't make it clear where the dark gods live, but he points his finger to the Australian bush, where Somers senses 'something big and aware and hidden':

> Something big and aware and hidden! He walked on, had walked a mile or so into the bush, and had just come to a clump of tall nude, dead trees, shining almost phosphorescent with the moon when the terror of the bush overcame him. He had looked so

long at the vivid moon, without thinking. And now, there was
something among the trees, and his hair began to stir with
terror, on his head. There was a presence. He looked at the
weird, white, dead trees, and into the hollow distances of the
bush.[49]

This sensation is what Jack in *The Boy in the Bush* experiences, to
whom the bush is alive and mysterious.

> There is something mysterious about the Australian bush. It
> is absolutely still. And yet, in the near distance, it seems alive.
> It seems alive, and as if it hovered round you to maze you and
> circumvent you. There is a strange feeling, as if invisible, hostile
> things were hovering round you and heading you off.[50]

What, then, is the dark god in the bush? While most critics
politely ignore it, Keith Sagar argues that it is 'the demons of the
underworld', and then calls it in a self-contradictory manner 'a
gesture' which is 'vaguely associated with certain qualities of the
bush or the sea'.[51] John Middleton Murry, on the other hand,
ridicules the dark god and identifies it with 'Death himself'.[52] Sagar
seems to have adopted Murry's view and contends that Lawrence
had to 'imagine a triumph in death for consolation', as 'the inertia
and cowardice and life-hatred of his fellow-men made impossible
his triumph in life'.[53] Surely Somers and Jack turn to the dark god
for anything but death or 'a triumph in death'. It is very much the
opposite of what Murry and Sagar try to prove. Leo Gurko thinks
the dark god represents a kind of 'complex animism'.[54] Sagar,
Murry, Gurko and even T. S. Eliot, who classified Lawrence as a
modern heretic, seem to be taken in by the 'mysterious', 'weird'
and 'invisible' attributes of the dark god, but one cannot imagine
it as a god of superstition and of shamanistic nature.

Graham Hough calls the dark god 'a god of healing and life-
giving power'.[55] One certainly finds 'life-giving power' in it when
Jack meets his dark god in the bush and feels 'strange unknown
wells of secret life-force' and 'a great deep well of potency':

> Yes, in the wild bush, God seemed another God. God seemed
> absolutely another God, vaster, more calm and more deeply,
> sensually potent. And this was a profound satisfaction. To find
> another, more terrible, but also more deeply-fulfilling God

stirring subtly in the uncontaminated air about one. A dread
God. But a great God, greater than any known. The sense of
greatness, vastness, and newness, in the air. And the strange,
dusky, grey eucalyptus-smelling sense of depth, strange depth
in the air, as of a great deep well of potency, which life had not
yet tapped. Something which lay in a man's blood as well – in a
woman's blood – in Monica's – in Mary's – in the Australian
blood. A strange, dusky, gum-smelling depth of potency that
had never been tapped by experience. As if life still held great
wells of reserve vitality, strange unknown wells of secret life-
source, dusky, of a strange, dim, aromatic sap which had never
stirred in the veins of man, to consciousness and effect.[56]

The dark god here is the same God that Somers encounters:

And the greater mystery of the dark God beyond a man, the
God that gives a man passion, and the dark, unexplained blood-
tenderness that is deeper than love, but so much more obscure,
impersonal, and the brave, silent blood-pride, knowing his own
separateness, and the sword-strength of his derivation from the
dark God. This dark, passionate religiousness and inward sense
of an inwelling magnificence, direct flow from the unknowable
God, this filled Richard's heart first, and human love seemed
such a fighting for candle-light, when the dark is so much
better.[57]

Lawrence is eloquently groping for the real identity of his God
with so many different attributes: 'God, vaster, more calm and
more deeply, sensually potent'; 'a great God, greater than any
known'; 'more terrible, but also deeply-fulfilling God' with 'the
sense of greatness, vastness, and the newness'; 'a great deep well
of potency'; 'a great well of reserve vitality'; 'dark, passionate
religiousness and inward sense of an inwelling magnificence'.

With all these Lawrence in the end seems to present a picture of
what Tillich called God, which is 'the deepest ground of our being,
the depth of life itself'. In other words, Lawrence has gone a
roundabout way to describe what he earlier called the supreme
state of the reconciliation between the Law and Love or the perfect
moment of the Holy Ghost, which is also symbolised by the crown,
the rainbow, the phoenix, and the Great Peace.

Sometimes, as with Connie in *Lady Chatterley's Lover*, this God provides Lawrence with fulfilment and vitality, which he also finds in the dark root of the vast Egdon Heath, 'the primitive, primal earth, where the instinctive life heaves up'. Egdon Heath is identified with 'the sombre latent power that will go on producing', 'the deep black source from where all these little contents of lives are drawn'.[58] The tragedy of Clym, according to Lawrence, is that he 'identified himself with the community',[59] and neglected to 'reunite himself with the strong, free flow of life that rose out of Egdon'.[60] Clym's fatal mistake was that he wanted 'to improve mankind rather than to struggle at the quick of himself into being'.[61] Lawrence thinks that Clym should have known the truth that 'the greater part of every life is underground, like roots in the dark in contact with the beyond'.[62] Clym, in other words, betrayed his dark god. Hence Somers, who also made a grave mistake of trying to lead and enlighten society and humanity like Clym or Jesus in 'The Man Who Died', retreats in the end to the bush to be one with God and to 're-unite himself with the strong, free flow of life'.

Once in the bush, Somers, in touch with the dark god that 'made a man realise his own sacred aloneness', becomes complete and whole in the fulfilment of singleness. He has a moment of epiphany, like Mrs Moore in the Marabar Caves. But unlike Mrs Moore, Somers is fully aware of what has filled his heart in the bush: the dark, passionate religiousness and inward sense of an inwelling magnificence, direct flow from the unknowable God'. He gains not only the balance of the mind reconciled in the Law and Love, but the fullness of inner meaning ('the inward sense of inwelling magnificence'), which he found lacking in the empty city of Sydney. It is also what Lou in 'St Mawr' found in the mountain spirits of New Mexico.

V

Why then is this fulfilling god a dark god? In his moment of vision in the bush, Somers realises that 'the only thing to wait for is for me to find their aloneness and their God in the darkness'.[63] I think God is dark in the sense that he is 'the forever unrealisable'. God is dark, because of his attribute of 'the unknowable' and 'the unknown'. The unknowable God is dark, also because it is in 'the very darkest continent of the body'.[64]

Why is the bush God in the body? Lawrence says in his Edgar
Allan Poe essay that the Holy Ghost is 'inside us' ('It is the
multiplicity of gods within us make up the Holy Ghost').[65] Lawrence
repeats this view through Lilly in *Aaron's Rod*:

> You are your own Tree of Life, roots and limbs and trunk.
> Somewhere within the wholeness of the tree lies the very self,
> the quick: its own innate Holy Ghost. And this Holy Ghost puts
> forth new buds, and pushes past old limits, and shakes off a
> whole body of dying leaves.[66]

Even Jack's God whom he feels in the bush is really inside him.
'Because where you are alone you are at one with your God',
writes Lawrence in *The Boy in the Bush*, 'The spirit in you is God
in you. And when you are alone you are one with the spirit of
God inside you.'[67] Somers also locates his God in himself: 'The
only thing one can stick to is one's own isolate being, and the God
in whom it is rooted.'[68] There is no doubt that Lawrence definitely
finds his God in what Tillich refers to as 'the deepest ground of
our being'.

Why then must Jack go into the bush to talk to his mysterious
Lord?[69] Was he talking to himself in the bush under hallucination?
Why does Somers go into the bush for his God? Is it because 'God
doesn't just sit still somewhere in the cosmos' but 'He, too
wanders?'[70]

It is obvious that this God should not be taken literally but on a
symbolic level. In the essay on 'Benjamin Franklin' Lawrence calls
'the soul of a man' 'a dark and vast forest, with wild life in it,'[71]
which he calls his 'creed':

> 'That I am I.'
> 'That my soul is a dark forest.'
> 'That my known self will never be more than a little clearing in the
> forest.'
> 'That gods, strange gods, come forth from the forest into the clearing
> of my known self, and then go back.'
> 'That I must have the courage to let them come and go.'
> 'That I will never let mankind put anything over me, but that I will
> try always to recognize and submit to the gods in me and the gods in
> other men and women.'[72]

With this statement Lawrence makes clear that Somers' visit to the bush and to be alone, one with God is only a symbolic gesture for his complete return to his own, pure, balanced being, to gain that momentary state of the perfect union of dual forces in touch with the godhead.

The statement also clarifies why the symbolic morning star in *The Plumed Serpent* shines in the Mexican skies, the morning star which appears in the hour of dawn and the night, which, according to Lawrence, 'unites the vast universal blood with the universal breath of the spirit, and shines between them both'.[73] The morning star is, in short, another form of the rainbow, the crown, the Holy Ghost and the dark God. In *Apocalypse* Lawrence explains:

> The morning star was always a god, from the time when gods began. But when the cult of dying and re-born gods started all over the old world, about 600 B.C., he became symbolic of the new god, because he rules in the twilight, between day and night, and for the same reason he is supposed to be lord of both, and to stand gleaming with one foot on the flood of night and one foot on the world of day, one foot on sea and one on shore.[74]

Basically Lawrence adopts this morning star of dual principle as the symbol for the new religion of Quetzalcoatl (which is the dual god of the Quetzal and the Coatl – the eagle and the serpent).

Now one wonders why Lawrence keeps changing the names of his God. Lawrence has a perfect answer for this. According to him, 'Man creates a God in his own image, and the gods grow old along with the men that made them. . . . Gods die with men who have conceived them', and therefore, 'the gods must be born again'.[75] In this sense Quetzalcoatl is directly connected with Jesus while Christianity is being replaced by Ramón's new religion, which is presenting the same God in a different name, but this time in the native Mexican clothes and in the language which Mexican Indians would understand. The logic of setting up Quetzalcoatl as the brother of Jesus, both coming from the morning star, is based on the three gods being the Trinity. In a different place, in a different time, the God is created differently by a different people. The morning star shines in the Mexican skies, because, as Ramón believes, 'the hearts of living men are the very middle of the sky . . . [a]nd . . . God is . . . inside the hearts of living men and women'[76] or in 'the forest of the soul'. Thus 'God is only a great imaginative experience'.[77]

Lawrence made extensive and frequent journeys all over the world, sailing from one continent to another back and forth in search of various gods, almost like a pilgrim; but in fact what he had undertaken was a tireless and courageous exploration in 'the darkest continent of the body' in search of the very essence of godhead and the core of life.

Notes

1. Rananim was an ideal community that Lawrence wanted to build up with a group of friends. What his Utopia consisted of was rather vague. He never reached the stage of writing out its charter, except that he was definite in one thing – that he wanted to get away from the pressure of materialistic society. One of his letters reveals his scheme of the ideal community:

   > It is communism based, not on poverty, but riches, not on humility, but on pride, not on sacrifice but upon complete fulfilment in the flesh of all strong desire, not on forfeiture but upon inheritance, not on heaven but on earth. We will be Sons of God who walk here on earth, not bent on getting and having, because we know we inherit all things. We will be aristocrats, as wise as the serpent in dealing with the mob. For the mob shall not crush us nor starve us nor try us to death. We will deal cunningly with the mob, the greedy soul, we will gradually bring it to subjection.
   > We will found an order, and we will all be Princes, as the angels are.
   > We must bring this about – at least set it into life, bring it forth new-born on the earth, watched over by our old cunning and guided by our ancient, mercenary-soldier habits.   (Letter to Lady Ottoline Morrell, 1 February 1915, *Letters*, II, p. 273)

2. *Phoenix*, p. 514.
3. Ibid., p. 515.
4. Ibid.
5. 'Wedlock', *Complete Poems*, vol. I, p. 247.
6. A. J. L. Busst, 'The Image of the Androgyne in the Nineteenth Century' in *Romantic Mythologies*, ed. Iain Fletcher (London: Routledge and Kegan Paul, 1967) p. 38.
7. *Phoenix*, p. 450.
8. *Phoenix* II, p. 410.
9. Ibid.
10. *Phoenix* II, p. 371.

11. Ibid., p. 368.
12. Ibid., p. 373.
13. John Burnet, *Early Greek Philosophy* (London: A. and C. Black, 1892); Fragment 36 in Burnet's version (p. 136, with further discussion on pp. 166–9).
14. I maintain that Lawrence's dualism is derived from Heraclitus, but H. M. Daleski says in *The Forked Flame* (London: Faber and Faber, 1965) that 'there is no evidence that he had read *Early Greek Philosophy* when he first formulated his theory of duality in *Twilight in Italy* and the "Study of Thomas Hardy"' (p. 21, note 2). Daleski therefore believes that 'Lawrence's dualistic outlook was primarily the result of his own early experience' and that 'he turned later to Greek philosophers for confirmation of his ideas' (ibid.). Daleski does not specify which 'early experience' led Lawrence to his dualistic outlook. I doubt whether Lawrence ever turned to any philosopher 'for confirmation of his ideas'. On the contrary, if one reads a work for confirmation, it implies that one has already been acquainted with the contents of the book.

Daleski's misunderstanding mainly seems to come from his misguided assumption that Lawrence 'was interested in Burnet as early as 1916' (p. 21). The exact date, given in Edward Nehls, *D. H. Lawrence: A Composite Biography* (Madison, Wisconsin: University of Wisconsin Press, 1957) vol. I, p. 402, on which Daleski bases his argument, is 5 September 1916. Part of the letter reads:

> Has Maitland got Burnet's 'Early Greek Philosophers'? If he has, I should be *so* glad if he would lend it to me – I want to refer to it. Perhaps it is at Well Walk – I remember Margaret was reading it there.   (Letter to Dollie Radford, *Letters*, II, p. 652)

The letter seems to indicate that Lawrence knew the book and that he only wanted to 'refer to it'. By this time Lawrence had already finished *Women in Love*, in which he proposed the theory of dualism in the form of star-equilibrium.

It seems obvious that Lawrence read Burnet's book long before this. In his letter to Lady Ottoline Morrell, dated 19 July 1915 by the editors of the new *Letters*, Lawrence handsomely acknowledges his indebtedness to Greek philosophy:

> I shall write all my philosophy again. Last time I came out of the Christian Camp. This time I must come out of those early Greek philosophers. I am sure of what I know, and what is true, now, I am stronger in the truth, in the knowledge I have, than all the world outside that knowledge. So I am not, finally, afraid of anything.   (*Letters*, II, p. 367)

Another letter, written a few days earlier (again the letter is not dated and the date given is what the editors conjecture), makes it clear that Lawrence was subject to the strong influence of early Greek

philosophers: 'These early Greeks have clarified my soul'. In the same
letter he reveals his deep admiration for Heraclitus: 'I shall write out
Herakleitos, on the tablets of bronze' (letter to Bertrand Russell [14?
July 1915], *Letters*, II, p. 364). There is no doubt that Lawrence's idea
of 'equilibrium' and the ever-recurring movements of drawing together
and drawing asunder in dualism originated in Heraclitus: 'You must
couple together things whole and things not whole, what is drawn
together and what is drawn asunder, the harmonious and the
discordant' (Fragment 59: Burnet, *Early Greek Philosophy*, p. 136).

15. Burnet, *Early Greek Philosophy*, p. 138 (fr. 62) and p. 136 (fr. 43).
16. Cf. 'The Crown', *Phoenix* II, p. 366.
17. Ibid., p. 373.
18. D. H. Lawrence, *Women in Love*, ed. Charles L. Ross (Harmondsworth, Middx: Penguin, 1982) p. 270.
19. *Phoenix* II, p. 384.
20. Ibid., p. 382.
21. J. W. von Goethe, *Faust*, part 1, trans. Philip Wayne (Harmondsworth, Middx: Penguin, 1981) p. 67.
22. Virginia Woolf, *A Room of One's Own* (London: Hogarth Press, 1929) p. 147.
23. *Phoenix* II, p. 377.
24. Woolf, *A Room of One's Own*, p. 247.
25. *Phoenix*, p. 460.
26. Woolf, *A Room of One's Own*, p. 147.
27. *Phoenix*, p. 481.
28. Ibid., p. 447.
29. Ibid.
30. Ibid., p. 459.
31. Ibid., p. 460.
32. Paul Tillich, *The Shaking of the Foundations* (Harmondsworth, Middx: Penguin, 1962) p. 63.
33. *Phoenix*, p. 513.
34. Tillich, *Shaking of the Foundations*, pp. 63–4.
35. Thomas Hardy, *Tess of the D'Urbervilles*, ed. David Skilton (Harmondsworth, Middx: Penguin, 1978) pp. 145–6.
36. *Phoenix*, p. 514.
37. Ibid., p. 447.
38. Lawrence, *Women in Love*, p. 111.
39. Ibid., pp. 474 and 476.
40. D. H. Lawrence, *Kangaroo* (Harmondsworth, Middx: Penguin, 1950) p. 352.
41. *Phoenix*, p. 514.
42. Ibid., pp. 664–5.
43. Ibid., p. 665.
44. D. H. Lawrence, *Fantasia of the Unconscious* (London: Heinemann, 1961) p. 184.
45. Lawrence, *Kangaroo*, p. 78.
46. D. H. Lawrence, *The Plumed Serpent*, ed. Ronald G. Walker (Harmondsworth, Middx: Penguin, 1983) p. 103.

47. Lawrence, *Kangaroo*, p. 180.
48. Ibid., p. 294.
49. Ibid., p. 19.
50. D. H. Lawrence, *The Boy in the Bush* (Harmondsworth, Middx: Penguin, 1963) p. 320.
51. Keith Sagar, *The Art of D. H. Lawrence* (Cambridge: Cambridge University Press, 1966) p. 137.
52. John Middleton Murry, *Son of Woman* (London: Jonathan Cape, 1931) p. 256.
53. Sagar, *The Art of Lawrence*, p. 140.
54. Leo Gurko, 'Kangaroo: D. H. Lawrence in Transit', *Modern Fiction Studies*, x, 4 (1964) p. 349.
55. Graham Hough, *The Dark Sun* (Harmondsworth, Middx: Penguin, 1961) p. 139.
56. Lawrence, *The Boy in the Bush*, p. 255.
57. Lawrence, *Kangaroo*, p. 360.
58. *Phoenix*, p. 415.
59. Ibid., p. 414.
60. Ibid., p. 417.
61. Ibid., p. 414.
62. Ibid., p. 418.
63. Lawrence, *Kangaroo*, p. 361.
64. 'The Novel and the Feelings', *Phoenix*, p. 759.
65. D. H. Lawrence, *Studies in Classic American Literature* (Harmondsworth, Middx: Penguin, 1971) p. 87.
66. D. H. Lawrence, *Aaron's Rod* (Harmondsworth, Middx: Penguin, 1977) p. 344.
67. Lawrence, *The Boy in the Bush*, p. 153.
68. Lawrence, *Kangaroo*, p. 361.
69. Ibid., ch. 21.
70. 'On Being Religious', *Phoenix*, p. 727.
71. Lawrence, *Studies in Classic American Literature*, p. 17.
72. Ibid., p. 22.
73. Lawrence, *The Plumed Serpent*, p. 454.
74. D. H. Lawrence, *Apocalypse and the Writings on Revelation*, ed. Mara Kalnins (Cambridge: Cambridge University Press, 1980) p. 132.
75. Lawrence, *The Plumed Serpent*, p. 91.
76. Ibid., p. 391.
77. Lawrence, 'Introduction to *The Dragon of the Apocalypse* by Frederick Carter', *Apocalypse*, p. 51.

6

Life as a Four-Letter Word: a Contemporary View of Lawrence and Joyce

H. M. DALESKI

Surveying the contemporary scene in the world of British fiction in 1914, Henry James praised H. G. Wells and Arnold Bennett for having 'launched the boat' in which the most promising younger novelists were then setting out with a 'fresh play of oar', and he named these as Hugh Walpole, Gilbert Cannan, Compton Mackenzie and D. H. Lawrence, though he added that he found Lawrence hanging very much 'in the dusty rear'.[1] James Joyce was not even aboard that particular craft of fiction, but then *Dubliners* was first published only some months after James's essay was written. When we look back on the intervening years from the vantage point of 1985, however, I think it would be generally agreed that it is Lawrence and Joyce who are the major British novelists of the century. In Lawrence's centenary year, therefore, it seems fitting to couple him with Joyce, whose own centenary was marked a few years ago. In the popular imagination, of course, they have long been linked in very different terms – as the notorious authors of banned books, the purveyors of unmentionable four-letter words. Though tarred with the same brush, they did not regard themselves as pursuing similar aims in their treatment of sexual matters or in their use of such words, and they did not even agree as to what constituted pornography. 'Pornography,' said Lawrence, 'is the attempt to insult sex, to do dirt on it.'[2] 'Desire,' wrote Joyce in the Paris Notebook, 'is the feeling which urges us to go to something and loathing is the feeling which urges us to go from something: and that art is improper which aims at exciting these feelings in us . . .',[3] Stephen Dedalus, following this line of thought in *A Portrait of the Artist*, puts a name to such improper arts and calls them 'pornographical or didactic'.[4]

The difference of view apparent in these statements is suggestive of the more general difference between Lawrence and Joyce that I wish to pursue. For Lawrence what is at issue is the effect a given kind of writing may have on life, the way in which pornography may corrupt sexual attitudes. For Joyce what matters is the way feelings we have in life, desire and loathing, corrupt the art that arouses them. The characteristic feature of pornography for Joyce is for Lawrence the distinctive value of the novel: 'It is the way our sympathy flows and recoils that really determines our lives,' he says in *Lady Chatterley's Lover*. 'And here lies the vast importance of the novel properly handled. It can inform and lead into new places the flow of our sympathetic consciousness, and it can lead our sympathy away in recoil from things gone dead.'[5] For Lawrence the significance of the novel is its potential for changing our lives through the vital flow of sympathy it can impel. For Joyce the mark of true art is that it is static, that it has a capacity not for moving us but for arresting our feelings; and he believes that 'rest' is 'necessary for the apprehension of the beautiful',[6] and also for ensuring our proper and exclusive concern with the art. For the same reason he believed we should not be diverted from our contemplation of the art by the intrusive presence of the artist; and he therefore held, as Stephen asserts in a famous passage in *A Portrait of the Artist* which it seems reasonable to regard as reflecting Joyce's own views at the time, that 'the artist, like the God of the creation, [should remain] within or behind or beyond or above his handiwork, invisible, refined out of existence, indifferent, paring his fingernails'.[7] Lawrence, on the contrary, declared he could not 'bear art that you can walk round and admire. A book should be either a bandit or a rebel or a man in the crowd. People should either run for their lives, or come under the colours, or say *how do you do?*'; and he maintained that 'an author should be in among the crowd, kicking their shins or cheering on to some mischief or merriment'.[8]

These various statements indicate the degree to which Lawrence and Joyce stand in polar opposition to each other in their views of the nature and function of art. Lawrence's position may be pinpointed in his declaration that 'the novel is the one bright book of life'.[9] So far as I know, Joyce is not on record with a comparable proclamation, but in these days of creative criticism I hope I will be forgiven for imagining him as quietly asserting that life, after all, is a four-letter word. The assertion, at any rate, throws light on his practice, and it not only serves to focus the difference between him and Lawrence but also to suggest how this in effect anticipates the cleavage between rival critical schools or approaches today. The Lawrentian view, in its insistence on the meaning of literature, on its force for life and its relation to life, links up with a traditional critical stance, one that we may associate with the work of F. R. Leavis, whom it is appropriate to recall on this centenary occasion as Lawrence's first great champion. Joycean practice, on the other hand, in its steadily increasing reliance on verbal play that destabilizes meaning, on the free play of the signifier in its detachment from the signified and from a world outside the text, may be associated with the work of Jacques Derrida and the Deconstructionists. It is indicative of this association that a collection of articles called *Post-structuralist Joyce: Essays from the French* should recently have appeared in English, and that Derrida himself should be represented in it by a fifteen-page essay on two words in *Finnegans Wake*.[10] *Finnegans Wake*, indeed, is a monument to the deconstructionist credo that language by its nature is equivocal rather than univocal in effect, and that literary texts are accordingly 'unreadable' in the sense that they cannot be reduced to unequivocal meaning. *Finnegans Wake* doubtless also has some claim to being regarded as unreadable in a less esoteric sense.

Given this fundamental difference between Lawrence and Joyce, it seems worthwhile to explore the effect that their attitudes to their art had on their work as novelists. At first it appears that Joyce's devotion to the purity of his art gives him a distinct edge over Lawrence in the fineness of his renditions. The point may be illustrated by a comparison of climactic scenes in works which were more or less contemporaneous, *Women in Love*, written in 1916–17, and *A Portrait of the Artist*, published in 1916. The scene from *Women in Love* I have in mind is that at the inn (in the chapter 'Excurse') in which Ursula discovers Birkin 'one of the sons of God':

> And she was drawn to him strangely, as in a spell. Kneeling on the hearth-rug before him, she put her arms round his loins, and put her face against his thighs. Riches! Riches! She was overwhelmed with a sense of a heavenful of riches. . . .
>
> She traced with her hands the line of his loins and thighs, at the back, and a living fire ran through her, from him, darkly. It was a dark flood of electric passion she released from him, drew

into herself. She had established a rich new circuit, a new current of passional electric energy, between the two of them, released from the darkest poles of the body and established in perfect circuit. It was a dark fire of electricity that rushed from him to her, and flooded them both with rich peace, satisfaction. . . . He stood before her, glimmering, so awfully real, that her heart almost stopped beating. He stood there in his strange, whole body, that had its marvellous fountains, like the bodies of the sons of God who were in the beginning. There were strange fountains of his body, more mysterious and potent than any she had imagined or known, more satisfying, ah, finally, mystically–physically satisfying. She had thought there was no source deeper than the phallic source. And now, behold, from the smitten rock of the man's body, from the strange marvellous flanks and thighs, deeper, further in mystery than the phallic source, came the floods of ineffable darkness and ineffable riches.[11]

It is the narrative voice that lets Lawrence down here. The narrative focus in the quoted passage is Ursula, for it is she who has the mystical experience, which is quite properly presented from her point of view. The artist, however, far from being refined out of existence, is very much in among the crowd, busy kicking their shins and shouting out loudly. The dissonance is felt the more strongly in that Ursula's own voice has been caught so memorably in her fight with Birkin that immediately precedes this scene, and it is still ringing in our ears when the couple reach the inn. But when her opening, exclamatory announcement of the riches she has discovered in his loins is followed by her recognition of a 'source deeper than the phallic', a recognition that is made dependent on the biblical appurtenances of the sons of God and the smitten rock, we are reminded of another well known biblical story and cannot help feeling that, though the hands are the hands of Ursula, the voice is the voice of the novelist. And Lawrence is so thumpingly insistent here because he is intent on making a point. He is setting himself against what he saw as a destructive tendency in relations between the sexes, the widespread desire in the world outside the novel for fusion, which Birkin (in distinctively Lawrentian tones) has shortly before denounced: 'Fusion, fusion, this horrible fusion of two beings, which every woman and most men insisted on, was it not nauseous and horrible anyhow, whether it was a fusion of the spirit or of the emotional body?'[12] Ursula's recognition at the inn is an essential prerequisite for the establishment, in contradistinction to the prevailing mode, of 'star-equilibrium' between her and Birkin, the sort of equilibrium, we are told, which 'alone is freedom'.[13] It is because Birkin and Ursula are intended to be exemplary in this regard, to serve as models in their sexual relationship, that Lawrence is ready to force that recognition on Ursula – to force it on her at all costs. The cost is considerable, manifested not least in a loss of verbal resource. Since the experience is repeatedly said to be 'ineffable' and is later referred to as 'untranslatable',[14] the attempt to render it in words was probably misguided anyway; but Lawrence proves to be singularly inept. Ursula previously says that she is 'not taken in by [Birkin's] word-twisting',[15] and Lawrence does not fare much better with us. When 'a dark fire' is said to 'flood' the couple, we infer that the fire must be dark because it has been doused. Birkin does not just stand but is made to stand 'in his . . . body', which is not only revealed as 'strange' but (mercifully) as 'whole'. When we are told that Ursula's heart 'almost stopped beating' at this point, the cliché is not redeemed in being elicited by Birkin's awful reality. And the nature of the ineffable experience is not clarified for us by Lawrence's falling back on miracle, both biblical and secular, to evoke it, verily smiting language to produce his flood of electric darkness.

The scene from *A Portrait of the Artist* which I wish to adduce for comparison is that in which Stephen Dedalus encounters the wading girl. This too is a climactic scene in the novel, for it sets the seal on Stephen's discovery of his vocation; it, like the scene at the inn, is also presented as a mystical or quasi-mystical revelation; and Stephen's experience carries with it a freight of extraliterary value for the author and so is of as much personal significance to Joyce as Ursula's to Lawrence. The effect, however, is markedly different:

There was a long rivulet in the strand: and, as he waded slowly up its course, he wondered at the endless drift of seaweed. Emerald and black and russet and olive, it moved beneath the current, swaying and turning. The water of the rivulet was dark with endless drift and mirrored the highdrifting clouds. The clouds were drifting above him silently and silently the seatangle was drifting below him; and the grey warm air was still: and a new wild life was singing in his veins. . . .

A girl stood before him in midstream, alone and still, gazing out to sea. She seemed like one whom magic had changed into the likeness of a strange and beautiful sea-bird. Her long slender bare legs were delicate as a crane's and pure save where an emerald trail of seaweed had fashioned itself as a sign upon the flesh. Her thighs, fuller and softhued as ivory, were bared almost to the hips where the white fringes of her drawers were like featherings of soft white down. Her slateblue skirts were kilted boldly about her waist and dovetailed behind her. Her bosom was as a bird's soft and slight, slight and soft as the breast of some darkplumaged dove. But her long fair hair was girlish: and girlish, and touched with the wonder of mortal beauty, her face. . . .

– Heavenly God! cried Stephen's soul, in an outburst of profane joy.[16]

ust prior to this scene, Stephen has a vision of Daedalus flying above the sea and wonders whether his own 'strange name' is 'a prophecy of the end he had been born to serve'.[17] That end is then graphically imprinted on his consciousness by his encounter with the girl. Joyce avoids having to assert the meaning of the experience by making the scene speak for itself. He does so through an art of epiphany, the bodying forth of inner meaning through the rendering of external detail in a way which focuses attention not only on the object but on the precision of the language in which it is manifested. The 'new wild life' Stephen gives himself to as he wades up the rivulet is defined for us by the 'endless drift' around him, the drift of seaweed and water and clouds. Stephen, that is, here opts for a kind of life that is viewed as endless flux, change, and motion – in contradistinction to the still, stable fixity of the life in a religious order that he has rejected. The girl whom he then sees, it is suggested, is herself part of the flux of life, for she bears its sign on her flesh which is marked by the 'emerald trail of seaweed'. At the same time in her stillness she is detached from the flux around her. In her 'mortal beauty', the girl thus images for Stephen what the artist sets out to do in his work, to capture flux in stillness, to strike it into stability. The bird imagery projects a similar tension of opposites: like a bird poised for flight, the girl is instinct with life and motion, but at this moment she is held in an utter stillness. Stephen's calling on God in 'an outburst of profane joy' signifies his conversion to a new religion, to the worship of such beauty.

The significance of the encounter is thus subtly communicated to us, not demonstratively proclaimed, but nonetheless the quoted passage makes us wonder whether the delicate purity of Joyce's art, like that of the girl's thigh, is not violated by its own trail of grosser matter. What are we to make, for instance, of those thighs which are 'softhued as ivory', of that bosom which is 'as a bird's soft and slight, slight and soft as the breast of some darkplumaged dove', and of that face which is 'touched with the wonder of mortal beauty'? Does the overly lush, rhapsodic quality of the prose – and this becomes even more cloyingly intense in the subsequent page and a half which completes the chapter – betray the presence of an author insistent in his own way on large effects? We might well be inclined to think so if we judged by this scene alone, but the rest of the novel makes clear that Joyce has eschewed even so minimal a sign of presence as a distinctive voice of his own, regularly adapting his style to the various phases of Stephen's development. If the prose here mirrors Stephen's adolescent fervour, it is by way of a merging of narrative voice and narrative focus, a merging that enables Joyce – even at so crucial a moment – to stand away from his protagonist and expose him, if ever so little, to irony.

The technique that Joyce first used extensively in *A Portrait of the Artist* is employed to even more striking effect in the first half of *Ulysses*, where the narrative is made to reflect the very different styles of Stephen and Bloom. Both Stephen and Bloom are strongly individualised as a result, and they are presented with such massive solidity in this part of the novel that they remain magnificently immune to subversion when they are subsequently subordinated to other interests. An initial sign of things to come is provided by the newspaper captions in the 'Aeolus' chapter; and what follows in the second half of the narrative is Joyce's attempt, in pursuit of imitative form, to adapt his style not to a perceiving consciousness as formerly but to the contours of his subject matter. The effect is curious. It is as if, having previously managed to refine himself out of narrative existence (in so far as that is possible) Joyce now seeks to return to his created world, and does so – like a god – by means of the word. Once the word-play begins in earnest, it is undoubtedly the presence of the word-player as an obtrusive and intrusive entity that comes to dominate the narrative. What is even more disturbing than that pervasive presence is the sense we now get of a crumbling of the novelist's artistic discipline that manifests itself in play for its own sake.

The 'Oxen of the Sun' chapter is representative of this tendency in the second half of the novel. It is a moot point whether anything is gained – other than the exhibition of the novelist's verbal skills – by Joyce's attempt to make his parodies of developments in English prose style parallel the development of the embryo and presumably too (though the connection here is tenuous) of Mrs Purefoy's labour and the birth of her child. An intellectual pattern may no doubt be imposed on the narrative material, but it is not evocative of the subject. Certainly Mrs Purefoy herself disappears behind the parodies. One cannot help thinking, by contrast, of the chapter in *The Rainbow* which deals with the birth of Lydia Brangwen's son. The 'moaning cry of [the] woman in labour' reverberates throughout this section of the narrative, 'vibrating through everything' and terrifying her daughter Anna, who feels 'lost in a horror of desolation'.[18] And the cry is set not against the complexly varied tones of English prose styles but against the simple sounds that calm Anna when Tom Brangwen takes her into the barn, the 'noise of chains running, as the cows lifted or dropped their heads sharply; then a contented, soothing sound, a long snuffing as the beast ate in silence'.[19] Joyce's oxen, however, move their heads to a different rhythm, and the chapter in *Ulysses* becomes a kind of glorified literary competition, with the reader vainly left trying to identify the parodied styles. The parodies, it must be said, are often very good and very funny; but not infrequently the humour is strained, relying heavily on the defamiliarisation of such everyday phenomena as bee stings – 'the traveller Leopold', we are told:

[comes to] the house of misericord [to be] healed for he was sore wounded in his breast by a spear wherewith a horrible and dreadful dragon was smitten him for which he did do make a salve of volatile salt and chrism as much as he might suffice

– or tins of sardines:

And there was a vat of silver that was moved by craft to open in the which lay strange fishes withouten heads though misbelieving men nie that this be possible thing without they see it natheless they are so. And these fishes lie in an oily water brought there from Portugal land because of the fatness that therein is like to the juices of the olive press.[20]

At times, moreover, though a joke begins well, there is a degener ation into what can only be called a schoolboy humour, as in the following instance:

Greater love than this, [Stephen] said, no man hath that a man lay down his wife for his friend. Go thou and do likewise. Thus, or words to that effect, said Zarathustra, sometime regius professor of French letters to the university of Oxtail.[21]

Joyce is so remorseless in the patterns he imposes on his materials and the verbal games he makes them yield that often what he generously gives with one hand he tightfistedly takes back with the other. The 'Cyclops' chapter is a case in point. Bloom's encounter with the Citizen, as it comes to us in the account of the unnamed first-person narrator in this chapter, is perhaps the most vivid episode in the novel, and the presentation of the racy, colloquial, down-to-earth style of this narrator is a triumph of dramatic mimesis. Joyce's Homeric pattern, however, leads him to seek to evoke the Cyclops not only by means of this narrator's immediate rendering of the Citizen's violent bigotry, his one-eyed view of things, but also through the provision of a second narrator whose inflation of everything he talks about (in a literary style the novelist labelled 'gigantism') is intended to suggest the giant as well. But the inflation tends to gallop away with itself, as in this description of the Citizen: 'The figure seated on a large boulder at the foot of a round tower was that of a broadshouldered deep-chested stronglimbed frankeyed redhaired freely freckled shaggy-bearded widemouthed largenosed longheaded deepvoiced bare-kneed brawnyhanded hairylegged ruddyfaced sinewyarmed hero.'[22] And all too often Joyce, like a schoolboy again, seems incapable of stopping once launched on a given course. Shortly after the above description of the Citizen, for example, we are told that he carries with him 'the tribal images of many Irish heroes and heroines of antiquity', whose names are then duly listed. In this catalogue the humour of the unexpected names that are ɪcluded in it speedily wears thin, but the list itself goes drearily ɪn and on and on:

Cuchulin, Conn of hundred battles, Niall of nine hostages, Brian of Kincora, the Ardri Malachi, Art MacMurragh, Shane O'Neill, Father John Murphy, Owen Roe, Patrick Sarsfield, Red Hugh O'Donnell, Red Jim MacDermott, Soggarth Eoghan O'Growney, Michael Dwyer, Francy Higgins, Henry Joy M'Cracken, Goliath, Horace Wheatley, Thomas Conneff, Peg Woffington, the Village Blacksmith, Captain Moonlight, Captain Boycott, Dante Alighieri, Christopher Columbus, S. Fursa, S. Brendan, Marshall Mac-Mahon, Charlemagne, Theobald Wolfe Tone, the Mother of the Maccabees, the Last of the Mohicans, the Rose of Castille, the Man for Galway, The Man that Broke the Bank at Monte Carlo, The Man in the Gap, The Woman Who Didn't, Benjamin Franklin, Napoleon Bonaparte, John L. Sullivan, Cleopatra, Savourneen Deelish, Julius Caesar, Paracelsus, sir Thomas Lipton, William Tell, Michelangelo, Hayes, Muhammad, the Bride of Lammermoor, Peter the Hermit, Peter the Packer, Dark Rosaleen, Patrick W. Shakespeare, Brian Confucius, Murtagh Gutenberg, Patricio Velasquez, Captain Nemo, Tristan and Isolde, the first Prince of Wales, Thomas Cook and Son, the Bold Soldier Boy, Arrah na Pogue, Dick Turpin, Ludwig Beethoven, the Colleen Bawn, Waddler Healy, Angus the Culdee, Dolly Mount, Sidney Parade, Ben Howth, Valentine Greatrakes, Adam and Eve, Arthur Wellesley, Boss Croker, Herodotus, Jack the Giantkiller, Gautama Buddha, Lady Godiva, The Lily of Killarney, Balor of the Evil Eye, the Queen of Sheba, Acky Nagle, Joe Nagle, Alessandro Volta, Jeremiah O'Donnovan Rossa, Don Philip O'Sullivan Beare.[23]

ɪhe list is typical of much of the play in the second half of the ɪovel, a kind of play that, in its self-gratification and self-indulgence ɪnd self-consciousness, seems if anything to be a playing with self. ɪs Lawrence has said, 'It really is childish, after a certain age, to ɪe absorbedly self-conscious.'[24]

It is not merely that Joyce's word-play is often tiresome; on ɪccasion it is even subversive of his own art. The Gerty MacDowell ɪction of the 'Nausicaa' episode is akin to a short story, in which ɪyce essays to catch the life of the young girl portrayed. This section, it will be recalled, is throughout written in unrelenting appalling cliché, the undiluted language of the woman's magazine. The technique adopted admittedly succeeds in projecting Gerty romantic and sentimental, living in a banal and unreal world which she seeks to turn herself into the heroine of a novelette; and the language in which she has her being is exposed as a vehicle for obscuring and distorting reality. The trouble is that the language of cliché is by definition secondhand and superficial – and inadequate to depict anyone in ways worth attending to. What lacking is any penetration to the area beneath the cliché in which Gerty lives, the area of her real pain and suffering. Instead we a given a pathos that is wholly derived from a plot surprise – as the ending of a Maupassant story – when Gerty is ultimately see to limp away from the scene of Bloom's onanistic admiration her. In this instance, life in Joyce has indeed become the word b at the cost of his losing touch with a more profound apprehensie of it.

Gerty MacDowell, of course, is only a minor character in *Ulysse* and in the same work the novelist certainly shows a capacity f memorable female portraiture in his evocation of Molly Bloom, b nonetheless I think that the presentation of Gerty is symptoma in a way that becomes more and more pronounced in Joyce. Mab Pervin, in Lawrence's story 'The Horse Dealer's Daughter', whi appeared in the collection *England, My England* in the same ye as *Ulysses*, is comparable to Gerty in a number of respects. She t is not representative of the author's major work; she, like Gert has strong pretensions to gentility; and she is confronted ev more starkly with the prospect of being left on the shelf, whi Bloom concludes will be Gerty's fate. Lawrence, however, do not focus on the language of Mabel's responses or h inexpressiveness – though her silences when she refuses to answ her brothers' questions are the first indication of her feeling hopelessness. The story begins with her brother Joe's asking h what she is going to do with herself when they all leave the fami home, and for Lawrence the issue is what she is going to do wi her life. When immediately afterwards the big draught-horses pa the house, 'swinging their great rounded haunches sumptuously' it is intimated what she has been defrauded of; and her sense deprivation proves to be so acute that it leads to her attempt drown herself in a nearby pond. She is rescued by the your doctor, who revives her, and then removes her wet clothes ar dries her, wrapping her naked in some blankets. When she comes ound, she elicits from the doctor that it is he who has both saved nd undressed her; and then follows an astonishing moment: 'Do ou love me, then?' she asks, and putting her arms round him, laims possession of him.[26] Mabel tacitly demands that he accept he responsibilities of touch, for in more than one sense he has ouched her into life. The doctor is 'amazed, bewildered, and fraid'[27] because consciously he has related to her only as to a atient, but he is slowly drawn to recognise and act on the deeper neaning of what he has done. Nor is it only to her that life is iven. Earlier in the day he has been mesmerised by her, and hough he is 'feeling weak and done', life is said to '[come] back nto him' as he looks at her, and he then feels 'delivered from his wn fretted, daily self'.[28] In the end, it is – quite simply – life that ney both choose, and that is celebrated in the story.

Connie Chatterley is another character in Lawrence who is ouched into life when she feels she is steadily '[going] cold from ead to foot'.[29] Her deathly chill is ultimately attributable to the nportance she has attached to words. In her youth it is talk 'that natters] supremely';[30] and, for her, sex is 'a final spasm of self-ssertion, like the last word'.[31] It is in this spirit that she marries lifford, but she eventually recoils from the way he turns 'every-ning into words': 'How she hated words, always coming between er and life'.[32] In the end she takes to visiting the pheasant coops : Wragby every day, for by then the hens are 'the only things in ne world that [warm] her heart'. It is spring, and Lawrence evokes ne force of the vibrant new life in the wood with a miraculous hrase that requires no biblical elaboration: the leaf-buds on the azels are said to be 'opening like the spatter of green rain'.[33] He okes it too in the 'perky chicken' that is 'tinily prancing round front of a coop', engaged in 'the game of living',[34] the prancing, its unexpectedness, effortlessly catching the strength of even nat minuscule life. What Connie herself is made to feel in relation the pheasants is strikingly suggested when, on another occasion, ne keeper gives her a chick to hold:

'There!' he said, holding out his hand to her. She took the little drab thing between her hands, and there it stood, on its impossible little stalks of legs, its atom of balancing life trembling through its almost weightless feet into Connie's hands. But it lifted its handsome, clean-shaped little head boldly, and looked

sharply round, and gave a little 'peep'. 'So adorable! So cheek
she said softly.

The keeper, squatting beside her, was also watching with
amused face the bold little bird in her hands. Suddenly he sa
a tear fall on to her wrist. . . .

He turned again to look at her. She was kneeling and holdi.
her two hands slowly forward, blindly, so that the chick
should run in to the mother-hen again.[35]

The chicken, with its 'little stalks of legs', is so much a part of t
springing new life of the wood that Connie, when its life trembl
into her, pulsating into her through her hands, is made poignan
aware of her own emptiness and barrenness. When she holds h
hands 'slowly forward, blindly', it is not only her tears that bli
her; the way she lets the chicken go enacts a mute recognition th
her own hold on life is slipping, that she can no longer hold it
her hands, so to speak.

As with Joyce's epiphanies, no authorial comment is needed
underline the significance of such moments, though in Lawren
meaning is elicited not through an arrested contemplation, as
Stephen's encounter with the girl, but through symbolic action,
in Connie's holding and releasing of the chicken. Inde
Lawrence's use of symbolic action as a technique has given
some of the finest scenes in modern literature – one thinks (thou
endless examples come at once to mind) of Will's entry into Linco
Cathedral or of Ursula and Skrebensky's dancing under the mo
in *The Rainbow*; of Gerald's handling of the mare at the railw
crossing or of Birkin's stoning of the moon's reflection in *Wom
in Love*. In all these cases it is a deep life-force that is manifested
the symbolic action, and both for better or for worse, it is t
meaning of the act for a character's life that the art reveals. It is
art, we might say, that is most profoundly engaged – like t
chick – by the game of living, not the play of words. Lawren
certainly has his weaknesses, as I have indicated, but they are t
defects of his intensities, and in 1985 his words remain as lively
ever.

otes

1. Henry James, 'The New Novel', *The Future of the Novel: Essays on the Art of Fiction*, ed. Leon Edel (New York: Vintage Books, 1956; first published 1914) pp. 260–1.
2. 'Pornography and Obscenity', *Phoenix*, p. 175.
3. *The Critical Writings of James Joyce*, ed. Ellsworth Mason and Richard Ellmann (New York: Viking Press, 1973) p. 143.
4. James Joyce, *A Portrait of the Artist as a Young Man*, text as edited by Chester G. Anderson and Richard Ellmann, in *The Portable James Joyce*, ed. Harry Levin (Harmondsworth, Middx: Penguin, 1977) p. 471.
5. D. H. Lawrence, *Lady Chatterley's Lover* (Harmondsworth, Middx: Penguin, 1961) p. 104.
6. James Joyce, 'Paris Notebook', *The Critical Writings*, p. 144.
7. Joyce, *A Portrait of the Artist*, p. 483.
8. Letter to Carlo Linati, 22 January 1925, Moore, II, p. 827.
9. 'Why the Novel Matters', *Phoenix*, p. 535.
10. See Jacques Derrida, 'Two Words for Joyce', *Post-structuralist Joyce: Essays from the French*, ed. Derek Attridge and Daniel Ferrer (Cambridge: Cambridge University Press, 1984) pp. 145–59.
11. D. H. Lawrence, *Women in Love*, ed. Charles L. Ross (Harmondsworth, Middx: Penguin, 1982) pp. 395–7.
12. Ibid., p. 391.
13. Ibid., p. 402.
14. Ibid.
15. Ibid., p. 387.
16. Joyce, *A Portrait of the Artist*, pp. 432–4.
17. Ibid., pp. 430–1.
18. D. H. Lawrence, *The Rainbow*, ed. John Worthen (Harmondsworth, Middx: Penguin, 1981) pp. 111–12.
19. Ibid., p. 116.
20. James Joyce, *Ulysses* (Harmondsworth, Middx: Penguin, 1983) p. 384.
21. Ibid., p. 390.
22. Ibid., p. 294.
23. Ibid., p. 295.
24. 'Surgery for the Novel – Or a Bomb', *Phoenix*, p. 518.
25. D. H. Lawrence, 'The Horse Dealer's Daughter', *The Complete Short Stories*, vol. II (London: Heinemann, 1958) p. 442.
26. Ibid., pp. 452–3.
27. Ibid., p. 453.
28. Ibid., p. 448.
29. Lawrence, *Lady Chatterley's Lover*, p. 117.
30. Ibid., p. 7.
31. Ibid., p. 8.
32. Ibid., p. 96.
33. Ibid., p. 117.
34. Ibid., p. 118.
35. Ibid., p. 119.

7

Lawrence of Etruria

SIMONETTA DE FILIPPIS

One begins to realise how old the real Italy is. . . . Life is s
primitive, so pagan, so strangely heathen and half-savage. . .
Wherever one is in Italy, either one is conscious of the presen
or of the medieval influences, or of the far, mysterious gods (
the early Mediterranean. Wherever one is, the place has i
conscious genius. . . . The expression may be Prosperpine, (
Pan, or even the strange 'shrouded gods' of the Etruscans.[1]

This passage outlines the profound symbolic meaning Italy hel
for D. H. Lawrence, as a country where primitive pagan life wa
still alive, where the ancient gods were still alive, where the pa
was still living in the present. Lawrence also explains the meanir
his journey through Italy had for him:

for us to go to Italy and to *penetrate* into Italy is like a mo
fascinating act of self-discovery – back, back down the old way
of time. Strange and wonderful chords awake in us, and vibrai
again after many hundreds of years of complete forgetfulness.

The charm of Italy, the mystery of Italy one has 'to *penetrat*
represents a way towards the discovery of the pagan elements i
oneself, a search for the unconscious vital chords of man; almost
sexual journey towards the sources and depths of life.

Here we have two of the principal keys to the understanding (
Lawrence: his relation to Italy and his unending need to travel.

After 1912 Lawrence spent a third of his life in Italy, and Ita
became a constant source of inspiration for his work.

Italy represented to Lawrence everything England was no
freedom, the pagan landscape, the source of primitive passion

he authenticity of life, the way towards re-birth. England, by contrast, was the symbol of a mechanical, corrupt society ruled by hypocrisy, intellectualism, power and money.

The idealised vision of Italy and the dramatic rejection of England were, of course, too extreme to be completely true. As a matter of fact, we know that Lawrence often sharply criticised Italy and the Italian people; that he did not consider the whole of Italy to be savage and primitive, and that he disliked Venice, avoided Rome, hated Capri, Messina and Cagliari. In addition, we must not forget that his last novel, *Lady Chatterley's Lover*, the climax of his artistic search and ideological achievement, the novel which contains the very essence of his message, although written in Italy, is set in England.

Places, for Lawrence, were important for their 'spirit', for what they meant and could symbolise. It is equally important, therefore, for us, to consider the itinerary of Lawrence's travels in order to grasp the profound meaning of his philosophical and ideological journey. We can trace the route of his travels through the characters of his novels and stories between 1919 and 1925: Alvina and Aaron leave England to go to Italy; the Somerses move to Australia; Kate and Lou travel down to Mexico and New Mexico; Juliet, in search of a better climate for her health, leaves the States for Italy.[3]

Like Lawrence, these characters abandon their original country, deadened by industrial civilisation, for unspoilt places where man and nature still respond to the sensual call and to the religion of the blood and the sun. Italy is therefore the place Lawrence and his characters choose as the first stage of their quest for a more authentic and vital way of life; Italy is the place they go back to when the need to immerse themselves again in European culture becomes urgent.

Towards the end of his life, Lawrence felt restless again and decided to leave Italy but in effect his miserable health allowed him only to go to a sanatorium in France where he died on 2 March 1930.[4] It is certainly revealing, however, that he entrusted his final prophetic message of love and re-birth for his fellow-countrymen and for the entire world to Connie and Mellors, who, in England, in the depths of the woods and under the reviving rain, discover the vitality and freedom of love and life in close and natural communion with the cosmos.

Towards the end of the novel, Connie goes to Venice, but 'she found nothing vital in France or Switzerland or the Tyrol or

Italy. . . . it was all less real than Wragby. Less real than the awfu
Wragby!'[5]

Lawrence's journey is over. His characters can return to England
having found in themselves what they had been looking for; and
to England, to Lawrence's country, they bring his prophetic
message. However, it is also true that Connie and Mellors develop
into symbols and come to life on a mythical level, which releases
them from any such national characterisation and makes them
'universal' – just like Lawrence, who, although profoundly English
is a writer whose art goes beyond a particular space and time and
reaches a wider dimension.

Lawrence spent three periods in Italy, all at crucial times in his life
and at key moments of his artistic journey.

In 1912 Lawrence decided to leave England and his job as a
teacher. Both acts came to symbolise for him a rejection of industrial
society and of the limitations and meanness of bourgeois life. Like
some of his characters, Lawrence found in his love for a woman
the necessary courage and strength to break his bonds and the
social conventions. His romantic elopement with Frieda towards
the south, crossing the Alps on foot with hardly any money,
brought them to Lake Garda, in northern Italy, and in the north
of Italy they lived for two years until they went back to England
in 1914 for Frieda's divorce.[6]

While Lawrence's personal experiences of those two years
generated a literary response and inspired some of his poems, the
play *The Fight for Barbara*, and the later novel *Mr Noon*, his
impressions of the places he saw and of the people he met in
northern Italy are reflected in some essays which were later recast,
and published in 1916 under the title *Twilight in Italy*, the first of
the three travel books Lawrence wrote about Italy.

In these sketches, as in the rest of his travel writing, Lawrence's
approach is personal, direct, impressionistic: like a painter,
Lawrence observes the landscape, watches the people and their
way of life, the churches, the houses, and then depicts his
impressions, making expert use of colours, shades and chiaroscuro:

The Italian people are called 'Children of the Sun'. They might
better be called 'Children of the Shadow'. Their souls are dark

and nocturnal. . . . Going through these tiny chaotic backways
of the village was like venturing through the labyrinth made by
furtive creatures, who watched from out of another element.
And I was pale, and clear, and evanescent, like the light, and
they were dark, and close, and constant, like the shadow.[7]

Light and shadow, then, a contrast which reflects the wider
opposition of two different cultures, one of the many forms in
which Lawrence expressed his dualistic vision of life.

What Lawrence conveys in these Italian sketches is the virginal
and unspoilt beauty of the Italian landscape, untouched by modern
civilisation, and the impression that the ancient culture was still
alive in the people, in their sensual attitude to life and their natural
way of relating to each other.

Having returned to England in 1914, the Lawrences were forced
to remain there by the outbreak of the First World War. These
were painful and humiliating years for D. H. Lawrence, married
to a German and subjected to what he considered a degrading
medical scrutiny and rejection. In this period he longed to go back
to Italy, which he thought of as a paradise lost, and whither
he returned as soon as he was allowed, in 1919, after the end of
the war. He knew that he could not live in England any longer,
and yet he had mixed feelings at his departure, perhaps similar to
those he gave to Alvina when she sails away towards Italy and
glances back, for the last time, at her grey, dead country:

All was very still in the wintry sunshine of the Channel.
So they turned to walk to the stern of the boat. And Alvina's
heart suddenly contracted. She caught Ciccio's arm, as the boat
rolled gently. For there behind, behind all the sunshine, was
England. England, beyond the water, rising with ash-grey,
corpse-grey cliffs, and streaks of snow on the downs above.
England, like a long, ash-grey coffin slowly submerging. . . .
Her heart died within her.
Never had she felt so utterly strange and far-off. . . . She felt
she could not believe it. It was like looking at something
else. What? It was like a long, ash-grey coffin, winter, slowly
submerging in the sea. England?

She turned again to the sun.[8]

For their second sojourn the Lawrences also turned to the sun: they chose the south of Italy and rented a villa near Taormina, in Sicily, where they stayed until 1922, leaving it only for short trips. One of these took them to Sardinia in 1921; the strong impression and charm that wild island exerted on Lawrence is expressed in his second travel book, *Sea and Sardinia*. In his typical style made of neat touches of colour, Lawrence depicts the landscape, the places, the social environment, the people and their habits, noticing that strange aloofness and reserve of the Sardinians, a different people from the rest of the Italians. As in all his writings, Lawrence takes here the opportunity to express his vision of the world, contrasting nature and industry, the old primitive culture and the modern mechanised civilisation.

During this second Italian period, Lawrence went beyond the mere observation of landscapes and people, and immersed himself in Italian culture, language and literature. To this period belong his translations of the novels and stories by the Sicilian author Giovanni Verga;[9] in Verga Lawrence found a writer who had depicted in his work the island and its culture whose mysterious charm he himself had tried to penetrate, although it is characteristic that Lawrence's interpretation reflects his own ideological position and literary sensibility.

In 1922, in one of their periodic moods of disillusionment, the Lawrences left Italy: 'I am weary of Taormina, and have no desire to stay in Sicily or in Europe at all',[10] wrote Lawrence on 2 January 1922. Taking the opportunity of an invitation to visit America, they sailed first for Ceylon; then they tried Australia. Finally they settled in New Mexico where they stayed until 1925, when Lawrence felt drawn back to Europe and to the Mediterranean. This time he chose central Italy and rented a villa near Florence.[11]

Lawrence had already been to Florence, for a short time, in 1919 and 1920, and had been struck by Michelangelo's statue of David in the Piazza della Signoria. Both in a short essay entitled 'David', after the biblical character, and in *Aaron's Rod*, in a chapter called 'Florence', Lawrence describes the statue of David as 'the genius of Florence', and sees the city as constituting a watershed between north and south:

> northerners must love Florence. Here is their last point, their most southerly. The extreme south of the Lily's flowering. . . . Florence, the flower-town. David![12]

David and Florence seem to contain the elements of the two different civilisations: the cold, christian North, and the warm, pagan South.

Is this the reason why Lawrence, the man from the North, chose Florence for his third Italian sojourn, as a fusion between his northern origin and culture and his drive towards and idealisation of the South? Was it a way to come to terms with the real modern world around him, to stop running away from his own present, and to give up searching for far-away places where natural and primitive life becomes, paradoxically, an artificial alternative for an educated Englishman and for all the civilised westerners to whom Lawrence preached his beliefs?

During his Tuscan period (April 1926–June 1928), Lawrence wrote a number of short essays about Florence ('Fireworks in Florence'), Tuscany ('Flowery Tuscany'), the Italians ('Man is a Hunter') and, above all, about his own ideology ('The Nightingale', 'Germans and English'). From this period also dates the most interesting, and perhaps one of the most beautiful, books among his prose works, his third travel book about Italy, *Etruscan Places*, written in 1927 as a result of a short trip made through the ancient Etruscan cities of Cerveteri, Tarquinia, Vulci and Volterra. This very stimulating and lively little book is, like *Twilight in Italy*, a collection of six essays; its original title, *Sketches of Etruscan Places*, better indicates the nature of a book which, in fact, includes only half of the originally planned sketches. The other six essays were never written because the deterioration in Lawrence's health prevented him from making a second trip to the Etruscan places, and the book remained unfinished (it was published, post-humously, by Secker, in 1932).

The first signs of Lawrence's interest in the Etruscans appear in the poem 'Cypresses', written in September 1920 at Fiesole (Tuscany), and published in the collection *Birds, Beasts and Flowers* (1923). The poem contains the germ of all the main elements of Lawrence's interpretation of the Etruscans later developed in *Etruscan Places*. At the time, Lawrence had not formulated a clear vision of the Etruscan world and the tone of the poem reflects his uncertainty, particularly by its opening series of unanswered questions:

> Tuscan cypresses,
> What is it?
>
> Folded in like a dark thought
> For which the language is lost,
> Tuscan cypresses,
> Is there a great secret?
> Are our words no good?
>
> The undeliverable secret,
> Dead with a dead race and a deep speech, and yet
> Darkly monumental in you,
> Etruscan cypresses.
>
> Ah, how I admire your fidelity,
> Dark cypresses!
>
> Is it the secret of the long-nosed Etruscans?
> The long-nosed, sensitive-footed, subtly-smiling Etruscans,
> Who made so little noise outside the cypress groves?[13]

The cypresses are seen, then, as the monumental remains of what Lawrence describes as those 'slender, flickering men of Etruria, / Whom Rome called vicious' (lines 34–5). Whether they were vicious, or whether their life-style was 'only evasive and different, dark, like cypress-trees in a wind' (line 42), Lawrence does not know; he can only conjecture that the Romans were wrong, 'For oh, I know, in the dust where we have buried / The silenced races and all their abominations, / We have buried so much of the delicate magic of life' (lines 59–61).[14]

The first essay of *Etruscan Places*, 'Cerveteri', opens by resuming the debate about the supposed viciousness of the Etruscans.

Lawrence questions this assertion on the part of Roman writers but is not really anxious to prove their mistake or bad faith; he is not interested in the non-demonstrable virtue of the Etruscans, and, in fact, he would not like to discover that they *were* virtuous:

> Myself, however, if the Etruscans were vicious, I'm glad they were. To the Puritan all things are impure, as somebody says. And those naughty neighbours of the Romans at least escaped being Puritan.[15]

The scant information about Etruscan culture appealed to Lawrence's curiosity and gave him the opportunity to interpret freely the Etruscan remains in terms of those symbols which best expressed his own ideas. So, he considered the Etruscans as the repositories of the 'delicate magic of life', of the 'great secret of life', of the 'old wisdom'.[16] Not surprisingly for someone who had been looking for an authentic and natural way of living, Lawrence portrays the Etruscans as embodying deep, spontaneous, vital communion with the cosmos and representing a dramatic antithesis to the mechanical, corrupted modern world.

That the Etruscans became the vehicle for a pre-existent thought is confirmed by the fact that Lawrence's belief in an ancient lost wisdom appears as early as the writing of *The White Peacock* where we find a passage which is clearly echoed in 'Cypresses':

> snowdrops are sad and mysterious. We have lost their meaning. They do not belong to us, who ravish them. . . . [Cyril to Lettie] '. . . Emily says they belong to some old wild lost religion – They were the symbols of tears, perhaps, to some strange hearted Druid folk before us.' 'More than tears,' said Lettie 'More than tears, they are so still. Something out of an old religion, that we have lost. . . . They belong to some knowledge we have lost, that I have lost, and that I need. I feel afraid. They seem like something in fate. Do you think, Cyril, we can lose things from off the earth – like mastodons, and those old monstrosities – but things that matter – wisdom?'[17]

The contrasts between the Etruscans and the Romans in the past, and the parallel with the simple peasants and the arrogant Fascists in the present, form the structure within which Lawrence builds his image of the Etruscan world; from it he proceeds to a wider contrast of past and present comparing the ancient Etruscan phallic consciousness with the modern world of mechanical industrialisation and intellectualism.

The Tuscan peasants are considered by Lawrence to be the direct offspring of the Etruscans, rather than of the Romans; they have the same 'physicality', the same warmth as their ancestors. The women of Cerveteri, for example, stimulate Lawrence's imagination:

> And in the full, dark, handsome, jovial faces surely you see the lustre still of the life-loving Etruscans! There are some level Greek eyebrows. But surely there are other vivid, warm faces still jovial with Etruscan vitality, beautiful with the mystery of the unrifled ark, ripe with the phallic knowledge and the Etruscan carelessness!   (p. 35)

Similarly, the faun-face shepherd met in the *Vini e Cucina* at Cerveteri with his 'brown, rather still, straight-nosed face' (p. 16) and 'a queer young fellow . . . a black, black beard on his rather delicate but *gamin* face, and an odd sort of smile' (p. 156) met on the Vulci ruins, recall those Etruscan features he had described years before in 'Cypresses'.

Very differently depicted is the Fascist policeman who asks for Lawrence's passport in Tarquinia, 'A real lout [who] half excused himself in a whining, disgusting sort of fashion' (p. 47). Lawrence shows his contempt for the Fascist régime and its ambition to revive the glorious Roman past, by refusing to visit the museum in Civitavecchia because 'all it contains is Roman stuff, and we don't want to look at that' (p. 47), and considering a 'sheer effrontery' the Roman salute some girls in Volterra make at him:

> a salute which has nothing to do with me, so I don't return it. Politics of all sorts are anathema. But in an Etruscan city which held out so long against Rome I consider the Roman salute unbecoming, and the Roman *imperium* unmentionable.
>
> (pp. 175–6)

Lawrence had previously complained that some Fascist officials in Tarquinia had saluted 'in the Fascist manner: *alla Romana*! Why don't they discover the Etruscan salute, and salute us *all'Etrusca*! (p. 54) and he tried to find out what the Etruscan salute could have been like, by observing the figures on the walls of the painted tombs; in the Tomb of the Leopards one couple on the banqueting couch were, he concluded, 'looking round and making the salute with the right hand curved over, in the usual Etruscan gesture' (p. 75).

Etruria and Rome are contrasted in the past, with implications for the present, as aspects of two opposing visions of the world: the Etruscan culture (and by extension the modern Tuscan peasantry) is all physicality, spontaneity, vitality; the Romans (and by extension the Fascists) were dominated by their 'will-to-power' and their continual life-denying behaviour. Soon after visiting the Etruscan places, Lawrence wrote to his mother-in-law expressing the sense of vitality which emerges from those funerary monuments:

> The Etruscan tombs are very interesting and so nice and lovable. They were a living, fresh, jolly people, lived their own lives without wanting to dominate the lives of others.[18]

This general interpretation of the Etruscan people emphasises some of those major qualities which were central in Lawrence's own ideology. When writing *Etruscan Places*, Lawrence has the opportunity to go into smaller details, to analyse the single elements of a painting, to discover their most hidden meanings; and, in this process, the Etruscan remains often become an attractive vehicle for discussing his own beliefs.

Even in the internal structure of Etruscan society and hierarchy Lawrence finds a correspondence with his theory of 'natural aristocracy':

> The clue to the Etruscan life was the Lucumo, the religious prince. Beyond him were the priests and warriors. Then came the people and the slaves. People and warriors and slaves did not think about religion. There would soon have been no religion left. They felt the symbols and danced the sacred dances. For they were always kept *in touch*, physically, with the mysteries.   (p. 93)

The Etruscan people, he felt, responded physically with their bodies and with their blood to the religious mysteries and that saved their religion from being spoilt by the imposition of rationality: it was not intellectual knowledge; it was the phallic consciousness and the sensual awareness which, for Lawrence, was lost after the time of the biblical king David:

> We have lost almost entirely the great and intricately developed sensual awareness, or sense-awareness, and sense-knowledge, of the ancients. It was a great depth of knowledge arrived at direct, by instinct and intuition, as we say, not by reason. It was a knowledge based not on words but on images. The abstraction was not into generalisations or into qualities, but into symbols. And the connection was not logical but emotional.[19]

Lawrence seems to find evidence of this in Etruscan art, even in the simple architecture of the tombs of Cerveteri:

> with those easy, natural proportions whose beauty one hardly notices, they come so naturally, physically. It is the natural beauty of proportion of the phallic consciousness, contrasted with the more studied or ecstatic proportion of the mental and spiritual Consciousness we are accustomed to.   (p. 25)

That Lawrence was providing an interpretation in terms of his own ideology becomes clear when one recalls that since the autumn of 1926 he had been engaged in the writing of *Lady Chatterley's Lover*, a work which he describes in a letter dated 15 March 1928 as:

> a nice and tender phallic novel – not a sex novel in the ordinary sense of the word. . . . I sincerely believe in restoring the other, the phallic consciousness, into our lives: because it is the source of all real beauty, and all real gentleness.[20]

If every religion has its own rituals and images, symbols are the main language of communication in a non-intellectual religion like the Etruscan. The sensual, mysterious quality of Etruscan life and religion, its 'physicality', speaks mainly through the use of two symbols, the phallic stone (the *cippus*), and the stone house (the *arx*), which were placed at the entrance of the tombs at Cerveteri according to the sex of the dead person. These, for Lawrence, indicate the essence of their beliefs and way of life:

the phallic symbol. Here it is, in stone, unmistakable, and everywhere, around these tombs. Here it is, big and little, standing by the doors, or inserted, quite small, into the rock: the phallic stone! . . . By the doorway of some tombs there is a carved stone house, or a stone imitation chest with sloping lids like the two sides of the roof of an oblong house. . . . The stone house . . . suggests the Noah's Ark without the boat part: . . . the Ark, the *arx*, the womb. The womb of all the world, that brought forth all the creatures. The womb, the *arx*, where life retreats in the last refuge.   (pp. 29–30)

Before seeing the Etruscan symbolic phallic stone, Lawrence had adopted that challenging symbol in his own figurative work, attributing to it a profound vital meaning:

I . . . put a phallus, a lingam you call it, in each one of my pictures somewhere. And I paint no picture that won't shock people's castrated social spirituality. I do this out of positive belief, that the phallus is a great sacred image: it represents a deep, deep life which has been denied in us, and still is denied.[21]

This Lawrence wrote on 27 February 1927 to Earl Brewster, his Buddhist American friend who, only a few weeks later, was his companion on the Etruscan tour.

It is not surprising that Etruscan art had a marked influence on Lawrence's paintings. This is particularly evident in a painting like *Dance Sketch* (probably made in January 1929) where the pale body of the woman and the reddish man – the typical colours of the Etruscan male and female figures – dance a sort of pagan dance, joined also by a dancing goat intended to stand for the god Pan. The painting reproduces the movements Lawrence had observed in the many dancing figures painted in the Etruscan tombs; particularly, his description of a man and a woman dancing on the walls of the Tomb of the Feast, recalls the main elements of his own 'dance sketch':

Wildly the bacchic woman throws back her head and curves out her long, strong fingers, wild and yet contained within herself, while the broad-bodied young man turns round to her, lifting his dancing hand to hers till the thumbs all but touch. They are dancing in the open, past little trees, and birds are running, and

a little fox-tailed dog is watching something with the naïv
intensity of the young.   (p. 77)

Dance as represented in Etruscan paintings assumes for Lawrenc
a much wider meaning and becomes an expression of the Etrusca
vision of the world and of their religion of life which Lawrence
once again, contrasts with our modern civilisation; the Etrusca
dance is:

> a dance that surges from within, like a current in the sea. It is a
> if . . . they drew their vitality from different depths that we ar
> denied. . . . Behind all the dancing was a vision, and even
> science of life, a conception of the universe and man's plac
> in the universe which made men live to the depth of thei
> capacity.   (pp. 88–9)

Lawrence was then deeply inspired by his view of the Etruscan
when he preached his phallic-cosmic mysticism based on the sens
of 'touch'. He often found this quality represented in the Etrusca
paintings of Tarquinia and he poetically describes this in a scen
from the Tomb of the Painted Vases which shows a man and
woman lying on the banqueting couch:

> Rather gentle and lovely is the way he touches the woman unde
> the chin, with a delicate caress. That again is one of the charm
> of the Etruscan paintings: they really have the sense of touch
> the people and the creatures are all really in touch. It is one o
> the rarest qualities, in life as well as in art. There is plenty o
> pawing and laying hold, but no real touch. In pictures especially
> the people may be in contact, embracing or laying hands on on
> another. But there is no soft flow of touch. . . . Here, in thi
> faded Etruscan painting, there is a quiet flow of touch that unite
> the man and the woman on the couch, the timid boy behind
> the dog that lifts his nose, even the very garlands that han
> from the wall.   (pp. 83–4)

The concept of touch as a means of physical and pre-ment
communication is a major theme in *Lady Chatterley's Lover*, th
novel which reflects, on a fictional level, the same ideology tha
Lawrence expresses in *Etruscan Places*.

The absence of 'touch' is represented in Sir Clifford who

throughout the novel, embodies the negatives of modern society: industrialism, intellectualism, mechanicism. In the second chapter of the novel, Connie still sticks 'passionately' to the lame Clifford:

> But she could not help feeling how little connexion he really had with people. . . . He was not in touch. He was not in actual touch with anybody, . . . Connie felt that she herself didn't really, not really touch him; perhaps there was nothing to get at ultimately; just a negation of human contact.[22]

Clifford's opposite, Mellors, in the second chapter from the end, formulates that 'religion of touch', the inner reality and mystery of which he had gradually penetrated together with his lover:

> Sex is really only touch, the closest of all touch. And it's touch we're afraid of. We're only half-conscious, and half alive. We've got to come alive and aware. Especially the English have got to get into touch with one another, a bit delicate and a bit tender. It's our crying need.[23]

Here Lawrence is specifically addressing his fellow-countrymen who, more than others, need a re-birth. In 'A Propos of *Lady Chatterley's Lover*' Lawrence shows England, even more directly, the path towards re-birth:

> If England is to be regenerated . . . then it will be by the arising of a new blood-contact, a new touch, and a new marriage.[24]

Lawrence had written the first two versions of his prophetic novel between October 1926 and February 1927. Two weeks before his Etruscan tour he had expressed his intention to 'go over' his novel again,[25] and in a letter to his English publisher, Secker, on 17 August, he asserted his intention 'to write a continuation of it, later'.[26] In December 1927 Lawrence began his third and final version of *Lady Chatterley's Lover*, a 'new' novel rather than 'a continuation'.[27] The Etruscan tour therefore falls right in the middle of the long process of writing the novel and was a decisive experience.

Lawrence had gradually developed, through the years and through his writings, his own image of the world and had travelled round the globe trying to find his 'Rananim': in the new Australian

continent, in the old Mexican civilisation, among the America
Indians. Those cultures, however, were too different and alien
accommodate fully and deeply someone whose formation wa
imbued with the major influences of western civilisation.

Visiting the Etruscan cities, Lawrence saw his own belie
objectified in the paintings, in the phallic stone, in the Ark, ar
his vision itself suddenly became clearer. The Etruscan world la
in a past where Lawrence could recognise his own cultural roo
and identify a sense of vitality which, through the centuries, ha
gradually been sapped and had finally been irretrievably lost.

Lawrence began to paint seriously again in November 1926 ar
commented: 'It's rather fun, discovering one can paint one's ow
ideas and one's own feelings'.[28] Observing the Etruscan painting
he therefore tried to decipher their figurative language, whic
expressed their ideas and their feelings. Even though the Etrusca
language had been lost, and their literature had not survived, the
'old secret' was not lost to Lawrence's eyes. Through his ow
'structure of feeling' he recovered and absorbed it, giving re-bir
to it in his prophetic novel.

Lawrence had finally *'penetrated'* into Italy, going 'back, ba
down the old ways of time', finding in the Etruscan past the re
meaning of life, of that vitality which continued even after deat
in the underworld, expressed in the gaiety, and brightness of th
colours, of the dances, of the music which accompanied the funer
ceremonies – the vitality and naturalness which is at the origin
the world and that Lawrence describes simply and poetically
Etruscan Places:

> Brute force crushes many plants. Yet the plants rise agai
> The Pyramids will not last a moment compared with the dais
> And before Buddha or Jesus spoke the nightingale sang, ar
> long after the words of Jesus and Buddha are gone into oblivic
> the nightingale still will sing. Because it is neither preaching n
> teaching nor commanding nor urging. It is just singing. And
> the beginning was not a Word, but a chirrup.   (p. 57)

Notes

1. D. H. Lawrence, *Sea and Sardinia* (Harmondsworth, Middx: Penguin, 1976) pp. 130–1.
2. Ibid.
3. Cf. *The Lost Girl* (1920), *Aaron's Rod* (1922), *Kangaroo* (1923), *The Plumed Serpent* and *St. Mawr* (1925), 'Sun' (written in 1925 and published in *The Woman Who Rode Away and Other Stories* in 1928).
4. After leaving Italy (June 1928), Lawrence took a few short trips to Switzerland, France, Mallorca and Italy again; however, he always stayed in hotels, never settling down. The only place the Lawrences rented was Villa Beau Soleil, at Bandol in France (October 1929) from where Lawrence moved to the sanatorium at Vence (February 1930) for his 'longest journey'.
5. D. H. Lawrence, *Lady Chatterley's Lover* (Harmondsworth, Middx: Penguin, 1974) p. 266.
6. Lawrence and Frieda arrived on Lake Garda in September 1912 and rented a villa at Gargnano where they lived until the end of March 1913; the period April–September 1913 was divided between Germany and England; at the end of September the Lawrences settled at Lerici on the Ligurian coast where they stayed until June 1914.
7. D. H. Lawrence, *Twilight in Italy* (Harmondsworth, Middx: Penguin, 1976) p. 26.
8. D. H. Lawrence, *The Lost Girl*, ed. John Worthen (Cambridge: Cambridge University Press, 1981) p. 294. The first 200 pages of this novel, entitled 'The Insurrection of Miss Houghton', were written in Italy, between January and March 1913; Lawrence started working on the novel again in February 1920, when he was back in Italy, and finished *The Lost Girl* at the beginning of May 1920. Dr Worthen, in his 'Introduction', explains that Lawrence could not work on the novel during the war years because the manuscript had been left in Germany; he had access to it again only in February 1920 and took up what, in fact, was to become a 'new' novel (cf. pp. xix–xxxii). Was it a mere coincidence that Lawrence could not finish a novel he had started in Italy until he had returned to Italy? Did Lawrence need to draw direct inspiration from the Italian environment to finish a novel whose protagonist chooses the primitive natural life of 'the dark half of humanity' in the Abruzzi mountains?
9. Lawrence translated *Mastro Don Gesualdo* and *Little Novels of Sicily* (February–April 1922); the Introductory Note to *Mastro Don Gesualdo* was written in March 1922 and later developed into a full-length Introduction (May 1927); the translation of *Cavalleria Rusticana and Other Stories*, started in August 1922, was completed in August–September 1927.
10. Letter to E. H. Brewster, *Letters*, IV, p. 155.
11. The Lawrences stayed in Ceylon just over a month (13 March–22 April 1922); then they lived in Australia for the period May–August 1922, and in September they went to New Mexico. On 14 July 1925 Lawrence

wrote to his sister Emily: 'I feel very much drawn to the Mediterranean again' (Moore, II, p. 847).

12. 'David', *Phoenix*, p. 61. Cf. also D. H. Lawrence, *Aaron's Rod* (Harmondsworth, Middx: Penguin, 1962) p. 253. According to tradition Florence derived its name from the abundance of flowers in the place where the town was situated; the lily, as the noblest flower, was chosen to be its symbol and it appears on the coat of arms of the city.

13. 'Cypresses', *Complete Poems*, p. 296.

14. Cf. L. D. Clark, *The Minoan Distance* (Tucson: University of Arizona Press, 1980) p. 381; Keith Sagar, *D. H. Lawrence: Life into Art* (New York: Viking, 1985) pp. 280–1; Billy T. Tracy, Jr, *D. H. Lawrence and the Literature of Travel* (Ann Arbor, Michigan: UMI Research Press 1983) pp. 94–5.

15. D. H. Lawrence, *Etruscan Places* (London: Secker, 1932) p. 12. Hereafter, references to the pages of this volume will be incorporated in the text.

16. Cf. 'Cypresses', *Complete Poems*; and 'Foreword' to *Fantasia of the Unconscious* (Harmondsworth, Middx: Penguin, 1978).

17. D. H. Lawrence, *The White Peacock*, ed. Andrew Robertson (Cambridge Cambridge University Press, 1983) pp. 129–30.

18. 14 April 1927; Frieda Lawrence, *'Not I, But the Wind . . .'* (London William Heinemann, 1935) p. 208.

19. D. H. Lawrence, *Apocalypse*, ed. Mara Kalnins (Cambridge: Cambridge University Press, 1980) p. 91.

20. Letter to Harriet Monroe, Moore, II, p. 1046.

21. Letter to E. H. Brewster, Moore, II, p. 967.

22. Lawrence, *Lady Chatterley's Lover*, pp. 16–17.

23. Ibid., p. 290.

24. *Phoenix* II, p. 508.

25. Letter to Nancy Pearn, 22 March 1927, Moore, II, p. 970.

26. *Letters from D. H. Lawrence to Martin Secker, 1911–1930* (privately published, 1970) p. 93.

27. See, for example, the letter to S. S. Koteliansky, 8 December 1927 Moore, II, p. 1025.

28. Letter to Dorothy Brett, 24 November 1926, University of Cincinnati Ohio.

8

The Sense of History in *The Rainbow*

MARK KINKEAD-WEEKES

A genuinely new possession is something which transforms the present. The insincere historicity of a culture which does no more than understand is a mere will to repeat the past; but a sincere historicity is a readiness to discover the sources which feed all life and therefore the life of the present as well.

Karl Jaspers, *Man in the Modern Age*

Without a felt relationship to the present, a portrayal of history is impossible. But this relationship, in the case of really great historical art, does not consist in alluding to contemporary events . . . but in bringing the past to life as the prehistory of the present, in giving poetic life to those historical, social and human forces which, in the course of a long evolution, have made our present-day life what it is and as we experience it.

Georg Lukács, *The Historical Novel*

The Rainbow is an historical novel – and if we have not read it so, it is despite the hint, in the pointed division of the opening chapter, which clearly asks for a double focus. From one angle, we are to see archetypal Men and Women in a timeless nature, outside history. The Brangwens, farming their borderland, reveal modes of being that are universal and 'from the beginning'; oppositions that provide a basic language for all the individual persons and particular conflicts that follow, so that we can compare and contrast three generations of lovers in unchanging terms and grasp the underlying nature of their relationships. However, the second section of the chapter begins pointedly with a date, 1840, and a marked change affecting the daily consciousness of the Brangwens,

121

the cutting of the Nottingham Canal across their lands. The novel will turn out also to be very much concerned, though in Lawrentian ways, with major changes in English life between 1840 and 1905: with effects of industrialism and urbanisation, with education, the emancipation of women, the decline of religion. From this angle the structure looks quite different. Instead of seeing the same conflicts reorchestrated (and so understanding them better), we have now to see each generation as very differently affected by historical development and social change. Moreover the movement *into* history is an important theme. We shall not find the 'hungry forties' or the Chartists in the world of the beginning: Tom's Marsh Farm is still relatively isolated and Lydia comes there as a refugee from history; but we can watch Anna and Will begin to enter the mainstream of their time; and Ursula and Skrebensky live in a fully historic world.[1]

It is not of course surprising that criticism should have concentrated on the archetypal ahistorical view. That is where the art seems most challenging and newly imaginative, sounding chords the whole work will orchestrate: there is the rich earth on which the Men are at one with the whole of nature, so that the life of each participates and is reflected in the other; there, conversely, is the road, the church tower on the hill, pointing up, out, beyond, to the town, the civilisation, the world of awareness, individuation, the separate self. Can the opposed visions, the conflicting impulses, the breadth and the height be *married*? We set out to discover how and why the marriage of opposites – present anytime, in everyone – becomes creative or destructive in the personal stories of Tom and Lydia, Will and Anna, Ursula and Skrebensky, as these shed light on one another; and we find a new kind of vision, demanding a new kind of art, a new attitude to 'character', new dimensions of symbol, rhythm, language. It is hardly surprising that we should tend to concentrate on such dimensions. But, for once, I propose to take the other view, and ask how exactly the novel sees the major changes in provincial middle-class life between 1840 and 1905, and in what sense one might make a serious claim for it as 'historical' fiction, in those terms.

The first surprise is to find an elaborate chronology. From three fixed points – the Polish insurrection of 1863; the wedding of Anna and Will on Saturday 23 December 1882;[2] and the outbreak of the Boer War in October 1899 – one can work backward and forward, using a multitude of particulars, to show that (apart from four easily explicable mistakes), Lawrence had a remarkably accurate sense of when as well as where he was on every page, far more than was necessary for novelistic purposes. Confidence grows when one works out that Ursula must have passed her London matric in 1900, and then finds 'June 1900' on her application form in the manuscript, though this has disappeared from the first edition. More extraordinarily, the novel might even help to date events outside. Lawrence based the outer shape of Will's career on that of Alfred Burrows, father of his fiancée Louie. James Boulton, writing of Alfred's woodwork classes in Cossall, and supposing Lawrence right that 'he' was about thirty at the time, puts the date at 1894.[3] But the novel's chronology says 1891 – and Wright's directory for 1891 mentions the new reredos carved for Cossall Church by 'the carving class'.[4] There may of course have been two carving classes; but one then discovers why a class might have begun in 1891; because it was in that year that such evening classes first became eligible for grants, so that there was a remarkable flowering just then.[5] It is not often that one can use a fiction to suggest the possibility of a factual correction to one of the most meticulous of scholars. Moreover, several revisions seem sensitive about chronology. For instance, Lawrence rightly decides that Skrebensky could not have hired a taxi to take Ursula for a drive in 1899.[6] Indeed, it is only by reading historically that one realises quite how exciting a 'coup' and a 'romance' that ride was meant to be. It was only just possible for the son of a Baron-Vicar of a local church to have got hold of a car from one of only three suppliers in Nottingham, and there were only 125 in the whole shire four years later.[7] But it was possible, because Nottingham was remarkably progressive; indeed several motor-cars had been locally manufactured before 1900, when the Automobile Club's famous expedition to popularise the motor-car came to town. Again, Lawrence oddly designates one of the books that Ursula and Maggie read in their lunch-break as 'some work about "Woman and Labour"'. He has a particular book in mind (hence the inverted commas), but also knows that Olive Schreiner's *Women and Labour* was not published until 1911, when he sent it to Louie, and this is a decade earlier.[8] Such concern for accuracy is remarkable, and there are very few anachronisms.[9] Lawrence does displace, by two or three years, some details of the Ursula story where it most closely approaches his own experience. Her accurately described tram-ride, for instance, from Ilkeston station to 'St. Philip's School

Brinsley Street' in 1900, obviously draws on Lawrence's own twice-weekly journeys to the Pupil Teacher Centre – but the tram-service only opened in 1903. Since he knew this very well, however, the licence is deliberate. Yet even if one conceded a tendency to displace memory to that extent, one would still be testing a fiction by extraordinary standards. Of course we need not think of him as some painstaking local historian – he could clearly draw for his third generation on his own memory; for the second on all he knew or had heard of the Burrows family; and for the first he had points of reference in well-known locals like the Polish refugee Baron von Hube, Vicar of Greasley,[10] and the Fritchley family who had farmed outside Cossall for 'over two hundred years' (as both Trueman's *History*[11] and *The Rainbow* put it). What does need insisting on, however, is that Lawrence's imagination was as densely 'historical' *in its nature* when he wrote *The Rainbow* as it was archetypal and 'mythic'.[12] There will therefore be a myriad of details which could say more than they seem to now, if only we hadn't lost the sense of date that Lawrence commanded. Tom Brangwen associates a Paisley shawl with his mother, precisely, because the pattern had its great vogue in the 1830s. More important, when Will rides a motorbike into 'Beldover'/Eastwood in 1902, an unworldly man has become remarkably up-to-date. (There were only 40 in the shire in 1903.[13]) Readers in 1915 could fine-tune as we cannot; and local readers still more so. Of course little Anna and her step-father found Derby's indoor market attractive. It still is, but when they went it was gleaming new.[14] And of course young Anna, determined to be a lady, would want to model herself on Princess Alexandra – for all Nottingham was full of her after the Prince opened the Castle Museum in 1878, when Anna was fifteen.

Given that his imagination was historical then, with what sense of pattern and diagnosis does Lawrence draw his Portrait of an Age?

'About 1840', canal, colliery and railway come together, to alter the life and consciousness of the Brangwens. The date may seem approximate short-hand, for a more gradual and complex process, but Lawrence chooses an actual spot – one can stand on it today[15] – in order to dramatise in a single vivid picture the essentials of industrial progress, and the picture turns out to be more accurately dated than appeared at first. A canal goes over a road on embankments and a bridge; through the arch is a colliery; there is a railway at the foot of Ilkeston hill; and a farm tucked away behind the embankment in pre-industrial England, yet within constant sight and sound of the Industrial Revolution in the midst of the countryside. Actually, 1840 was nearer the end of the canal-building age than the beginning; the Nottingham Canal had opened in 1796, and, with the Cromford and the Erewash canals, had opened up markets that gave the Erewash Valley coal-owners a competitive edge.[16] But when they were faced with the threat of a railway in Leicestershire which might turn the tables, the Valley coal-owners met at the Sun Inn in Eastwood, and as a result the Midland Counties Railway opened, in 1840, with an Erewash spur a few years later.[17] Vast new markets became available and an extraordinary mining, industrial, trading and population expansion began. So new bits of canal and new coal seams were opened, about 1840. Barber, Walker & Co. had taken over Cossall Colliery by 1844;[18] and it even seems that by 1836 a new route for the canal may have been cut (replacing a loop on the other side of Cossall Marsh whose embankment broke in 1823);[19] more steeply banked, and hence involving a narrow-arched aqueduct across the road which for the first time shut the Marsh Farm off from Ilkeston. Both Nottingham and Derby began a rapid industrial expansion. The Nottingham lace-curtain, that essential feature of Victorian respectability, went into factory-production in 1846, to be followed by bicycles, sewing-machines and motorbikes, all of which duly make their appearance in *The Rainbow*. Ilkeston had grown by only 1000 people in the fifteen years before 1846, but grew nearly as much in the next five. By 1881 (just before Will marries Anna) the 4500 of the 1840s had leapt to over 14,000; and in 1891 (when Will began those evening classes) it was nearly 20,000. Eastwood had 'the greatest increase of any parish in Nottinghamshire during the 19th century in population per square mile'.[20] So those houses spreading across the skyline at the end of the book were quite as spectacular and ugly a development as *The Rainbow* suggests.

On the other hand, the prosperity of the Marsh Farm, supplying that growing urban population, becomes readily intelligible. Though Lawrence does not spell it out, it is clear how there is business enough for a separate family butchery, and why the farm-Brangwens, as they prosper, go up the social ladder. If one reads historically, what seemed insignificant detail reveals a chain of implication. Take, for example, the generational significance of the engine. We now know why a demand for lace-designers for machine-production took Alfred Brangwen into the factory, to be followed by his son Will, until he escapes. But Tom's son, studying engineering in London via Nottingham High School, becomes a technocrat and manager. The prosperity that made Tom squire-like buys the education that turns his sons into gentlemen, on terms with the Big House. But we can also see an irony in making Skrebensky an engineer in the third generation, or rather, a Sapper. For in his world the Industrial Revolution has turned to war. The novel may end in 1905, but we know Anton will have to return from India to help engineer the destruction in Flanders. The passages which deal with the sprawling ugliness on the skyline, and the de-humanisation of the miners' lives in Wiggiston where Tom Junior is manager, are the one area where the book's socio-historical insight has been discussed. However, it has far too often been in isolation from the actual complexity of the fiction. The Lawrence of 1914–15 was by no means simply 'agin' the machine, as the *Study of Thomas Hardy*[21] made clear, and *The Rainbow* is very much aware of how the widening horizons of Ursula's generation relate to the mine and the factory. She has no intention of being poor; Lawrence knows perfectly well what has produced her mother's sewing machine, and the bicycles on which Ursula and Maggie tour the countryside. Most of all, we shall not understand Lawrence's diagnosis of the ills of industrialism and urbanisation without seeing how these connect with the revolution in education, which followed.

The first generation of Brangwens are only half-educated. Alfred goes to school in Ilkeston in the 1840s, but it is only in drawing that he shows any talent, hence the factory – though we see later that there was more to him. Frank soon goes into the butchery, and their sister marries a collier (there is no talk of her education). But the mother has ambitions for Tom and sends him to Derby Grammar School, which dates from the sixteenth century and offers the classical education of the old foundation. However, Tom cannot articulate, argue, or become mentally conscious. He has strong and delicate feelings, and an instinct for the order of mathematics; but he seems unable to develop intellectually, and is glad to give up and take over the farm at seventeen. Lydia had a governess in Poland but she too, despite the seeming progress-iveness of having been a nurse, is a physical and mystic being rather than an intellectual one. So their marriage, though the most uccessful in the book, carries in all its richness a sense of limitation, f human resources that have not yet opened out.

The second generation have far wider horizons. Young Tom ve saw going to Nottingham High, another sixteenth-century oundation; but in this more scientific age he goes on, not to lassical Oxbridge, but to London, almost certainly the Royal ichool of Mines which, with the School of Science, became Imperial College. There, in the eighties, 'some of the most energetic cientific and mathematic people' were indeed to be found, notably Huxley. We measure the contrast with his father, and how young om and his brother have become gentlemen. In the other family Vill, pulled into the lace factory behind his father, is neither a gentleman nor a success. Yet he too escapes his background because of the intensity of his self-education in the arts, which ligns him with another side of the new times. Fred may read Ruskin, but Will is an enthusiastic practitioner of the Gothic and he Pre-Raphaelite. His woodcarving becomes the link with the Morris-inspired Arts and Crafts movement, and he is ready for his hance when it comes. What had seemed peripheral and private urns out to be in the mainstream of its time. Out of the evening lasses and the summer holiday schools comes the post of Art and Handwork Instructor for the new County Education Department; xperimental classes in new Swedish methods of teaching manual lexterity in schools; and a role in the education of the underprivieged.

What still lags is the education of women; and here the chronology holds ironies which I for one had missed. Anna is better ducated than her mother, and has a more developed and critical ntellect, but she is born just too early to get the education she leserves. In 1872 she is sent to a Dame School, in ironic uxtaposition to the Education Act. She goes on to 'the High School' n Nottingham, founded in 1875, only the sixth to be created by he Girls' Public Day School Company,[22] but in its very earliest ears when it still resembles a young ladies' seminary. Even so, as Anna and Will argue about art and religion, we have a dramatic neasure of how the consciousness of the second generation of Brangwens has altered, and is becoming articulate. But in the third generation the change is spectacular. In 1892 Ursula is at no Dame School but one of the new kindergartens pioneered in Nottinghamshire by the progressive Inspector Abel, who makes n appearance in the novel.[23] Then she and all her siblings attend,

as they now must, a state school made free since 1891 – which
as well, since there are eight of them! Next, the eldest three go o
to the Girls' High, now risen in the world and firmly establishe
in a handsome lace-manufacturer's house – once again we se
connections between industry, wealth and education. Gudrun
headed for Art College, unlike her father, and his. Ursula's Londo
Matriculation will qualify her as a teacher, then take her to th
'Gothic' grandeur of the new University College of Nottinghar
with the chance of a degree – and we measure the full contra:
with her mother, and her grandmother. The difference in th
position of the three generations is carefully and dramaticall
plotted. Of course, Ursula's two years as a teacher also expose th
seamier side of the coming of free and compulsory education. Th
pushing-up of the leaving age to 12 in 1899 (13, by bye-law, i
Nottinghamshire)[24] created desperate over-crowding. That is wh
in 'St. Philips' the big-room has been glass-partitioned and thre
classes of 55–60 children each are being taught simultaneousl
Both school and (Ursula thinks) university have become lik
factories. So though the story of *The Rainbow* is essentially
widening circles – hence the two chapters thus entitled – the mo:
highly educated of all the Brangwen women is deeply disillusione
by her experience.

And the same is true of the other New Women, for we hav
also been talking about female emancipation. This had been centr.
to the novel from its earliest stage *The Sisters*, whose germ, Lawren
told Garnett, had even then been 'woman becoming individua
self-responsible, taking her own initiative.'[25] Ursula and Gudru
are only two of a number of emancipated women who, i
professional independence, freedom of ideas and morals, and th
demand for the vote, proclaim new conceptions of womanhoo
Winifred Inger seems the most 'advanced': the science studies
Newnham, the contempt of men, the critique of religion, th
friends who seem to conform to a smug provincial society but ar
inwardly raging. Her lesbian relation with Ursula is finally rejecte
by the girl, yet she had been a liberating and enriching influenc
But there is something half-hearted which emerges when sh
settles, open-eyed, for marriage with Tom Brangwen the min
manager; for domesticity within a system, both of which sh
had condemned. This says something about her times, but als
something about her: she is a compromised Diana, someho
only half-formed. Maggie Schofield has also become a competer

rofessional in a man's world, but in order to do so has had to ivide herself in two, so that paradoxically 'there was something ke subjection in Maggie's very freedom'.[26] Her personal life exists uite separately from her working life. And though she has dvanced ideas of love – that it is beyond law and must be plucked vhere it is found – she is unfulfilled, brooding, melancholy.)orothy Russell is a serious, intense suffragette, devoted to he cause that all these women support – though Ursula with awrence's reservation, that what really needs to be changed is he inner life of individuals, which can't be done by merely mending the political system. Dorothy's circle is also sexually iberated, though non-promiscuous. Yet here, too, freedom does iot seem to have brought fulfilment. Of all these, however, Ursula eems to embody the New Woman most powerfully. Her life seems o include them all with greater intensity than any: the education, he struggle for independence through work, the freethinking, the iberated sexuality, above all the passionate pursuit of the liberty o be herself and shape her life to her own wishes. This is the onstant impulse beneath all the violently contradictory phases of ier life: as she rides above the crowd or defines herself against her /oung lover; in her female relation with Winifred or the male world »f Brinsley Street School; in the world of the senses with Andrew ichofield or the world of the mind at university; in the passionate exuality with Skrebensky or the even more passionate aspiration vhich turns against and destroys him. In every phase the New Voman demands the freedom to create herself and her life. So vhen she staggers up the hill at the end, to miscarriage and)reakdown, she seems a bitterly ironic comment on the impulse owards new life of the Brangwen women at the beginning.

But to see why, and to establish the ultimate basis for Lawrence's liagnosis of what had happened since 1840 – from which one night hope to connect up his critique of industrialism, of the igliness of urbanisation, of the malaise of education, and the non-ulfilment of feminism – I think we need to see how it was the lecline of the religious sense that was the most significant of all to i writer who called himself 'a passionately religious man'.[27] The vorld of Tom and Lydia is destroyed by flood, but far from having)een sinful, it was a world in which the forces of divine creativity :ould build, in the human relation of man, woman and child, a House for the Lord. It was also a limited world in which whole limensions of human potential had not yet opened. But as a result

of the 'widening circles', as the century wears on, we see in th
novel how rational scepticism and scientific materialism not onl
bring about the decline of the church but also of the religious sens
itself. Anna pits against both a newly sharp critical intellect
exposing the reduction by the Victorian church of religion t
morality, and turning against Christian symbols and mysteries
scientific, literal materialism, to which her less intellectual an
articulate husband can find no answer. In Lincoln Cathedral he
resistance to Will's religious ecstasy and self-abandon reaches
climax, as she sets out to destroy his sense of mystic unity, in th
name of humanism, multiplicity, freedom. Her brother Fred studie
Huxley's agnosticism. Her brother Tom, the scientist and engineer
moves beyond the agnostic to the atheist. He becomes cynic an
hedonist; sardonic observer of the wife-swapping of the Wiggisto
miners and the reduction of their personal and family life i
subjection to the machine. His own display of domestic feeling
Ursula thinks, is a kind of sentimentality based on no commitmen
to any system of value. Winifred, scientifically educated, directs a
religion the other form of demythologising intellect, 'comparativ
religion'; seeing all religions as the deifying of man's own values
and his own impulses to submit to or identify with what are n
more than aspects of himself. Dr Frankstone, teaching biology a
university, will recognise nothing mysterious about the creativ
processes of life, which science will sooner or later explain an
codify. The mystic and religious side of Ursula rebels against al
these, her mother, her uncle, Winifred; and turns from Dr Frank
stone to see the cell under her microscope as a mysterious an
gleaming triumph of infinity. But she also makes love in he
father's church, and listens in scorn to the old hackneyed tale o
Genesis and the Flood and the Rainbow; for Ursula is a ferment o
contradiction. Like Anna with Will, she reacts against too-read
self-abandonment or inadequate selfhood in Skrebensky; but he
own aspiring self-assertion turns out to be even more destructive
beaked, like a harpy. Where the religious sense is not destroyed
it seems perverted.

As the novel's history moves into the twentieth century, then
it is not merely that the great promise of Victorian progress an
opportunity seems to have gone sour, or even that individual
have become hollow or destructive, marshy or brittle. Somethin
seems to have gone wrong with the very springs of human life
But to seek below the symptoms for the innermost cause, is to be

steadily forced back to the *other* way of looking, the archetypal vision of the Beginning. History, for Lawrence, is only to be finally understood in terms of the timeless deep-structure within personal stories, those basic and opposite impulses within all people and relationships: the impulse to be at-one with all created nature through the body and the senses; the opposite impulse to become individual, to know, and act upon the 'other', in separateness and differentiation. In one, we are aware of ourselves only in togetherness with nature and fellow man or woman; the other defines the self against the not-self, a process of individuation, self-conscious thought and utterance. One is stable; the other holds in change both threat and promise. As archetypal Men and Women give way to Tom and Lydia, the personal stories reveal both impulses conflicting in each, and both individuals unfulfilled. But with strange beauty and power they are drawn magnetically together like opposite 'poles'; and experience in marriage a kind of death and rebirth. Sexual relationship is a crucible of conflict, and it is intensely painful to 'die' to the old self and be transformed through the 'other'; yet from conflict and self-abandon springs rich new life. Out of the ashes of dead selves the lovers rise like phoenixes, more themselves each time; separate individuals, strangers, yet indissolubly bound together. Biblical language and symbol insist that we see this marriage of opposites as a religious mystery. In continual Genesis, man and woman create and recreate each other, and the tree of knowledge, by marrying the divine forces within and between them. They journey through the wilderness from exile, but meet as pillars of cloud and fire, passing through each other to create a rainbow-arch, a doorway to the Promised Land of new life beyond; with new freedom for man, woman and child. In marriage, rather than stone or wood or scroll, they build a House for the Lord to dwell in. Though a flood destroys their 'Old Testament' world, and Tom/Noah is drowned, he and she have laid hold of eternity.

Anna and Will partly re-enact this archetypal pattern – but with new strain on both sides. Anna tends to resist the movement towards the other: her greater individuality, wary intelligence, more developed self-consciousness make it harder to give or risk herself, as Lydia had done. Conversely Will, who seems assured because he is so unselfconscious, is over-ready to abandon himself and merge into the other, which betrays insufficiency of self. As she resists, he becomes insistent, clutching, predatory. As he demands, she resists more strongly. The creative conflict of opposites turns into a battle for domination which Anna, the more self-assured articulate individual, is bound to win. But having conquered, she dances her own fertility to the Lord, against the shadowy man in the doorway. She builds a house for herself on Pisgah, but doesn't enter the Promised Land or open it for Will. Indeed, as she pushes him off, he nearly drowns in the flood of his insufficiency, and only gradually develops some independent selfhood. Now we see how directly the greater potential and the lesser achievement are *related*. New dimensions and tensions of religion and art, intellect and spirit, opening out through history, mean that there is more to marry in the second generation – but also that it is more difficult to marry. The polarities become more extreme, and the increased one-sidedness in each begins to turn the conflict from creation to destruction.

Ursula in the third generation embodies all the opposites of her family at peak intensity, and with greater awareness than any. She is intensely visionary and intensely sceptical, spiritual and fleshly, arrogant and unfixed, emancipated and primitive, and it is her fate because of her generation to be conscious of herself in all these aspects. She also wins new freedom of choice. So we watch her trying continually to resolve her contradictions by pursuing one aspect of herself to the exclusion of others, but never finding the way to marry them: 'always the shining doorway was a gate into another yard, dirty, and active, and dead'.[28] She reacts one way and another, but none can fulfil because each reduces her complex being. In the three crises of her affair with Skrebensky we measure the escalating difficulty of the marriage of opposites, and the still greater antagonism that comes from asserting partial selves. When the young lovers dance at the wedding, it becomes a destructive contest in which Ursula, like her mother, is victrix. When Skrebensky returns from Africa, some years after the Boer War, Ursula is reacting against university and the life of the mind, and they achieve a purely sexual kind of consummation, mating their 'darker' sides. Inevitably, however, reaction sets in, and the terrible scene on the beach shows how Ursula cannot be satisfied while her infinitely aspiring 'bright' side is denied. Under an incandescent moon, beside a brilliant sea, she tries to force the opposite of what they had had, some consummation of intense awareness – and succeeds only in destruction, like a harpy. Then she tries to settle for domesticity, but that is to reduce herself still more. She has tried all the reductive ways; only the inclusive one remains, and Lawrence confronts her with it in that powerful last scene with the horses.

But first – how do these personal stories, in revealing deep-structure, illuminate the social history the novel has recorded? Here I believe Lawrence would have agreed with the Jaspers of my epigraph:

> A genuinely new possession is something which transforms the present. The insincere historicity of a culture which does no more than understand is a mere will to repeat the past; but a sincere historicity is a readiness to discover the sources which feed all life and therefore the life of the present as well.[29]

Just as we must see each generation of *The Rainbow* in a different context because of the history of society; so, conversely, we must understand the history of society in terms of 'the sources which feed all life, and therefore the life of the present as well'. It is no use 'understanding' history merely in terms of industrialisation, urbanisation, education, feminism; nor even their economic or political causes. If that is all, we shall merely repeat the past. For Lawrence, the 'sources which feed all life' – the natural universe, and man – must lie deeper, in those dialectically creative forces of the Beginning; the 'opposites' whose marriage produces Genesis and the Promised Land; and whose disjunction, the Cities of the Plain and the exile with the burning fiery furnace. So what underlies that ugly sprawl of housing on the skyline, without communal centre, is the atrophy of man's sense of organic beauty related to the natural landscape, and of togetherness with other men – the unifying impulse that is one essential pole of the dialectic of creative growth. Moreover, decay of the one must inevitably bring overdevelopment in the other: and there, plain to see, is the excess of rational intellect, obvious in those ugly lines and squares of housing, and the machine-industry which imposes human mind and will on nature and other men, shaping them to mere functions of 'idea'. If a man sees himself as an instrument and his passional and family life as a sideshow, there (again) is the twin loss: of natural being and relationship; and of individuality. The attack is not on the machine, which can enhance life if it is properly used by the living, but on the disease of man, his betrayal of the creative forces in nature and himself. If a school becomes a mechanical system of will and power, divorcing knowledge from being in both teachers and taught, it is bound to produce partial or split personalities, turning repression into rage, and discipline into brutal domination or rebellion. If essential human impulses are distorted or denied, the coming of universal education is a pyrrhic victory. If universities get governed by the utilitarian, the materialist, the commercial, turning knowledge merely rational, there will not only be sterility but the reaction to dark irrationality will be all the more extreme. If the novel's 'emancipated' women seem unfulfilled, it is not because the Lawrence of 1915 is anti-feminist, but because their feminism is still half-hearted. His dialectic needs each 'pole' to *be* itself as these women, in their time, have not yet managed; but equally, each can only become itself more fully by also accepting transformation from the 'other'. Yet the more self-conscious and cerebral the 'new' women become, the less capable they seem of marrying the other or risking the self. Above all for Lawrence, through the decline in the religious sense, people have lost touch with the primary creative energies. He is of no church or creed. Yet he sees truths in Christianity (which Christians do not understand), and above all in the 'sacred history' of the Bible which *The Rainbow* seeks to reinterpret into new language for 'God', i.e. those 'sources which feed all life, and therefore the life of the present as well'. And what of that 'present', in 1915? Surely, if the 'opposites' fail to marry, there is bound to be destructive violence. The increasing loss of individuality is dangerous in two ways. Will's inchoate lack of self turns evil when his need to merge or absorb is thwarted; Skrebensky can only conceive of himself as part of a collective, an army, a state seeking *Lebensraum*.[30] Others, insufficiently differentiated, marshy or clayey, identify with what they really despise. But overdeveloped individuals, assertive, domineering, are no less dangerous. Newly aggressive self-awareness and self-preservation resist challenge from the 'other' with increasing violence and destructiveness from Anna to Ursula. All these phenomena are not without point in a novel which reached its final state between November 1914 and June 1915.

Yet for Lawrence the creative sources of life are always there, in challenge and promise, and that is why Ursula must be made to meet them in the end. The encounter with the horses confronts the educated modern city girl, so ready now to deny the elemental forces in herself, with the unitary landscape of her grandfather, the big wind, the earth and looming trees, the rain, the power of nimals, the fire from their nostrils. But the summons is not to the merely elemental; it is, as always, to the marriage of opposites. The horses are an intensity of conflicting energies that cannot be denied or reduced, and must not be, in Ursula. But she now finds nature terrifying, and she cannot meet the abiding challenge to meet the 'other' and 'come through' to new life, beyond – which has always meant an agony like death in the self. At first she does manage to walk on, towards 'the high-road and the ordered world of man'[31] through the horses, but only by refusing to look or think or know, following her feet blindly and instinctively while her nerves and veins 'ran hot, ran white hot, they must fuse and she must die'.[32] But Ursula's modernity has everything to do with awareness, and to become aware of the horses is to increase the terror of self-risk. The old ways of instinct are gone by, but she *cannot* go through again in full consciousness. She runs away, climbs a tree, collapses, 'like a stone at rest on the bed of the stream'.[33] This is her Flood, and it almost destroys her. On the 'realistic' level she is pregnant, terrified, in shock, and she miscarries. But on a deeper level Lawrence suggests that she has failed, not only because of the inadequacy of Skrebensky, but also because she herself has seemed incapable of the marriage of opposites. Yet in her illness she diagnoses what is wrong: her self-projections and relationships have all been unreal entanglements, forced by her will. She must 'die' to her own self-assertion, and at last let go, trust herself nakedly to the sources which feed all life – but she is then reborn into a new world, the mysterious work of divine creation, as in Genesis. She must no longer try to manipulate herself, or others, but wait, for the coming of a Son of God, from the infinite and eternal to which she now belongs, 'within the scope of that vaster power in which she rested at last'.[34] The Rainbow is not achieved – but as she sees the sign in the sky it remains covenanted like the one in the Bible. Perhaps the promise is not the logical outcome of the story but an assertion of Lawrence's own revolutionary optimism breaking through in a language of assertion; but the one in the Bible was also gratuitous, and seen only by the reborn soul that has died to its old self in the Flood.

Finally the two kinds of reading are also dialectic, and to be married. The deep-structure view of men and women has to be embodied in personal stories, and these in turn seen as moments of consciousness and crisis in the whole inner and social history of their time. But conversely, consciousness in time, and of history, must always for Lawrence be transfigured by consciousness of the timeless and archetypal, or man will perish from an inadequate conception of his own nature and his world.

Yet to recognise the richness and power of fusing archetypal with historical vision in *The Rainbow*, is to recognise a degree of loss thereafter. For that richness of texture came from Lawrence's sense of still *belonging*, to a place, a culture, a history; and also to a literary community, an audience which could share and understand. The denunciation and destruction of the novel shattered these conditions for ever. No fiction like *The Rainbow* could come from Lawrence again. What did come, even in the 'continuation' of *Women in Love*, is not only 'another story' but necessarily another kind of story, which overtly renounces the sense of date and historical precision.[35] Of course there is gain as well as loss, a new apocalyptic and mythic intensity; a new sharpness of diagnosis and separation; and might-have-beens are always unprofitable – but a kind of imaginative loss there is, and only a fully historic reading of *The Rainbow* can bring out its nature and extent.

Notes

1. Graham Holderness ('its evolving generational structure has no realist or historical content') and John Worthen ('the historical conflicts of the nineteenth century are alien to the progression of the novel') seem to me to mar a good case on the first generation by generalising to the novel as a whole. Both point out, rightly, that Lawrence is not very interested in the work of the Marsh Farm – though we do get glimpses, and would have seen more had Lawrence not cut a fine ploughing scene from the manuscript. However, in chapter 5 of his *Study of Thomas Hardy*, Lawrence had argued that the real significance of work is not socio-economic but to do with the evolutionary development of consciousness and selfhood. So it is not surprising that work, too, should figure more in the second generation (though it will be Will's carving that is important rather than the lace factory) and most in the third generation, when it moves centre-stage in 'The Man's World'. See G. Holderness, *D. H. Lawrence: History, Ideology and Fiction* (Dublin: Gill and Macmillan, 1982) p. 186; D. H. Lawrence, *The Rainbow*, ed. J. Worthen (Harmondsworth, Middx: Penguin, 198?) p. 31. All page references will be given to the latter, cited as *The Rainbow* (Penguin, ed. Worthen).

2. Day and month are given, Lawrence, *The Rainbow* (Penguin, ed. Worthen) p. 167; the year is arrived at from the ages of all concerned but it turns out that 23 December was indeed a Saturday that year.

3. *Lawrence in Love: Letters to Louie Burrows*, ed. James T. Boulton (Nottingham: University of Nottingham Press, 1968) p. x.
4. C. N. Wright (ed.), *Directory of Nottingham and Twelve Miles Round*, 15th edn (Nottingham: J. Bell, 1891) p. 488, though the credit is given to a Mr Brand, who turns out to have been the clergyman.
5. D. Wardle, *Education and Society in Nineteenth-Century Nottingham* (Cambridge: Cambridge University Press, 1971) p. 95.
6. Manuscript, p. 449, 'called a taxi-cab'; first edition, p. 284, line 10 'had a motor-car'; so also Penguin edition, Worthen, p. 350, line 16.
7. 'Nottinghamshire Register of Motor Cars and Motor Cycles 1903', ed. P. A. Kennedy, *A Nottinghamshire Miscellany*, ed. J. H. Hodson et al., Thoroton Society Record Series, xxi (1962) pp. 65–79.
8. *Letters*, i, pp. 287–8.
9. Lawrence has Dorothy belong to the Women's Social and Political Union a year before it was founded; and Will could not have gone to the Empire Music Hall before 1897 – but these are rare examples, and not very significant.
10. He was the author of a history of Greasley, *Griseleia in Snotinghscire* (Nottingham: Murray, 1901), which contains a portrait of him; cf. *The Rainbow*, ch. 7. He claimed to have escaped the Russians by swimming the Vistula.
11. Edwin Trueman, *History of Ilkeston* (Ilkeston: John F. Walker, 1880) p. 98; cf. Lawrence, *The Rainbow* (Penguin, ed. Worthen), p. 72.
12. Perhaps the most spectacular illustration of this point, for me, was to be told by Louie Burrows's youngest sister that the flood at the Marsh Farm had actually occurred, when her mother was alone in the house with young children. There could hardly be a more striking example of the fusion of the biblical/symbolic with the historical.
13. 'Nottinghamshire Register of Motor Cars, 1903'.
14. The foundation stone is dated 16 February 1864.
15. On the A6096 Ilkeston to Eastwood road, just on the Ilkeston side of the turning to Cossall. The canal is choked and its old narrow-arched aqueduct has been replaced by an ugly new one; the colliery has gone; but the situation described in the novel is easily re-imagined from the canal bank.
16. Charles Hadfield, *The Canals of the East Midlands* (London, 1966) p. 55.
17. R. Leleux, *Regional History of the Railways of Great Britain*, vol. ix: *The East Midlands* (Newton Abbot: David & Charles, 1984) p. 143; E. G. Barnes, *The Rise of the Midland Railway* (London: George Allen & Unwin, 1966) ch. 1.
18. Alan R. Griffin, *Mining in the East Midlands* (London: Frank Cass, 1971) p. 53.
19. Frank Grafton Cook, *Some Notes on Cossall and its Past* (privately printed, 1971) pp. 4–5; cf. Greenwood's *Map of the County of Nottingham*, surveyed 1824–5, pub. 1826. But Ellis's map, also 1824–5, pub. 1825, portrays the existing situation, so the facts remain rather obscure. Trueman's *History of Ilkeston*, p. 99, records the bursting of 'the embankment close to this aqueduct' in 1823, so there was already an aqueduct of some sort by then.

20. Harry T. Moore, *The Intelligent Heart* (Harmondsworth, Middx: Penguin, 1960) p. 25.
21. D. H. Lawrence, *Study of Thomas Hardy and Other Essays*, ed. Bruce Steele (Cambridge: Cambridge University Press, 1985) pp. 36–7.
22. Wardle, *Education and Society*, p. 145; Geoffrey Trease, *Nottingham: A Biography* (London: Macmillan, 1970) pp. 202–3.
23. Wardle, *Education and Society*, pp. 100–1; Lawrence, *The Rainbow* (Penguin, ed. Worthen) p. 281.
24. W. H. G. Armytage, *Four Hundred Years of English Education* (Cambridge: Cambridge University Press, 1965) p. 186; and Wardle, *Education and Society*, p. 88. Those not allowed to leave lingered in Standard V, Ursula's class, hence its difficulties.
25. *Letters*, ii, p. 165.
26. Lawrence, *The Rainbow* (Penguin, ed. Worthen) p. 441.
27. *Letters*, ii, p. 165.
28. Lawrence, *The Rainbow* (Penguin, ed. Worthen) p. 487.
29. Karl Jaspers, *Man in the Modern Age* (London: George Routledge & Sons, 1932) pp. 139–40.
30. Ursula's anti-Imperialist arguments with Skrebensky about the Sudan and the British in India (Lawrence, *The Rainbow* (Penguin, ed. Worthen) pp. 356 and 513), together with her denunciation of his soldier's identification with 'the nation' (p. 357) may well have seemed particularly unpatriotic to the powers-that-be in 1915. These arguments show that the lovers have become part of political history too, by contrast with their parents and grandparents.
31. Lawrence, *The Rainbow* (Penguin, ed. Worthen) p. 541.
32. Ibid., p. 540.
33. Ibid., p. 543.
34. Ibid., p. 547.
35. Cf. 'I would wish the time to remain unfixed', in unpublished 'Foreword to *Women in Love*'; see the Random House Modern Library edition and *Phoenix* ii, p. 275.

9

The Midlands Imagination: Arnold Bennett, George Eliot, William Hale White and D. H. Lawrence

BRIDGET PUGH

When one considers the regional novel it is usual to take into account how novelists have used local material in their work. This is the approach taken by Phyllis Bentley in her booklet *The English Regional Novel* where she looks particularly at manifestations of regionalism in the elements of character, plot, setting, narrative and theme in the works of four major writers: Charlotte Brontë, George Eliot, Thomas Hardy and Arnold Bennett. She defines a regional novel as 'a novel which concentrating on a particular part, a particular region of a nation depicts the life of that region in such a way that the reader is conscious of the characteristics which are unique to that region and differentiate it from others in the common motherland'.[1] One cannot fault this definition; and there is much to be said for the manner in which Bentley investigates the regional influence in well-defined areas of her chosen novels. But, as I intend to show, this seems to me a limited approach because its emphasis is on the effect of the region on the literature and does not see it as intrinsic to the writing.

Another approach to regionalism, adopted by Lucien Leclaire in his *Bibliography of the Regional Novelists of the British Isles 1800–1950* and *Le Roman régionaliste 1800–1950*,[2] also has much to recommend it but is yet in some ways unsatisfactory. Leclaire lists exhaustively every work with a local setting that he could discover under headings like romance and history. This is valuable in that it attempts to illustrate how regionalism affects different modes of writing. But one can only dissociate oneself from any classification that places Lawrence in the category of 'Interpretative regionalism from 1920 to 1939' and sympathise with Leclaire's rueful declaratio partway through his book: confronted with hundreds of titles h admits that 'it will easily be conceived that such diversity entai for the systematic student of literature quasi-insuperable problem of classification'.[3]

The limitations of these two approaches reinforces my convictio that the starting point for the study of the regional novel shoul be the region. Furthermore, one can only really understand th regional influence by taking two groups of contemporary novel: one representing a given community and one quite apart from i and examining the differences between them to see if they ar significant.

In England it is not easy to find a group of novelists depicting shared community. In America there are accepted distinction between New York writers, writers of the Deep South, and writer of the Middle West. In England one might name the Mancheste school and think of Mrs Banks and Mrs Gaskell, or one coul perhaps talk of London writers, but definition by region has no been characteristic of the study of literature in this country. Thi does not seem wholly a matter of scale, since there are man variations in the landscape and atmosphere of areas of Englanc even if they are not separated by the vast distances characteristi of America. It seems, rather, a matter of habit.

In default of an already obvious grouping I decided to choos the Midlands as an area to study. I took the area to be that define by the *OED* so helpfully as 'the middle counties of England . . remote from the sea', the description is further developed as 'th counties south of the Humber and Mersey and north of th Thames, with the exception of Norfolk, Suffolk, Essex, Middlese Hertfordshire, Gloucestershire and the counties bordering o Wales'.[4] This area neatly disposes of the Celtic fringe and th problem of considering the complication of racial influence in th region, and leaves one with a population less settled and probabl more mixed than in other parts of the country.

Leclaire lists some twenty authors using this region within hi period of study, 1800–1950. But a novel does not acquire status a a regional novel merely by background. To exclude all novelist not, as Auster would have it,[5] absorbed in the region, I took fron Leclaire's list only those born and brought up in the area for a least the first twenty-one years of their lives. This meant omittin authors like Samuel Butler and Francis Brett Young who wer

ducated outside the region and were therefore subjected in their
ormative years to quite other influences, although they used the
egion in their works. It meant excluding Mrs Henry Wood, despite
er descriptions of the glove trade in her native Worcester, because
he too left the area on her early marriage. The numerous minor
ovelists, Woden, Murray, Prior, Moult, Parkes and Mordaunt
ust be omitted here for reasons of space, although they are
vorthy of consideration elsewhere as part of the pattern and fulfil
ne condition of being thoroughly imbued with a sense of the
egion. One is left with the names of four authors outstanding in
nemselves and thoroughly of the Midland area. They are Arnold
ennett, George Eliot, D. H. Lawrence and (curiously omitted
rom Leclaire's list) 'Mark Rutherford' or William Hale White.

The choice of the novelists dictated a time span. In 1858 David
Masson had seen the potentiality for the regional novel, pointing
ut in his book on British novelists that 'there are rich fields of yet
nbooked English life'.[6] George Eliot exploited this opportunity in
er *Scenes of Clerical Life* published in the same year. This and her
nsuing works are considered by Leclaire to be the first self-
onsciously regional novels in English literature. The year 1858
eemed a suitable starting point for this study, and 1928, which
aw the publication of *Lady Chatterley's Lover*, seemed an appropriate
nding.

Seventy years is a long period of time – a life span. It is a period
vhich encompassed literary fashions such as the Pre-Raphaelite
novement, the decadence of the end of the century, imperialist
vriting, the Celtic revival and a movement to cosmopolitan settings
hat started with Conrad and continued to the end of the period
nd beyond, providing new backgrounds where the regions had
•een exhausted. Bennett with his Parisian setting in *The Old Wives'
Tale* and Lawrence in *Kangaroo* and *The Plumed Serpent* are examples
of this last development. But on the whole it would be true to say
hat literary *fashions* passed the Midland writers by. Despite their
lifference in period they are remarkably homogeneous in their
ppreciation of Spencer's concept of an organic society nurturing
heir own provincial communities; in their interest in Carlyle's
understanding of the opposition between instinct and analysis and
ais finding in favour of instinct and in endorsing Ruskin's belief
hat the natural rather than the mechanical aspects of life should
prevail. The themes the Midland novelists pursued were timeless –
he marriage relationship, the problems, sexual and religious, of

the adolescent, the individual's right to personal fulfilment with
a restrictive society. Their treatment of these themes was natural
affected by their period. In sexual matters George Eliot is reticen
Lawrence is explicit and Bennett, as David Lodge has pointed o
in his analysis of the execution sequence in *The Old Wive
Tale*, obliquely uses obvious sexual imagery.[7] But despite the
differences of treatment they share an innate conservatism
matter, development and indeed in the structure of their nove
which exists even alongside the more provocative pronouncemen
and experiments of Lawrence.

They therefore form an interesting group to compare with the
more varied contemporaries. I compared them with those autho
writing between 1858 and 1928 who were on the reading list f
the students at Birmingham University studying for the first degr
in English. This superficial comparison suggested to me that the
were distinct similarities amongst the writings of the Midlan
group which united them and set them apart from other write
of their time. It would be absurd, of course, to suggest th
they do not have many of the same pre-occupations as the
contemporaries. *Felix Holt* which is a typical Midland novel h
also been described as a novel of the 1860s. None the less it is cle
that Bennett, Eliot, Lawrence and Hale White, at a level muc
deeper than setting, share enough qualities to set them apart
distinctly of the Midland region.

One might, of course, object here that it is not the region whic
is the unifying force in their works but a common admiratic
amounting to emulation of George Eliot. The connection betwee
her work and Lawrence's is a commonplace of literary scholarshi
The similarity between George Eliot and Hale White is also we
established. Basil Willey has pointed out that:

> Hale White as a novelist may be regarded as a minor Georg
> Eliot. The patterns of their inner lives were similar: from narrov
> intense provincial piety, through emancipation, to a hard-wc
> and precariously held religion of the heart and conscience. Bo
> had deep roots in their provincial past, both had tenaciou
> memories and the power to recreate the scenes and people
> their early lives. . . . Hale White returns to his Bedford,
> George Eliot to her Warwickshire towns and farms, with t
> sense that here he belongs, knows his bearings, understanc
> the language and thoughts of the inhabitants.[8]

Much the same could be said of Arnold Bennett and the Five Towns.

But there is little evidence that these writers were imitating George Eliot. D. H. Lawrence noted of novelists in general 'The usual plan is to take two couples and develop their relationships. Most of George Eliot's are on that plan. . . . I shall try two couples for a start.' But he was not sure that she was right in 'putting all the action inside'.[9] He came to the conclusion that one required both internal action in the manner of Eliot and external as in Fielding. William Hale White, who worked with George Eliot at Chapman's and described her as Theresa in *The Autobiography of Mark Rutherford* was admiring but not wholly uncritical of her: 'her brain seemed to rule everything'. He thought she must have had a heart but 'how much share that organ had in her utterances I never could make out'.[10] Margaret Drabble has pointed out that there are similarities in the situations of Bulstrode in *Middlemarch* and Titus Price in *Anna of the Five Towns*.[11] The similarity is clearly one of experience if not of art. Indeed Bennett, writing in his journal a year or so before he wrote *Anna of the Five Towns* listed George Eliot as one of the authors he had 'never even overlooked'.[12] What is most probable is that the connection between these authors is one of affinity with rather than imitation of George Eliot.

Certainly both Lawrence and Bennett admired William Hale White. A reviewer, writing in *The New Statesman* in 1923, states that Bennett declared *The Revolution in Tanner's Lane* to be 'the finest example of modern English prose'.[13] In his journal for 19 February 1914 he recorded:

I bought 'Autobiography of Mark Rutherford' and 'Mark Rutherford's Deliverance' in 7d editions at station. And in the night I had finished reading the latter. Very impressive and original. Fine style, no scheme of construction. As a continuous narrative extraordinarily amateurish. The man had no notion of fiction. But a work not easily forgotten. Full of wisdom and high things.[14]

'Wisdom' and 'high things' were very important to the novelists of the Midlands. Lawrence also admired Rutherford's high tone: 'I've read *The Revolution in Tanner's Lane* and find myself fearfully fond of Rutherford. I used to think him dull, but now I see he is so just and plucky and sound.'[15] Previously he had exclaimed

'How good he is! – so just, so harmonious.'[16] It is not, perhaps, surprising that White, who died in 1913 aged eighty-two had little to say about these younger writers.

It is, however, instructive to consider what they had to say about each other. Lawrence wrote to Arthur McLeod on 4 October 1912:

> I have read *Anna of the Five Towns* today . . . to be in Hanley, and to read almost my own dialect, makes me feel quite ill . . . I hate Bennett's resignation. Tragedy ought really to be a great kick at misery. But *Anna of the Five Towns* seems like an acceptance.[17]

Bennett recorded in his journal for 30 November 1920:

> I read Lawrence's new novel, 'The Lost Girl'. It would be absolutely great if it had a clear central theme and comprehensible construction. It doesn't end; it stops. But it is very fine indeed, the work of a genius. It held me. I read it in less than 24 hours.[18]

These are the comments of men who in their books were both dealing with the same problem, that of the 'odd woman' in a provincial town with limited opportunities for the only career open to her, marriage. And although they came up with opposing solutions of submission or escape, and very different treatments in the restrained realism of Bennett and the extravagant symbolism of Lawrence, the root of the matter they discussed was the same – their compassion for a thwarted individual in a provincial society.

So one comes back to the region and its influence on these four novelists. The first remarkable similarity about them is that they all share the same kind of imagination – what Bennett calls 'synthetic impressionism'.[19] It is what one might describe as a practical imagination. It is true that realism was the mode of their time and in this sense they are like their contemporaries. But *nowhere* does one Midland novelist dabble in fancy or fantasy. No Midland novelist evinces any of the inventive qualities of the imagination that one finds in Lewis Carroll or Jules Verne. Nonsense as Lear and Carroll demonstrated it was unknown to any of these writers. They were not even interested, apart from Lawrence's abortive schemes for Rananim, in projecting other worlds as were their contemporaries, Morris, Butler, Bellamy and eventually Huxley. Neither, apart from brief references to evolution or such medical advances as the use of digitalis in heart disease which George Eliot had learned from her Birmingham brother-in-law Dr Clarke, did they have any developed interest in science. Bennett and Wells are often compared as writers of realistic novels. But the soaring imagination of Wells' scientific fiction was beyond the reach of Bennett. He, like Eliot, Lawrence and Hale White preferred to reproduce the world they had experienced. It was a world where nonsense, fantasy, even scientific vision had no place – a real world.

The real world, as far as landscape was concerned, was the world in which they had grown up. Thus, in George Eliot's case, *Adam Bede* was set on the Derbyshire–Staffordshire border between Ellastone and Norbury where her father's family lived; *The Mill on the Floss* is largely set around Nuneaton; *Silas Marner* is set in the Midlands but it is not easy to identify the exact location; *Felix Holt* is set in Nuneaton and Coventry; and *Middlemarch* in Coventry. The introduction to *Felix Holt* with its magnificent description of the Midlands of England gives a broad general picture of the area. *Scenes of Clerical Life* is precise enough to identify Shepperton Church as Chilvers Coton; and Cheverel Manor, 'the castellated house of grey-tinted stone . . . the broad gravel-walk winding on the right, by a row of tall pines, alongside the pool'[20] is clearly Arbury Hall. William Hale White describes Bedford very precisely in the opening chapter of *Catharine Furze*, and has scenes from Ampthill and Bedford in *The Autobiography of Mark Rutherford, Mark Rutherford's Deliverance, The Revolution in Tanner's Lane* and *Clara Hopgood*. Arnold Bennett's connection with the landscape of the Five Towns is proverbial. But if one visits Burslem, the setting for books like *Anna of the Five Towns, The Old Wives's Tale, Clayhanger, Hilda Lessways, These Twain* and *The Card*, one is immediately struck by the detail of Bennett's reproduction of landscape. There is, as in *Anna of the Five Towns*, a gold angel on top of the Town Hall; there is a sloping run through the square that an intrepid boy like young Povey might take on his new bicycle. Similar fidelity to detail is to be found in Lawrence. It is well known that in *The White Peacock* and *Sons and Lovers* he was writing about Felley and Eastwood; that *Women in Love* is partly set in Moorgreen; and that *The Rainbow* gives an accurate picture of Cossall. But the exactness of his detail is only fully to be seen in old maps. There the boathouse by the lake in *Women in Love* is shown clearly; the two islets in Felley Mill pond can be seen and the path taken by the children in *The Rainbow* from Church Cottage to school becomes visible.

The fidelity of the Midland writers to their landscape is, then, everywhere apparent. One of the most illuminating illustrations of the similarity of their approach may be seen by comparing the decline of James Houghton's shop in *The Lost Girl* with the adaptations of Constance Baines's shop in *The Old Wives' Tale*. Both shops existed, in fact, the one in Eastwood High Street, the other in St Luke's Square, Burslem; and both had the alterations Lawrence and Bennett described. Such use of real happenings for fictitious purposes shows the practical imagination at its best. It is interesting to note that when George Eliot moved to Lincolnshire for the flood at the end of *The Mill on the Floss* she made topographical errors. The use of a well-known landscape generally guarded against such mistakes.

This practical imagination shows itself in many other ways. It is not surprising that all these writers should use the material they know best – their own lives. All four of the Midland writers wrote strongly autobiographical novels: George Eliot's *The Mill on the Floss*, D. H. Lawrence's *Sons and Lovers*, Hale White's *Autobiography* and *Deliverance of Mark Rutherford* and Arnold Bennett's *A Man from the North* and *Clayhanger*. Each describes the struggle of the author for emancipation from his environment with some details subtly altered: Paul Morel's route is through painting not writing; Mark Rutherford becomes a preacher as Hale White never did; while Bennett in one book shows a flight to London as his means of escape and in the other shows how time and experience eventually free his alter ego while adhering to the general truth of his own experience. Thus Tom Brangwen and Maggie Tulliver may be taken to illustrate their authors' struggle with sex, and in this, of course, they were of their time. Similarly, *David Copperfield, Father and Son* and *The Way of All Flesh* illustrate the frequency of the autobiographical mode in this period. But the fact that not one but all the Midland novelists used it is significant.

It was not only their personal experiences that they seized on as matter for their fiction: they used their whole community. Despite George Eliot's claim that her father's situation meant that she was familiar with all classes of society this is a community limited by class. In the writings of these four Midland novelists we meet neither the very rich nor the very poor. The height of society for them is represented by their fathers' employers; the depth is represented by the respectable working poor like the rustics in *Silas Marner*, the chapel folk in Bennett and Hale White or the miners in Lawrence. The community of the Midland novelists embraces the whole of the middle class but does not descend to the destitute or rise to the aristocrat.

As examples of this community these novelists all used real people as the basis of their characters. In her *Groombridge Diary* Hale White's second wife recorded 'Hale tells me he never created a character, never sat down to write without having somebody before his mind's eye.'[21] William Robertson Nicoll notes that the Rev. John Jukes was the original of the Rev. John Broad in *Tanner's Lane*.[22] Wilfred Stone has identified many others of his characters. Louis Tillier claims that *Anna of the Five Towns* reads like a *roman à clef* to Five Towns society, seeing as the prototype of Henry Mynors, J. W. Dean 'a remarkable teacher at Swan Square Sunday School' and connecting the cornet-playing revivalist with 'the cornet-playing Mr Middleton who often visited Burslem on missions'.[23] In the Baines family and in Auntie Hamps one sees portraits of Arnold Bennett's own relations. The same use of relations is to be found in George Eliot with the Tulliver aunts and the use of her father's family in the characters of the two Bede brothers. Her use of real people in *Scenes of Clerical Life* was so exact that characters in the scenes instantly recognised themselves. Marghanita Laski goes so far as to claim that *Silas Marner* 'is the only one of George Eliot's English set novels in which real-life resemblances have not been traced'.[24] As for Lawrence, his fidelity to fact in his portrayal of real characters meant that he was more than once threatened with legal action. But his use of his own family as the Morels, of the Chambers family as the Saxtons and the Leivers, and of the Barber family as the Crichs indicates his consistent use of real people in real situations. When comparing the Midland novelists in this respect it is quite interesting to see a link between the first and last of them. George Eliot's Adam Bede is a portrait of her father, and is depicted as being devoted to the church at Norbury and carving the reredos there. William Brangwen is a portrait of Alfred Burrows, father of Lawrence's one-time fiancée; he too is portrayed as being attached to the church at Cossall, and carves the reredos. Again the use of real characters in fiction was not unusual in the period 1858–1928. But all four of these writers are consistent in employing this practice.

Similarly they used local stories and events. The revolution did take place in Bedford Bunyan Meeting just as described in *The Revolution in Tanner's Lane*. Hetty Sorrel's relationship with Dinah Morris after the former had murdered her child had much to do with a case of infanticide in Nottingham related to George Eliot by her Aunt Samuel. The political events in *Felix Holt* reflect the riots in Nuneaton. The chapter 'The Child Man' in *Clayhanger* is taken from the memoirs of an early pottery worker. Keith Sagar has plausibly suggested that even the basis of *Lady Chatterley's Lover* may come from the true story of a member of the Arkwright family.

These local stories are, of course, couched in local dialect. It is natural that they should be, and interesting that the authors claimed to 'hear' their characters using local words. They use dialect in different ways, in George Eliot's case even different dialects in different books. Arnold Bennett's dialect words are largely confined to his accounts of the industrial world of the Potteries. George Eliot uses hers largely in dialogue. Lawrence uses his within the narrative as well as in his conversations. Hale White's use of dialect is more stylised than that of the others. But the significant fact is that their use of dialect is always individual-ised. They do not descend to the catch phrase, the 'Barkis is willing' form of expression. They knew the people they were writing about as individuals within their communities rather than as types.

One can perhaps link their use of dialogue with their use of place names. All of them attempted to disguise the real places they wrote about by the use of fictitious names. Again their technique varied. Lawrence used several names for the same places; so did George Eliot and Hale White. Arnold Bennett, on the other hand, was consistent in his use of place names from book to book thus building up a sense of continuity in his works. But they all shared the method of attempting to disguise what they were doing by using invented place names.

All this use of familiar matter serves to illustrate that the particular imagination of these novelists was practical but not inventive. Synthetic imagination is another way of describing it. It does not deal with the abstract – all these novelists are happier in dealing in terms of the concrete rather than the theoretical. It does not often see its material in terms of a wider world. It depicts the limited world they knew. But the reproduction of landscape and community, though common to them all, is not nearly as significant as the effect of landscape and community on their work. And it is well worth considering the kind of landscape which formed their shaping environment.

It was a moderate landscape, far away from the extremes of the Brontë country, Manchester, Wessex or the metropolis. George Eliot described how:

> In these midland districts the traveller passed rapidly from one phase of English life to another: after looking down on a village dingy with coal-dust, noisy with the shaking of looms, he might skirt a parish all of fields, high hedges and deep-rutted lanes; after the coach had rattled over the pavement of a manufacturing town, the scene of riots and trades-union meetings, it would take him in another ten minutes into a rural region. . . . The busy scenes of the shuttle and the wheel, of the roaring furnace, of the shaft and the pulley, seemed to make but crowded nests in the midst of the large-spaced, slow-moving life of homesteads and far-away cottages and oak-sheltered parks.[25]

Sixty years later Lawrence, writing of his childhood, described life as 'a curious cross between industrialism and the old agricultural England of Shakespeare and Milton and Fielding and George Eliot'.[26] One gets an impression of a mellow, cultivated countryside. Such industries as Eliot, White and Bennett described – ribbon making, metal working and potting – were on a relatively small scale where masters and men were quite closely related and often interchangeable. Lawrence in *Women in Love* laments the mechanisation of the mines which destroyed the relationship between employer and employee in his eyes. But much of his early work describes a butty system where the men directly responsible for the organisation of the work at the pit face worked with their team.

This was also a countryside of railways and canals. George Eliot and Hale White saw the beginning of the expansion of the railways, Hale White explaining 'I was born just before the Liverpool and Manchester Railway was opened.'[27] Lawrence was a true man of the railway age. The combination of easy terrain and the commercial expansion of the period meant that communication was easy throughout the Midlands. There were no communities cut off from their neighbours such as one might find in Wales, Cornwall, Scotland or Yorkshire.

The result is that there is very little sense of space or isolation in the Midland novels. People are always seen as part of a community. It is quite remarkable for any of the characters in these books to be alone. One is never conscious of them set against vast unpopulated tracts of countryside. Arthur Donnithorne, when distraught, is pictured as seeking solitude in Eagledale but this flight to the hills of Derbyshire is only described obliquely. Samuel Povey, returning from announcing to his mother-in-law that Constance is expecting a child after six years of marriage

> walked home . . . over the wavy moorland of the county dreaming in the heart of England. Night fell on him in mid-career, and he was tired. But the earth, as it whirled through naked space, whirled up the moon for him. . . . A wind from Arabia wandering cooled his face.[28]

Hale White, seeking for space around his characters could only just find it for them in the sky and stars.[29] Lawrence's characters have to escape out of the region to Mablethorpe or the South Downs if they wish to commune in solitude. Such escapes are rare. For the most part the characters in the Midland novels are confined by sheltered fields and small inter-connected communities.

The primary result of this is that all these novels lack a sense of scale. Hardy, who has many qualities in common with the Midland writers, is separated from them here. In his description of Egdon Heath at the beginning of *The Return of the Native* he sets his hero in a landscape so vast that it reduces men to the proportion of insects. This would be impossible in a Midland novel where the mildness of the countryside suggests that man is central. The novels illustrate man in control of the landscape. This does not mean that they are never at the mercy of accidents caused by powerful natural forces. Death by flood, quarry or mineshaft sometimes seems almost a concomitant of living in the area, but the landscape itself is neither inimical nor diminishing. Lawrence sums up its influence finely in *Apocalypse*: 'With us all is personal, landscapes and sky, these are to us the delicious background of our personal life and no more.'[30] A hostile universe has no part in a Midland novel. Man is the centre of this world.

An extension of this lack of wild country is the obvious lack of sea. Again there is no opportunity for the Midland novelist to show his creations pitted against the elements in a manner which gives a sense of the littleness of human life such as one gains from

Conrad. Although, by the time of Lawrence and Bennett, it had become the custom for quite modest families to take a seaside holiday and both Anna Tellwright and the Morels are described as so doing, these are conventional experiences and such sense of freedom as these visits suggest is limited and fleeting. Only Hale White was conscious that in the distance, over the fens, the 'sea was a corrective to the littleness around me'.[31]

This was not only a littleness of spirit. Within their daily lives the Midland writers could have had no consciousness of the wider world that proximity to a large port brings. There is no awareness within these communities of far-off countries. But if they were unaware of foreign places they were very aware of the effect of a foreigner in their midst. The foreigner is a device every Midland novelist uses. Characters like Ladislaw in *Middlemarch*, Lydia Lensky and Skrebensky in *The Rainbow*, Ciccio in *The Lost Girl*, the Caillauds in *The Revolution in Tanner's Lane*, even Chirac in *The Old Wives' Tale*, serve to introduce fresh viewpoints into the novels. Often they are liberators proclaiming different sexual mores. They play significant roles in the books, but they represent an idea rather than an alternative community. If Midland novelists wished to introduce their heroines to a wider world they sent them, in true English tradition, southward. Dorothea, awakening to awareness of physical life amongst the statues of Rome, prepared a path that many others trod, including Alvina and Aaron. Sophia, of course, came back from her Parisian experiences untouched. But apart from her all these escapees show the difficulty of achieving any sense of freedom within the narrow constraints of that Midland community.

And if the outlook of the characters in the novels is bounded by a lack of space it is equally bounded by a limited perspective in time. Nowhere is there a place where a Midland novelist writing of his region betrays a consciousness of any earlier period of history than that immediately preceding his own. Here again it is instructive to look at Hardy and to consider the use he made of Stonehenge in *Tess of the D'Urbervilles* and of the Roman amphitheatre in *The Mayor of Casterbridge*. The difference between these unchanging monuments and the momentous but passing events which take place within them informs what happens with a sense of perspective the Midland novels lack. Midland writers are never aware of far distant periods, perhaps because there are so few prehistoric or Roman sites in the area to suggest them.

The sense of history in the Midland novels is in itself interesting.
Leavis makes a great point of the way in which Eliot and Lawrence
share a sense of 'essential English history'.[32] This is a sense also
characteristic of Hale White and Bennett. All four writers present
an experience of the region they describe in terms of a kind of folk
memory which extends backwards into the reminiscences of their
parents or even grandparents. They are, in this, probably quite
realistic in representing the historical consciousness of their characters as being like that of the German peasant of whom 'it must not
be supposed that the historical piety . . . extends to anything not
immediately connected with himself'.[33]

The result of this attitude is that although the Midland writers
are adept at giving the reader an impression of what it was like to
live in their time and even the time of their parents and grandparents, their perspective is always intensely personal. To the pure
historian the picture they give is biased in the cause of their art
and often inaccurate: thus George Eliot in *Felix Holt* purports to
describe one Reform Bill but her account has overtones of another.
But to the local historian they are a mine of reliable information. If
one finds Lawrence describing a dame school in Cossall one is
unsurprised to find the evidence for it in contemporary directories
although local people may have long forgotten its existence.

To sum up it appears that all the Midland writers would have
accepted the advice given by Arnold Bennett in *How to Become an
Author* in 1903:

> The action . . . should spring out of the characters and the
> characters should spring out of the general environment. By the
> environment I mean the place or places where the action is to
> pass, the general class and sort of people involved and the broad
> effect of landscape and other surroundings.[34]

In acknowledging these guidelines these writers produced characters not always without aspiration but generally practical, materialistic to the degree of fully appreciating the value of a competency
but for ever unaware of their insignificance when set against the
larger perspectives of the world, the universe and time.

There are many other aspects of characterisation which these
novelists share. Their humour is generally ironic, concerned with
the weaknesses of human nature. Pretentiousness seems its main
butt. Their knowledge of their own community prevents them

from descending to caricature or stereotype in even the most minor characters – they knew their people too well to see the poor merely as figures of fun or their misers – Silas Marner or Ephraim Tellwright – as Scrooges. Thirdly they were always concerned with the respectable. There are no criminal classes in the Midland novels. Crimes, of course, there are in many of them – infanticide, fraud, wife murder, common theft. But these are crimes committed by ostensibly law-abiding members of the community. Perhaps one can argue that the small, ordered social groups of the area provided a form of natural surveillance that made the growth of criminal gangs unlikely. Dickens and Conrad might be fascinated by the criminal and the anarchist. But the novel of sensation was a very long way from the Midland novels.

Another aspect of the sensational – the supernatural – is also absent from these works. Except for some examples of rural superstition in *Adam Bede* and *Silas Marner*, an excursion into spiritualism in *The Glimpse* and a few short stories of the supernatural written by Lawrence for collections of ghost stories, the realms of faery, ghosts, hobgoblins and extra-sensory perception in general do not appear in any Midland writing.

This absence can be explained in several ways. It might be environmental. An examination of a map of superstitions shows that the Midlands offer far fewer examples of such beliefs than the more remote parts of the country. Even the folk hero of the region, Robin Hood, is essentially practical. It might be that the supernatural was not a popular literary mode at that time although *The Woman in White, Edwin Drood, Puck of Pook's Hill, The Turn of the Screw* and Hardy's all-permeating Fates show that it was certainly not unknown to the contemporaries of the Midland writers. The most probable explanation for this lack of the super-stititous is a religious one. And here we come to the heart of the quality which sets the Midland novelists as a group conclusively apart from their contemporaries. They were all, as Valentine Cunningham said of George Eliot, 'open to Dissent',[35] Dissent which, as Katherine Tillotson put it, is often 'part of the genius of place'.[36]

The religious experience of all these writers was, despite the difference of their periods, very much alike. They were all assailed by doubt, all rejected religion at about the age of twenty-two, yet all retained some residue of their previous religious conviction throughout their lives. Dissent, the principal key to the similarity between these novelists, manifests itself in a different way in each writer. Hale White and Bennett were most affected by it in its institutional form in the Strict Baptist group at Bedford and the Methodists at Burslem. Lawrence and George Eliot seem to have been more affected by it in its experiential form through conversion. But Dissent is the key.

It was, of course, a major factor in their environment. Valentine Cunningham writing in *Everywhere Spoken Against* pointed out that Dissent was dominant in all the *mining* counties; in three of the main manufacturing counties (the exceptions were Staffordshire and Warwickshire); in Derby and Nottinghamshire (partly mining and partly agricultural); and in only one agricultural county (Bedfordshire).[37] It is fascinating to see how the Midland novelists fit into this distribution. William Hale White comes from Bedfordshire, the one agricultural county dominated by Dissent. He belonged to the Bunyan Meeting there. Of him Basil Willey wrote that he was:

> the best interpreter of the provincial non-conformity of his time. It is from this world that he derives most of his richest material as a novelist, and nobody – not even George Eliot or Arnold Bennett – has etched more sharply some of its characters or traced more subtly the filaments linking its various levels, spiritual and social, into an ordered hierarchy.[38]

Arnold Bennett came from Staffordshire which was not as a county dominated by Dissent although his particular area was. It would be hard to better his description of the stultifying effect of a narrow Methodist upbringing on a character in the dramatic last paragraph of *Anna of the Five Towns*:

> Some may argue that Anna, knowing she loved another man, ought not to have married Mynors. But she did not reason thus; such a notion never even occurred to her. She had promised to marry Mynors, and she married him. Nothing else was possible. She who had never failed in duty did not fail then.[39]

It was this renunciation which appalled Lawrence. His case in relation to Dissent is somewhat different. He was brought up a Congregationalist in an area Cunningham describes as dominated by Dissent. His books are not so directly concerned with chapel

ociety as are the works of other writers in this group. But the
mainspring of his writing comes from his revolt against the
restrictions which the non-conformist conscience set upon the
achievement of the full potential of the individual. Where the earlier
writers illustrated the limiting effect of this religious environment,
Lawrence cried out against it. He seems in fact, to belong to an
earlier, more robust tradition of non-conformity when it promised
a deeper and more abundant life than that permitted by the narrow
institutions portrayed by White and Bennett. In Lawrence one
sees, particularly after he denied his Congregationalist roots, the
nonconformist as seeker. He was pre-eminently a pilgrim in
Bunyan's mould. He did not use the language or conventions of
the early Dissenters but in his seeking after truth he remained one
with them throughout his life.

It is apparently difficult to fit George Eliot into this neat scheme
of things for her family was, of course, Anglican. But she clearly
was deeply influenced by her school teachers, Miss Lewis, an
evangelical, and Miss Franklin whose father was minister of Cow
Lane Baptist Chapel in Coventry. In adolescence her views were
extremely puritanical and led to a renunciation of the world which
included refusing such ordinary pleasures as going to the theatre
with her brother.

Although all four of these writers rejected Christianity they all
returned to an approximation of it. Basil Willey applied the term
'religionless Christianity' to William Hale White but Wilfred Stone
pointed out he always continued to use the name of God.[40] George
Eliot in later life admitted:

I have not returned to dogmatic Christianity – to the acceptance
of any set of doctrines as a creed, and a superhuman revelation
of the Unseen – but I see in it the highest expression of the
religious sentiment that has yet found its place in the history of
mankind and I have the profoundest interest in the inward life
of sincere Christians in all ages.[41]

Bennett, in describing the rigid Sabbatarianism of his youth, pointed
out: 'It was inevitable that religion should come to be unalterably
connected in my mind with the ideas of boredom, injustice and
insincerity', although he elsewhere admitted that 'the oftener I
read the Sermon on the Mount the more deeply I am convinced
that here is the final practical wisdom'.[42] Lawrence wrote to Robert

Reid in 1907 that he could not believe in the divinity of Jesus
Christ, but he spent much of his life in pursuit of a replacement
divinity.[43] And he was highly appreciative of the sense of wonder
he derived from his early religious training. In 'Hymns in a Man's
Life' he wrote:

> I think it was good to be brought up a Protestant: and among
> Protestants, a Nonconformist, and among Nonconformists a
> Congregationalist. Which sounds pharisaic. But I should have
> missed bitterly a direct knowledge of the Bible, and a direct
> relation to Galilee and Canaan, Moab and Kedron, those places
> that never existed on earth. And in the Church of England one
> would hardly have escaped those snobbish hierarchies of class
> which spoil so much for a child. And the Primitive Methodists,
> when I was a boy, were always having 'revivals' and being
> 'saved', and I always had a horror of being 'saved'.[44]

Most importantly he spoke of Congregationalists as Independents,
as men without ritual belonging to a group where 'Thirty-six years
ago men, even Sunday School teachers, still believed in the fight
for life and the fun of it.'[45] He was a Dissenter in a different mould
from the other Midland writers in precisely the ways which he
listed in this essay. He retained throughout his life a sense of
wonder, he was always sternly independent and impatient of
outward show and he adhered to a belief in the importance of not
merely existing but enjoying life.

It would be interesting and profitable here to consider how much
and how similarly the accounts of clerical figures, religious festivals
and social meetings based on church and chapel contributed to the
quality of the works of the Midland writers. But it is more important
to consider the fundamental implications of Dissent for them.

Their class in part separated them from the Hellenic tradition of
thought. Dissent embedded them firmly in the Hebraic. It left them
all with a sense of sin, of the inevitable punishment that follows
wrong-doing and also with hope of salvation, redemption for those
who seek the truth. Despite their rejection of religion these concepts
remain important to them. It depended on their temperament
and, in part, their time whether they emphasised one or both of
these attitudes.

The first of these – found also in the belief in cause and effect in
Charles Bray's *The Philosophy of Necessity*[46] – is meticulously worked

ut in *Middlemarch* where the characters all sow what they reap. It
; a doctrine ironically referred to in *The Old Wives' Tale* where
amuel Povey meditates on his cousin Daniel's murder of his
runken wife:

> For many years he, Samuel, had seen in Daniel a living refutation
> of the authenticity of the old Hebrew menaces. But he had been
> wrong, after all! God is not mocked! And Samuel was aware of
> a revulsion in himself towards that strict codified godliness from
> which, in thought, he had perhaps been slipping away.[47]

awrence followed this doctrine on a much broader basis. To him
ilfilment of an individual's potential was right, denial of life the
ltimate wrong. And in his works those who sought their own
:uth were rewarded, those who denied it punished. He is perhaps
1e most outright Dissenter of the four.

Where this doctrine of cause and effect is dominant, chance and
1te can play little part. Coincidences and mishaps there are in
lenty in these novels. But a moral order which rewards the good
nd punishes the bad is the overriding force; although that moral
rder has to be extended in Lawrence's case to include his perfectly
alid stance that it is the seekers after truth who should be
ewarded, the followers of false gods who are destroyed.

All these facts suggest that there is a distinctive Midland novel.
: is a novel which appears to be characterised by a painstaking and
aithful reproduction of life in the area. It describes a community,
rdered and moderate, part rural and part industrial and so
opulated, so lacking in topographical extremes that it lacks a
ense of space and wildness, an acceptance of the smallness of the
1dividual set against the universe. It is a community concerned
vith recent history and unaware of the immensity of time. Morally
)o it is without extremes. There are no criminal classes. Over-
iding goodness or evil are non-existent. Fantasy is excluded from
1e lives of the members of this society. The characters are, on the
vhole, of much the same class, they share the same limited
spirations and are varied only by the introduction of foreigners
vho serve as a device to widen the horizons of this indigenous
opulation. There is no group of writers comparable with them
vriting during the same period. It is reasonable to suggest that
1ese writers have so much in common that they may be seen as
lustrating a form of the collective unconscious which represents

the underlying spirit of the Midlands of their time and that th
undoubted originality which each displays grows from a commo
root.

Notes

1. Phyllis Bentley, *The English Regional Novel* (London: George Allen an
   Unwin, 1941) p. 1.
2. Lucien Leclaire: *A General Analytical Bibliography of the Regional Noveli*
   of the British Isles, 1800–1950 (Clermont-Ferrand: Imprimerie G.
   Bussac, 1954) and *Le Roman régionaliste dans les Iles Britanniques, 180*
   1950 (Paris: Les Belles Lettres, 1954).
3. Leclaire, *Le Roman régionaliste*, p. 122.
4. *Oxford English Dictionary* (Oxford: Oxford University Press, 1970) v
   p. 424. The Midland counties are Derbyshire, Staffordshire, Nottin
   hamshire, Leicestershire, Rutland, Worcestershire, Warwickshi
   Northamptonshire and Bedfordshire.
5. Henry Auster, *Local Habitations: Regionalism in the Early Novels of Geor*
   Eliot (Cambridge, Mass.: Harvard University Press, 1970) p. 20. Aust
   quotes F. W. Morgan's article 'Three Aspects of Regional Consciou
   ness' in *The Sociological Review*, xxi (1939) p. 84: 'absorption in
   particular locality; absorption, not merely interest'.
6. David Masson, *British Novelists and their Styles* (Cambridge, 185
   p. 220.
7. David Lodge, 'Arnold Bennett: *The Old Wives' Tale*' in *The Modes*
   Modern Writing: Metaphor, Metonymy and the Typology of Modern Literatu
   (London: Edward Arnold, 1979) pp. 27–35.
8. Basil Willey, 'Mark Rutherford' in *More Nineteenth-Century Studies:*
   Group of Honest Doubters (New York: Harper and Row, 1966) p. 189.
9. 'E.T.' (Jessie Chambers), *D. H. Lawrence: A Personal Record*, 2nd ed
   ed. J. D. Chambers (London: Cass, 1965) pp. 103, 105.
10. Mark Rutherford, *The Autobiography of Mark Rutherford and Ma*
    Rutherford's Deliverance, ed. Basil Willey (Leicester: Leicester Universi
    Press, 1969) p. 125. Hereafter referred to as Rutherford, *Autobiograph*
11. Margaret Drabble, *Arnold Bennett* (London: Weidenfeld and Nicolso
    1975) p. 97.
12. 15 October 1896; *The Journals of Arnold Bennett*, ed. Newman Flow
    (London: Cassell, 1932) i, p. 18.
13. *The New Statesman*, 13 October 1923, pp. viii–x.
14. *Journals of Arnold Bennett*, ii, p. 83.
15. Letter to Arthur McLeod, 2 December 1912, *Letters*, i, p. 482.
16. Letter to Arthur McLeod, 28 November 1912, ibid., p. 481.
17. Ibid., p. 459.
18. *Journals of Arnold Bennett*, ii, p. 280.
19. 29 September 1896; *Journals of Arnold Bennett*, i, p. 16.
20. George Eliot, 'Mr. Gilfil's Love Story', *Scenes of Clerical Life*, ed. Dav
    Lodge (Harmondsworth, Middx: Penguin, 1973) p. 133.

21. Dorothy V. White, *The Groombridge Diary* (London: Oxford University Press, 1924) p. 66n.
22. Nicoll made the identification in *British Weekly*, 9 July 1896, p. 185. White challenged it in a letter (signed 'Reuben Shapcott') in *British Weekly*, 30 July 1896, p. 232.
23. Louis Tillier, *Studies in the Sources of Arnold Bennett's Novels* (Paris: Université de Paris, thèse complementaire, 1952) p. 30.
24. Marghanita Laski, *George Eliot and her World* (London: Thames and Hudson, 1973) p. 79.
25. George Eliot, *Felix Holt the Radical*, ed. Peter Coveney (Harmondsworth, Middx: Penguin, 1972) pp. 79–80. (First published 1866.)
26. D. H. Lawrence, 'Nottingham and the Mining Countryside', *Phoenix*, p. 135.
27. Rutherford, *Autobiography*, p. 2.
28. Arnold Bennett, *The Old Wives' Tale*, ed. John Wain (Harmondsworth, Middx: Penguin, 1983) p. 204. (First published 1908.)
29. Mark Rutherford, *Miriam's Schooling*, 4th edn (London: T. Fisher Unwin, n.d.; first published 1890) pp. 135ff.; *Catharine Furze*, 4th edn (London: T. Fisher Unwin, 1894; first published 1893) p. 181. See also Basil Willey, *More Nineteenth-Century Studies*, pp. 217ff.
30. D. H. Lawrence, *Apocalypse and the Writings on Revelation*, ed. Mara Kalnins (Cambridge: Cambridge University Press, 1980) p. 76.
31. Rutherford, *Autobiography*, p. 34.
32. 'Lawrence knows and renders . . . what have been the conditions of his own individual development; to be brought up in the environment of a living tradition – he is recording, in his rendering of provincial England, what in the concrete this has meant in an actual civilization. As a recorder of essential English history he is a great successor to George Eliot' [F. R. Leavis, *D. H. Lawrence: Novelist* (Harmondsworth, Middx: Penguin, 1964) p. 110].
33. George Eliot, 'The Natural History of German Life', *Essays of George Eliot*, ed. T. Pinney (London: Routledge and Kegan Paul, 1963) p. 278.
34. Arnold Bennett, *How to Become an Author* (London: C. A. Pearson, 1903) p. 135.
35. Valentine Cunningham, *Everywhere Spoken Against: Dissent in the Victorian Novel* (Oxford: Oxford University Press, 1975) p. 9.
36. Kathleen Tillotson, *Novels of the 1840s* (Oxford: Oxford University Press, 1971) pp. 88–91. Valentine Cunningham claims that 'some form of Dissent is frequently part of the "genius of place" that Kathleen Tillotson has discussed' (Cunningham, *Everywhere Spoken Against*, p. 74).
37. Cunningham, *Everywhere Spoken Against*, p. 70.
38. Basil Willey, 'Introduction' to Rutherford, *Autobiography*, p. 10.
39. Arnold Bennett, *Anna of the Five Towns* (Harmondsworth, Middx: Penguin, 1967) p. 235. (First published 1902.)
40. Basil Willey uses the phrase 'religionless Christianity' in the 'Introduction' to Rutherford, *Autobiography*, p. 17; Wilfred Stone, *Religion and Art of William Hale White (Mark Rutherford)* (Stanford: Stanford University Press, 1954) p. 67.

41. George Eliot, letter to François d'Albert-Durade, 6 December 1859; *The George Eliot Letters*, ed. Gordon S. Haight (New Haven and Yale: Yale University Press, 1954–78) III, p. 231.
42. Arnold Bennett, 'My Religious Experience', *Sketches for Autobiography*, ed. James Hepburn (London: George Allen and Unwin, 1979) pp. 168–9, 176.
43. 'At the present moment I do not, cannot believe in the divinity of Jesus'; letter to Revd Robert Reid, 2 December 1907, *Letters*, I, p. 40.
44. D. H. Lawrence, 'Hymns in a Man's Life', *Phoenix*, II, p. 600.
45. Ibid., p. 601.
46. 'I would show that the mind of man is not an exception to Nature's other works; that like everything else it has received a determinate character; that all our knowledge of it is precisely of the same kind as that of material things, and consists in the observation of its order of action, of the relation of cause and effect' [Charles Bray, *The Philosophy of Necessity; or the Law of Consequences as Applicable to Mental, Moral and Social Science* (London: Longman, 1841) p. 8].
47. Bennett, *The Old Wives' Tale*, pp. 250–1.

10

Skinning the Fox: a Masochist's Delight

CLAUDE SINZELLE

Barthes has compared the literary text to an onion with no core, no ultimate secret, but an infinite number of layers.[1] Now, if 'The Fox'[2] has already been peeled like an onion, the skin of this animal remains rather puzzling. The heroine refuses to wear it. There is a gap here and this is where 'the pleasure of the text', however unwholesome it may be, is to be sought.[3]

The peeling of 'The Fox' has led so far to two systems of interpretation: the phallic and the pre-oedipal. All studies of this tale before Judith Ruderman's[4] were variations on the theme of the phallic fox and the problems it raised. Indeed, this system of interpretation is the most conspicuous, the one propounded by the implied author. The power of Eros in nature is threatened by the repressive forces of civilisation; the fox can no longer live in the 'motherland', he is sacrificed. The only solution for the man–fox is exile, the Lawrentian solution *par excellence*. Banford must be annihilated because she stands for the evil forces of civilisation. But, as Daleski has shown, this is an unnecessary crime. Henry's power over the woman fascinated like a rabbit in front of the fox (p. 148) is such that one does not see why it is necessary to kill Banford except that, as in *The Plumed Serpent*, the 'master of death' is 'the Lord of life' to whom the heroine must submit.[5] It seems that this is a defensive fantasy underlying all the Leadership novels. The phallic system of interpretation is closely linked, as Lawrence Jones has shown, to the theory expounded in *Fantasia of the Unconscious*, a theory which justifies the ways of Lawrence to Woman – Woman must submit to the aggressive male sensual will.[6] In support of the phallic interpretation Vickery pointed out that Henry's omnipotence is derived from what Lawrence found in Frazer, especially the conception of the primitive hunter who mimes his actions in his imagination and, by killing the totem-animal, conquers March's soul and makes her submit to his will.[7] But this fantasy of magic omnipotence seems to be the symptom of a regression to an early stage in the child's development and Henry's victory is a Pyrrhic one. Our hero cannot achieve his aims with March even when the obstacle represented by Banford has been removed. March is never 'won' after all and, as usual, the story ends in indecision and suspense, Canada being at the foot of the rainbow.

We are faced with a very common scenario in Lawrence, especially in the Ladybird tales: the dominating woman must be brought to her knees, figuratively and literally. After Banford's death, March sinks down at Henry's feet, helpless and submissive, and she must now look up at her lord and master (p. 153) while in previous scenes the fox and Henry looked up at her (pp. 88, 95). Like the kneeling scenes in 'The Captain's Doll' and especially in 'The Ladybird' where there are two, this suggests that the Lawrentian solution consists in inverting the roles. The man's omnipotence is borrowed from the woman and the woman is always a mother-image. Judith Ruderman's pre-oedipal interpretation of 'The Fox', corresponding to the second layer of meaning, is incontrovertible. Let us summarise her arguments. What a strange 'phallic' hero, this 'boy' or 'youth', so often compared to a puppy or a cub, in quest of a home rather than a woman (pp. 100, 103, 115), the two women being older than he is! And how can one account for the raw fantasy of the two women's breasts, one with 'tiny iron breasts' and the other with breasts which he hopes are 'soft . . . under the tunic' (pp. 131–2) without having recourse to the two mother-images, one 'good' and the other 'bad'? In the oft-quoted letter to Katherine Mansfield written at the time of the first version of 'The Fox', noting that 'Frieda is the devouring mother', Lawrence draws the conclusion that 'a woman must yield some sort of precedence to a man', thus revealing his constant strategy.[8] In 'The Fox', not only is there a matricide but, as Judith Ruderman has shown, Henry becomes March's devouring mother: he wants her 'asleep, at peace in him' (p. 157). 'The Fox' is the story of the devoured devourer and Lawrence was probably conscious of this interpretation. This is corroborated by the references to Frazer in the first dream where the fox is both a principle of fertility and a principle of destruction.[9] It seems that Lawrence propounds a phallic reading of the tale while being aware that this system of interpretation is only a defensive scenario against the devouring mother. But at this pre-oedipal level, the text is a palimpsest and by scraping off the upper layers one finds elements which seem to have deeper roots in Lawrence's unconscious. There are obsessional images which were already present in his early works.

MASOCHISM

Emile Delavenay has studied the masochistic component of Lawrence's personality as it appears in the early works, and especially the 'masochian' structure of 'The Shades of Spring' in the light of Deleuze's study of Masoch.[10] He has also raised the problem of the relationship between the obsessional images and the 'interpretive structure' through which the author integrates them in his work.[11] Among the obsessional images he quotes there is the rabbit, associated with March in 'The Fox'. In 'Cruelty and Love' the speaker of the poem identifies with a masochistic virgin who both desires and fears to be raped by the rabbit-killer. In 'The Fox', Lawrence's fascination with March fascinated by the fox and wishing to be mastered by a tyrant (from the start the fox '[masters] her spirit', p. 89) may be a compulsive repetition of this situation.

There are two levels in masochism: neurosis and perversion. Behind the spectre of the oedipal mother of *Sons and Lovers* which reappears in 'The Fox' hides the oral mother of what Edmund Bergler calls 'psychic masochism'.[12] But this will leave us with a number of elements which fit in with a masochian scenario.

PSYCHIC MASOCHISM

What distinguishes 'The Fox' from the other two tales is that we are faced with two women, a couple with homosexual characteristics, one of whom plays the part of the husband and the other that of the wife, an 'Oedipal camouflage' which, according to Bergler, masks the deepest layer of the lesbian structure, a pre-oedipal oral masochism, and explains March's thirst for punishment, her 'injustice-collecting'.[13] Bergler's central idea, developed in *The Basic Neurosis*, is that all neuroses have an oral basis. The lesbian structure is only one form of the 'triad of the mechanism of orality' of oral neurotics.[14] Bergler's thesis establishes a link between masochism and oral regression. Unfortunately he studies 'The Fox' as if Lawrence had meant to make a clinical study of a lesbian couple. This amounts to ignoring Henry's role in his relationship with the two women and the role of Lawrence himself. By analogy with the case of Mrs M. in the chapter of *The Basic Neurosis* devoted to lesbianism,[15] we might conclude that Henry, in becoming involved with a homosexual woman, is also an 'injustice-collector' and suffers from psychic masochism. Moreover, what makes the tale so fascinating is precisely the link between the author and the patterns of relationships between the characters. If March is Henry's 'good mother', at another level March and Henry's relations with Banford echo those of Lawrence with his mother.

Banford's emotional blackmail with March reminds us of the call of the grey-haired 'beggar-woman', the ghoulish mother of the early poem 'End of Another Home Holiday', and March's inner conflict echoes the tension between filial love and the need for independence which was so acute in Lawrence.

Forever, ever by my shoulder pitiful love will linger,
Crouching as little houses crouch under the mist when I turn.[16]

The narrator finds Banford pitiful when she is sobbing ('her poor, thin hands', p. 136) and when Henry re-enters the sitting-room with March and finds Banford crouching by the fire, she becomes for him a witch, the incarnation of evil (p. 140). The ghoul of the poem is now recognised as evil, crouching like the farmstead which 'crouched blackly' on the night when Henry killed the fox (p. 121). The call of the beggar-woman is fatal for the son: she must die for him to live (p. 152). It is just as fatal for March who is also afraid of Banford and feels secure only with Henry (p. 141). At the end of the tale, Henry wonders whether he should not have left Banford and March to kill one another.

The matricide in 'The Fox' recalls that of *Sons and Lovers* where the mother had to die for the son to survive. In both cases the son and the daughter are accomplices in the act of euthanasia. Henry only finishes off the work initiated by March (the second dream and the cutting of the tree). In both cases the dying mother's hair is 'brown and grey'.[17] In 'The Fox' March, who is often described wearing muddy shoes, compares hers to those of Banford: 'My boots are a good bit too big for you, and not half dainty enough' (p. 130). In *Sons and Lovers* the mother's 'sexual' shoes are clean and dainty.[18] The matricide committed by the son with the assistance of the daughter is necessary to 'release' the oedipal son. But even in the novel, the oral mother appears beneath the oedipal mother, as is shown by the way she is killed. Paul waters down the milk to make it less nourishing (p. 476) and then poisons it with an overdose of morphia, a way of retaliating upon the 'bad' mother. This is a symptom of regression to the oral stage. In 'The Fox' there is a pervasive emphasis on food and the appetite of Henry and Banford. Food is scarce and often inadequate. Even the hens have digestive trouble. Contrary to Henry who has a voracious appetite (pp. 96, 100), Banford begins to lose hers and to waste away when she starts feeling jealous (p. 116). Henry helps to replenish the larder by killing rabbits and birds, wild ducks or pigeons (pp. 101, 118), animals which are associated respectively with March (the rabbits) and Banford (the birds). In *Sons and Lovers* Paul calls his dying mother 'my pigeon' (p. 475) and he sees 'marks of rabbits and birds in the white snow' at the time when he thinks his mother will die that very day (p. 477). When Banford learns that Henry and March have decided to marry, the reader is told about the colour of her hair and her loss of appetite; she is compared to a shot or sick bird; Henry goes out with a gun and comes back at nightfall with a rabbit and a pigeon and the narrator tells us that 'March seemed to flourish in this atmosphere', as if she unconsciously rejoiced in the prospect of Banford's death (p. 118). In *Sons and Lovers* Mrs Morel grows chrysanthemums in her garden and among these Paul prefers the yellow to the white ones which had been given by Miriam, which leads us to suppose that the yellow ones are associated with the mother (p. 395). In 'The Fox' when Henry spies on the two women climbing the hill, he is revolted by the bunch of yellow chrysanthemums carried by 'the Banford'. Moreover, he would make her eat them, he would feed her only with flowers (p. 129).

At first sight, it seems that we are faced with the first three of the 'septet of baby fears', i.e. 'fear of being starved, devoured, poisoned'.[19] The mechanism is apparently simple: it amounts to retaliating upon the starver, the devourer, the poisoner. Lawrence kills the mother with her own weapons. Banford's hospitality backfires and in *Sons and Lovers* the milk is watered down, then poisoned and returned to the sender. But according to Bergler, there is no direct connection between the child's aggression and the fear of the mother's retaliation, and the 'mechanism of orality' at work in adult oral neurotics is not an expression of unconscious wishes, but rather 'a complicated *inner defense mechanism*, created by the unconscious ego'.[20] Thus 'the writer does *not*, in his work, *express his unconscious wishes and fantasies*' but, 'under pressure of his unconscious guilt feelings, he gives expression to his unconscious *defense against these wishes and fantasies*'.[21]

In the perspective of the 'triad of the mechanism of orality' in neuroses,[22] one could postulate a three-layer structure:

(1) Masochistic desire to be 'starved' or rejected by the mother.[23]
(2) First defence: *I* do not refuse food, but *my mother* refuses to feed me. Hence my aggressiveness and my refusal to feed her.
(3) Second defence: I do not refuse to feed her: she refuses to feed herself.

In 'The Fox', the second defence, the one which is most accessible to consciousness, is the most conspicuous (Henry only takes away Banford's appetite) but the pseudo-aggressive first defence emerges when Henry thinks of feeding the 'bad' mother only with flowers. The context is significant. The primitive hunter's magic omnipotence is at work in this scene where Henry begins to apply the omnipotence of his thoughts:

> And if looks could have affected her, she would have felt a log of iron on each of her ankles as she made her way forward. 'You're a nasty little thing, you are,' he was saying softly, across the distance. 'You're a nasty little thing. I hope you'll be paid back for all the harm you've done me for nothing. I hope you will – you nasty little thing. I hope you'll have to pay for it. You will, if wishes are anything.'   (p. 129)

Now, it is at the weaning stage that 'the fantasy of autarchic omnipotence' collapses.[24] Hence Henry's extraordinary aggressiveness towards Banford in this scene which culminates in the fantasy of the women's breasts, Banford with her 'iron breasts' refusing to feed her baby.

As one finds these two layers in 'The Fox', one is led to postulate the existence of the deepest layer: the repressed oral masochism, completely inaccessible to consciousness. The middle layer is then a pseudo-aggressive defence against the desire to be cast off. As Bergler sensibly remarks, this layer belongs to fantasy, not to reality: if mothers starved their babies, they would not stand a chance of surviving to be neurotics.[25] Henry's voracity is a mask for his repressed masochistic desire to be 'starved' or cast off. His unconscious masochistic desire appears most clearly in his determination to enter a home where he is not wanted. Lawrence too had a knack of trespassing upon people's intimacy, thus unconsciously prompting them to cast him off so that he could feel indignant while revelling in the delicious feeling of being betrayed. Like the man–fox, he was an intruder in quest of a Judas whom he invariably found.

HOW TO MAKE GOOD USE OF THE MASOCHIAN FANTASY

Neurosis is not perversion. The defence mechanisms of neurosis prevent pleasure from being consciously felt as is the case with the pervert.[26] But perverse tendencies may underlie the neurotic symptoms. The interpretation of 'The Fox' in the light of psychic masochism leaves a great number of elements unexplained which fit in with a masochian interpretation, even if Lawrence does not allow March to play the part of Venus in Furs. In 'The Fox' one finds the rites of the hunt, the conquest of a fur, the rite of crucifixion and rebirth, the exclusion of the father, the fetishistic denial that the mother has no phallus, and the 'oral mother' who is at the core of the masochian fantasy. In other words, what Delavenay, using Deleuze's theory, discovered in 'The Shades of Spring' is also to be found in 'The Fox' even if it is buried under the other layers of meaning and may be warped by their pressure. My thesis is that the masochian fantasy is not played out to the end simply because Lawrence uses it in a desperate attempt to escape from the bad mothers by usurping the power of the 'good mother' specific to this fantasy.

It seems that the characters function on different levels, inside different systems. At the level of psychic masochism, whether one sees only the enacting of a lesbian relationship as Bergler did in his study of 'The Fox' or whether one takes into account the whole pattern of relationships involving the protagonists and the author,

March functions as Banford's daughter. At another level March
and Banford are substitutes for the split image of the pre-oedipal
mother as 'good' and 'bad'. But in Banford's case, this role is very
precarious since she is not so much a surrogate mother as the very
image of the oedipal mother which had already appeared in *Sons
and Lovers*. In his Freudian interpretation of *Sons and Lovers*, Weiss
has shown that the conscious image of the mother is pure and
strictly virtuous[27] and that, for the oedipal man, women remain
mother surrogates, a means of overcoming the incest barrier being
to separate the love object from the lust object which must be
debased.[28] Applying what he found in Ernest Jones's study of
Hamlet, he showed that Miriam and Clara derive from the splitting
of the mother-image into the virgin and the harlot.[29] If one applies
these divisions to 'The Fox', one finds that Banford is the equivalent
of Mrs Morel and March of Clara. Banford is not a substitute for,
but the very image of, the oedipal mother, sexually pure and
virginal. She watches over the fire like a vestal (p. 92) and, before
going to bed, she regularly tells Henry to see that the fire is safe
(p. 113). Now, the 'sexual fire' metaphor is not rare in Lawrence
and reappears in 'The Fox', for example when March is 'burnt'
by Henry's kiss (p. 115). In March's second dream, Banford is
eventually dressed like a vestal, with the 'ruddy, fiery' fox skin
over her white nightdress (p. 123). On the other hand March's
'sexual' shoes are muddy (pp. 91, 108, 130) and she does the 'dirty'
work outside (p. 132). Moreover, she becomes 'accessible' only
when she is debased, when she dresses like a prostitute, i.e.
wearing a *crape* dress and black *silk* stockings. Indeed we know
that Frieda 'was not permitted to wear silk or dainties' and that
Lawrence objected to women's wearing crape which he found
'prostitutey'.[30] No wonder March feels 'unpeeled and rather exposed', 'almost improper' (p. 134). And this in spite of the fact that
she usually is not over-concerned with sexual mores: she said she
did not care what people might say about their taking Henry as
lodger (p. 99). At the oedipal level, Banford would be the image
of the mother and March her debased substitute. But the problem
with the oedipal interpretation is that it cannot explain why, when
March as mother surrogate is 'debased', hence 'accessible', Henry
is sexually inhibited. Even at the pre-oedipal level, it seems that
March can be the good mother only when she is dressed in the
'armour' which makes her inaccessible: 'But March, under her
crude, fast, workman's tunic, would have soft, white breasts, white

and unseen' (p. 132). The mother-image in March is composite and unstable, both 'good' and 'bad'. By using the masochian fantasy, Lawrence tries to make of March a good mother, an attempt which is bound to fail.

Banford, as the image of the real oedipal mother, belongs to what Lacan calls '[the order of] the real' while March and Henry are fantasy characters who belong to 'the symbolic [order]'. According to Deleuze, 'the art of masochism is the art of phantasy'[31] and the father, abolished in the symbolic order, reappears only at the periphery of the fantasy, together with the oedipal mother, in a hallucinatory form, a 'return of reality as experienced in the order of the real'.[32] Thus Banford, the spectre of the real oedipal mother, hence linked to the father, is on the border of or even outside the fantasy while March and Henry are at its core. For the masochist there are only mother-images in the symbolic order; the functions of the father are transferred on to these images and, in the masochian myth, 'the father is and always has been abolished'.[33] This is the case in 'The Fox' where the father is 'already abolished', as is the dying oedipal mother of *Sons and Lovers*, like wood which is already dead before being cut. The grandfathers are dead before the beginning of the action. Banford's father appears briefly at the time of Banford's death and his weak constitution echoes that of his daughter: both suffer from rheumatics in the shoulder (p. 147).

Deleuze finds in Masoch three types of women 'corresponding to the basic mother-images: the primitive, uterine, hetaeric mother of cloaca and marsh; the oedipal mother, image of the lover who will enter into relations with the sadistic father as his victim or his accomplice; and in between these two, the oral mother, mother of the steppes, great nurturer and death-dealer'.[34]

There are two bad mothers at the periphery of the fantasy, the primitive, uterine mother and the oedipal mother, and one good mother, the oral mother who is 'the core of the phantasy' and in which are condensed the functions of the other two.[35] Finally, the oral mother who is the essential feature of masochism, must be both tender and cruel, 'cold, maternal, severe', 'an ideal of coldness, solicitude and death'.[36] It is the role that the masochist wants his torturess to play, a role which March plays up to a point, but which she stops playing when she refuses to wear the fox skin and wears instead 'prostitutey' clothes, i.e., those of the hetaeric mother. In so far as the functions of the other two are idealised and concentrated in the oral mother,[37] the 'sadistic' functions of the oedipal mother being transferred on to the 'cruel' oral mother, March should encompass, within the fantasy, the three mother-images. But one notices an imbalance in 'The Fox'. While Banford, as 'bad' oedipal mother linked to the 'sadistic' father, is outside the bounds of the masochian fantasy, March is essentially an unstable compound of the 'good' oral mother and the 'bad' primitive, uterine, hetaeric mother. She is first and foremost the primitive mother, corresponding to the type of 'the Grecian woman, the pagan, hetaera or Aphrodite, the generator of disorder' who endangers man by claiming the equality of the sexes and who is hermaphrodite.[38] Dressed in men's clothes, she looks like a graceful young man (pp. 86, 103) and she does a man's job. We shall see later that she is also the primitive mother in the guise of the mother of the marshes, a most scary image for Lawrence.

Our fox is hung up by the heels before being crucified (pp. 124–5). There are many ritual scenes in Masoch and the rites of suspension and crucifixion are frequent. In the crucifixion, 'it is the Mother who puts the Son on the cross', ensuring his 'resurrection as a parthenogenetic second birth'.[39] As in the rite of the hunt, Banford is excluded, only March and Henry are involved. Hence the 'secret bond' between them which excludes 'everybody else' (p. 131), 'everybody else' including the Father. Indeed on the cross, 'it is not so much the Son who dies as God the Father, the likeness to the father in the son'.[40] Genital sexuality, inherited from the father, is 'foresworn and sacrificed', the 'new man' is reborn 'from the woman alone'. Thus castration makes incest possible and is the origin of a second birth, the birth of the man 'without sexual love'.[41] Genital sexuality is indeed absent in 'The Fox'. Henry cannot make love to March, even when she has taken off her 'armour' to play the part of the hetaeric mother. When March becomes 'accessible' and when he feels 'a man, no longer a youth' (p. 133), he is sexually inhibited by his new feeling of responsibility (pp. 133, 138). This feeling of responsibility is only a moral alibi: the 'new man' is a man 'without sexual love'.

There are allusions to the crucifixion of Henry himself in the text. The night when he kills the fox, he goes through a grove of hollies (p. 121) and when he enters the house after having dis-covered the secret bond between March and himself, his face is compared to holly berries (p. 132). Now holly, with its white flowers, red berries and sharp prickles is a traditional emblem of the birth and of the Passion of Christ. In the following scene there is a glancing reference to the Last Supper although the words are not capitalised in the text (p. 134). Henry has found his Judas in March who refuses to wear the fox skin and later proposes in her letter to send it back to him, thus breaking the masochian contract. In the scene describing Henry's reaction to her letter, he is indirectly compared to Christ through the image of the thorn in the flesh.[42]

The father is excluded from the masochian symbolic order and the good mother, the oral mother is provided with the phallus through the fetishist's disavowal: 'No, the mother does not lack a phallus'.[43] The fur is one of Masoch's most common fetishes. By refusing to wear the fur, March refuses the phallus which the masochist wants her to have. When in the second dream March has qualms about allocating the fur to Banford ('She knew that it wasn't right, that this was not what she should have', p. 123), the sentence can be read with a stress pattern implying that it is what March herself should wear. March stands in front of the suspended dead fox as she usually stands in front of Henry, 'her foot trailing aside, one hip out' (p. 124 and pp. 105, 113, 114). The narrator's comment 'its poor brush falling backwards' suggests castration. In the following paragraph, the description of the fox is focalised through March. She finds the tail of the fox 'wonderful' and she passes her hand slowly down it. This might suggest a ritualistic process through which she acquires the potency of the phallic object (perhaps through the blood which stains her hand). The exclamatory sentence 'And he was dead!' might suggest that the father in the son is killed, a prerequisite for the parthenogenetic rebirth of the son as the man devoid of genital sexuality. The later allusions to the crucifixion of the fox and of Henry fit in with this interpretation, as well as Henry's metamorphosis into a 'new man' after this scene.

Both with Henry and with Banford, March behaves like the tyrant in the masochian fantasy, 'cold, maternal, severe', 'an ideal of coldness, solicitude and death'. With Banford she is 'always outspoken and rather scolding in her tenderness' (p. 129). Her eyes are 'shy and sardonic at once' (p. 86). She has the same ambivalent attitude when she speaks to Henry about the dead fox: 'Partly she was so shy and virgin, and partly she was so grim, matter-of-fact, shrewish' (p. 125). There is in March a disavowal of sensuality which fits in with the ideal of the oral mother. This is what makes her such elusive game for the hunter:

If he wasn't careful, she would just simply mock at the idea. He knew, sly and subtle as he was, that if he went to her plainly and said: 'Miss March, I love you and want you to marry me' her inevitable answer would be: 'Get out. I don't want any of that tomfoolery.' (p. 104)

It is significant that Henry does not use this cunning strategy in the following scene: he rushes to propose to March, thus provoking the violent reaction he consciously dreaded: 'Don't try any of your tomfoolery on me' (p. 106). Such a woman is difficult to catch, even using mesmerism like a primitive hunter, and is never really caught. Indeed, Henry is, like Masoch, in search of an elusive tyrant:

Balked! Balked again! Balked! He wanted the woman, he had fixed like doom upon having her. He felt that was his doom, his destiny, and his reward, to have this woman. She was his heaven and hell on earth, and he would have none elsewhere. (p. 144)

'His heaven and hell on earth': this is the object of Henry and Masoch's quest, and their doom.

In the second dream, March behaves with Banford as the oral mother, nurturer and death-dealer. Her tender solicitude towards 'her darling Jill' must not make us overlook that she kills her through her dream. March is a tender killer who, inside the dream, buries her child. The size of a wooden box suggests that Jill's body is that of a child. Henry and March had carried in the logs and March carried them 'on her breast as if they were some heavy child' (p. 108). Judith Ruderman's pre-oedipal interpretation is compatible with the masochian interpretation: the oral mother is both nurturer and death-dealer. What Masoch adds to this image of the mother is the theme of coldness, ice, frost, hence Deleuze's subtitle: 'coldness and cruelty'.[44] Henry kills the fox on a 'frosty December night' (p. 121) and 'big stars [are] snapping outside' just before he hears the fox (p. 118). The word 'snapping' is used in a rare sense, meaning 'sparkling', and it may connote 'snatching with teeth' in this context. In the third paragraph of the description of the dead fox, cruelty and cold, biting and ice are associated: 'Wonderful silver whiskers he had, like ice-threads' (p. 124). The spoon-shaped or spatula-shaped muzzle which seems to fascinate the narrator as much as March, with its cruel white teeth underneath, might be the *vagina dentata* which seems to have obsessed Lawrence. The biting cold is castrating. In the preceding paragraph we are shown March fascinated by the whiteness and softness of the fox's belly, both associated with snow: the simile 'white and soft as snow his belly' is repeated. It is as if March were projecting the coldness of the castrating oral mother on to the dead fox. The words 'white' and 'soft' are used again in Henry's evocation of the 'good mother''s breasts (p. 132). March's throat also is white and soft and her arms, 'strong and firm muscled' (p. 133), remind us of Masoch's muscular heroines.

What is most striking in Lawrence's two fantasy characters is that they are like mirror images of each other. March and Henry are both the quarry and the hunter. Both carry a gun and hunt the fox. Indeed, even when she is under the spell of the fox, March still goes out with the gun (pp. 89–90). On Henry's arrival she holds on to the gun until Banford tells her to put it down (p. 94), at a time when she identifies Henry with the fox (p. 93). Both saw the logs for the fire. If March paints swans (pp. 87, 110), Henry thinks of spending his first night at 'the Swan' (p. 94). Both have red hands (pp. 110, 114). Both are linked with the mud (pp. 108, 148). Both cut the *male* dead tree which kills Banford ('his base . . . he did not fall', p. 146). The felling of the male tree could be interpreted as the exclusion of the father as well as prefiguring the death of the oedipal mother linked to the father. March and Henry are endowed with the power of life and death: March through her dream, Henry by actually killing Banford. Henry, like March, assumes some of the characteristics of the oral mother, both soft and cruel:

> And with *awful softness* he bent forward and just touched her neck with his mouth and his chin.
>
> 'Don't!' she cried . . . 'What do you mean?' . . . It was as if she was killed.
>
> 'I mean what I say,' he persisted *softly and cruelly*   (italics added; p. 107)

When he leans out of the carriage window, there is 'no emotion on his face' and his eyes are compared to those of a *she*-cat: 'like a cat's when suddenly she sees something and stares' (p. 142). The sexes seem to be all mixed up.

It is as if the features which make up the image of the oral mother in the masochian fantasy were distributed among the two protagonists, and this can be accounted for in terms of Deleuze's theory. Starting from the opposition made by Daniel Lagache between the *narcissistic ego–ideal ego* and *superego–ego ideal* systems which he applies respectively to masochism and sadism,[45] Deleuze finds in masochism a twofold process of desexualisation and resexualisation. Through disavowal the ego abjures sexuality and rejects the superego, both inherited from the father and 'entrusts the mother with the power to give birth to an "ideal ego" which is pure, autonomous and independent of the superego' while there simultaneously takes place 'resexualization . . . in the narcissistic ego, which contemplates its image in the ideal ego through the agency of the oral mother',[46] the ego using 'the mother-image as a mirror which can reflect and even produce the "ideal ego" as a narcissistic ideal of omnipotence'.[47] In 'The Fox', the narcissistic omnipotence of the totem hunter is only the reflection of the narcissistic ideal of omnipotence represented by the oral mother in the mirror. Henry, a fantasy character, is only a reflection of March in so far as the latter is endowed with the omnipotence of the oral mother. He imitates March's actions: she is the first to smell and hunt the fox, saw the logs, cut the tree and kill Banford. 'The narcissistic ego contemplates the ideal ego in the maternal mirror of death.'[48] After the crucifixion of the fox and the murder committed by March through her dream, Henry, 'liberated from the superego as from sexuality',[49] can kill Banford himself. As a prerequisite, March had to become the oral mother, 'the death-image' in the mirror. But not only does Henry imitate the oral mother, he usurps her power. Both with the fox and with Banford, March only initiates the deadly process, Henry finishes it, as he finishes cutting the tree. Lawrence superimposes fantasy upon fantasy: he offers the oral mother the phallus, the power to deal death, the better to take it back. He makes Henry offer March the fur and takes it back by making her refuse it. But a usurped power is precarious, all the more as March is an unstable compound of the primitive mother and the oral mother. By not allowing her to play the role of Venus in furs, of the oral mother, to the end, Lawrence makes her relapse into primitive hetaerism.

Deleuze has pointed out that Masoch's three feminine types come from the three Bachovian eras (Aphroditic hetaerism, matriarchy, patriarchy):

The first is the hetaeric, Aphroditic era, born in the chaos of luxuriant marshes, characterized by multiple and fickle relationships between men and women, but in which the feminine principle predominates, the father being 'Nobody'.[50]

It is generally assumed that Lawrence had an indirect knowledge of Bachofen and owed something to his ideas.[51] According to Bachofen, while 'matriarchy reveres the ear of grain and the seed corn', 'hetaerism finds its principle embodied in the vegetation and animals of the marshy lowlands, which become its chief gods', 'the unbidden wild growth of mother earth' being 'manifested most abundantly and luxuriantly in the life of the swamps'.[52] Hence, perhaps, March's name (the mother of the marshes). Moreover, she paints swans and water-lilies (pp. 87, 110). Now, water animals and plants are always associated, in Lawrence's imagination, with the mud of marshes, the phosphorescence of the moon (in the dark March is 'almost phosphorescent', p. 106), the 'Aphrodite of the foam', symbols of the forces of corruption and dissolution in 'The Ladybird' and in *Women in Love*.[53] Aphrodite of the foam is associated in 'The Ladybird' with 'white love', i.e., self-conscious love, as it already was in *Twilight in Italy*.[54] Now, we find her again in the famous scene in *The Plumed Serpent* in which Lawrence makes his heroine renounce clitoral orgasm through which the woman seeks her 'conscious satisfaction'. Kate must kill 'in her' the 'Aphrodite of the foam'.[55] Daleski has cogently argued that the new way of love advocated by Henry in 'The Fox' (p. 154), which demands that the woman be passive, is a means of exorcising (excising?) the abominable Aphrodite of the foam.[56] In 'The Ladybird', the Aphrodite of the foam must die *in* Daphne (pp. 72, 76). In the same way, Henry gives the phallus to March for her to destroy it in her. But, taking it back from her, be becomes the oral mother who tries to swallow up the hermaphroditic Aphrodite ('He wanted her asleep, at peace in him', p. 157). The masochian fantasy allows the Lawrentian hero to usurp the oral mother's power in a desperate attempt to annihilate the primitive mother, the Aphrodite of the foam which haunted Lawrence from the time of *Twilight in Italy* to that of *The Plumed Serpent*. In 'The Ladybird', the phallic omnipotence of the Lawrentian dark sun is derived from the omnipotence of the moon, of the Aphrodite of the foam. But death has the last word in love, Woman remains to the end of the image of death. The lily, the water-lily and the lotus associated with Lady Daphne[57] foreshadow the swan song at the end of the story. In 'The Fox', the killing of the oedipal mother is of no avail. The dreadful mother-image is like the Lernean hydra. Lawrence may well try to cut off one of the monster's heads: other heads spring up again in the marsh of his unconscious.

Notes

1. Jonathan Culler, *Structuralist Poetics* (London: Routledge & Kegan Paul, 1975) p. 259.
2. D. H. Lawrence, 'The Fox', *Three Novellas* (Harmondsworth, Middx: Penguin, 1982). All references in the text are to the Penguin edition of the works of D. H. Lawrence.
3. 'L'endroit le plus érotique d'un corps n'est-il pas *là où le vêtement bâille?*' [Roland Barthes, *Le Plaisir du Texte* (Paris: Editions du Seuil, 1973) p. 19].
4. Judith G. Ruderman, '"The Fox" and the "Devouring Mother"', *DHL Review*, x (1977) pp. 251–69.
5. H. M. Daleski, 'Aphrodite of the Foam and *The Ladybird Tales*', in *D. H. Lawrence: A Critical Study of the Major Novels and Other Writings*, ed. A. H. Gomme (Hassocks: Harvester Press, 1978) p. 154.
6. Lawrence Jones, 'Physiognomy and the Sensual Will in "The Ladybird" and "The Fox"', *DHL Review*, XIII (1980) pp. 1–29.
7. John B. Vickery, 'Myth and Ritual in the Shorter Fiction of D. H. Lawrence', *Modern Fiction Studies*, v (1959) pp. 80–2.
8. 5 December 1918, *Letters*, III, p. 302.
9. Judith Ruderman ('"The Fox" and the "Devouring Mother"', pp. 258–9), refutes Vickery's arguments using the references to Frazer to support the phallic interpretation. Another source for the fox's burning tail and the corn might be the Old Testament: Samson, after being betrayed by Delilah, punishes the Philistines by setting fire to the foxes' tails in order to burn their corn (Judges xv, 4–5).
10. Emile Delavenay, 'D. H. Lawrence and Sacher-Masoch', *DHL Review*, VI (1973) pp. 119–48; Gilles Deleuze, *Présentation de Sacher-Masoch – Le Froid et le Cruel*; avec le texte intégral de La Vénus à la Fourrure (Paris: Editions de Minuit, 1967), trans. by Jean McNeil as *Masochism: An Interpretation of Coldness and Cruelty* (New York: George Braziller, 1971).
11. Delavenay, 'D. H. Lawrence and Sacher-Masoch', p. 121.
12. Edmund Bergler, *The Basic Neurosis: Oral Regression and Psychic Masochism* (New York: Grune & Stratton, 1949).
13. Edmund Bergler, 'D. H. Lawrence's "The Fox" and the Psychoanalytic Theory on Lesbianism', in *A D. H. Lawrence Miscellany*, ed. H. T. Moore (London: Heinemann, 1961) pp. 47–53. Hereafter cited as *Miscellany*.
14. Bergler, *Basic Neurosis*, pp. 4–5.

15. Ibid., pp. 237–42, especially p. 239.
16. *Complete Poems*, p. 63.
17. Lawrence, 'The Fox', p. 116; *Sons and Lovers* (Harmondsworth, Middx: Penguin, 1962) p. 457.
18. The shoe being 'a symbol for the female genitals' [Daniel A. Weiss, *Œdipus in Nottingham: D. H. Lawrence* (Seattle, Washington: University of Washington Press, 1962) p. 64]. See also Lawrence, *Sons and Lovers*, p. 152: 'Mrs Morel was one of those naturally exquisite people who can walk in mud without dirtying their shoes. . . . He . . . thought them the most dainty boots in the world, and he cleaned them with as much reverence as if they had been flowers.'
19. Bergler, *Basic Neurosis*, p. 19.
20. Ibid., p. 19 and p. 13.
21. Ibid., p. 187.
22. The 'five-layer structure' in Bergler's article on 'The Fox' (*Miscellany*, pp. 51–2) includes the two superego vetoes. The basic lesbian structure has in fact three layers only. Cf. Bergler, *Basic Neurosis*, pp. 237–8: 'The peculiar nature of the clinical Lesbian conflict consists of the fact that a three-story structure is unconsciously erected: *masochistic injustice collecting*, warded off by *pseudo-hatred*, secondarily warded off by *exaggerated pseudo-love* towards a representative of the infantile image of the mother. . . . Lesbians use the man–wife (father–mother) disguise as a covering *defensive* cloak.'
23. 'In later years, the reproach of "starvation" is modified into that of being refused' (Bergler, *Basic Neurosis*, p. 20). Bergler dispels a common misunderstanding by distinguishing sharply between the *clinical* picture and the *genetic* picture of psychic masochism. The genesis of masochism is explained thus: the child wants to get, then he is refused or *fancies* that he is refused; he becomes all the more aggressive as his fantasy of omnipotence is challenged; then, if he is to become a masochist, because of his guilt he eventually turns his aggression against himself and derives masochistic pleasure from it ('libidinisation' of guilt). It is at this moment that the *clinical* picture starts: the superego 'objects to this peculiar type of infantile pleasure'. As a result the ego creates 'secondary defenses' which constitute the 'mechanism of orality' (pp. 3–4). Injustice collectors 'create or misuse' situations in which somebody representing the oral mother refuses their wishes (p. 5). They themselves provoke 'a situation of being refused' (p. 12). Originally, every baby wants to get, not to be refused: 'Nobody denies that oral neurotics were, once upon a time, babies who wanted to get. As adult neurotics they reproduce the situation 'Bad mother refuses'. What they repress deeply is their masochistic enjoyment of that refusal' (p. 8).
24. Bergler, *Basic Neurosis*, p. 3.
25. Ibid., pp. 9, 19–20.
26. Ibid., pp. 12, 216.
27. Weiss, *Œdipus in Nottingham*, p. 40.
28. Ibid., p. 62.
29. Ibid., pp. 48–9.

30. Anecdote told by Cecily Lambert Minchin, the 'original' of Banford, in *D. H. Lawrence: A Composite Biography*, ed. Edward Nehls, vol. I (Madison, Wisconsin: University of Wisconsin Press, 1957) p. 465.

31. Deleuze, *Présentation de Sacher-Masoch*, p. 59(58). Page references to the American edition will be given in brackets after the references to the French edition.

32. Ibid., pp. 57–8(57): 'It would therefore be thoroughly misleading to confuse the phantasy that comes into play in the symbolic order and the hallucination that represents the return of reality as experienced in the order of the real. Theodor Reik quotes a case where all the "magic" vanishes from the masochistic scene because the subject thinks he recognizes in the woman about to strike him a trait that reminds him of the father.' [Translation modified.]

33. Ibid., p. 56(55). Translation modified.

34. Ibid., p. 49(49). Translation modified. Quoted by Delavenay, 'D. H. Lawrence and Sacher-Masoch', p. 138.

35. Deleuze, *Présentation de Sacher-Masoch*, p. 59(58).

36. Ibid., pp. 45(45), 50(49).

37. Ibid., p. 55(54).

38. Ibid., p. 42(42).

39. Ibid., p. 84(84). Translation modified.

40. Ibid. Translation modified.

41. Ibid., p. 87(86–7). Through a process of disavowal, 'sexual pleasure . . . is interrupted, deprived of its genitality and transformed into the pleasure of being reborn' (ibid.). We shall see later that in masochism there is a twofold process of desexualisation and resexualisation. Without the latter the masochist would not experience any pleasure. But this resexualisation in the narcissistic ego has nothing to do with genital sexuality which is abjured. See ibid., p. 112(113).

42. II Corinthians XII, 7. As in the story 'The Thorn in the Flesh', the Lawrentian hero finds his strength in his weakness.

43. Deleuze, *Présentation de Sacher-Masoch*, p. 109(110). See also pp. 28–9 for a good study of the process of disavowal in fetishism.

44. One finds in Masoch the Lawrentian myth of the North and the South, respectively associated with Christianity and paganism (ibid., p. 48(47)).

45. Ibid., p. 110(111).

46. Ibid., p. 109(110).

47. Ibid., p. 110(111). Translation modified.

48. Ibid., p. 112(113).

49. Ibid.

50. Ibid., p. 47(46–7). My translation. J. J. Bachofen, *Das Mutterrecht* (Stuttgart: Krais & Hoffmann, 1861).

51. Delavenay, 'D. H. Lawrence and Sacher-Masoch', p. 148, n.53; Martin Green, *The von Richthofen Sisters* (London, 1974) pp. 81–4; James F. Scott, 'Thimble into Ladybird: Nietzsche, Frobenius, and Bachofen in the Later Work of D. H. Lawrence', *Arcadia*, XIII (1978) pp. 161–76.

52. *Myth, Religion, and Mother Right: Selected Writings of J. J. Bachofen*, trans.

Ralph Manheim (Princeton, N.J.: Princeton University Press, 1967) p. 97.

53. D. H. Lawrence, 'The Ladybird', passim; *Women in Love*, esp. the passage about the 'dark river of dissolution', pp. 192–3; the passage about the swan in 'The Crown', *Phoenix* II, p. 403.

54. 'Aphrodite, the queen of the senses, she, born of the sea-foam, is the luminousness of the gleaming senses, the phosphorescence of the sea, the senses become a conscious aim unto themselves. . . . But also there is the Aphrodite-worship. The flesh, the senses, are now self-conscious' [D. H. Lawrence, *Twilight in Italy* (London: Heinemann, 1956) p. 35].

55. 'She realized, almost with wonder, the death in her of the Aphrodite of the foam: the seething, frictional, ecstatic Aphrodite. . . . And there was no such thing as conscious "satisfaction". What happened was dark and untellable. So different from the beak-like friction of Aphrodite of the foam, the friction which flares out in circles of phosphorescent ecstasy, to the last wild spasm which utters the involuntary cry, like a death-cry, the final love-cry' [D. H. Lawrence, *The Plumed Serpent* (Harmondsworth, Middx: Penguin, 1961) p. 439].

56. Daleski, 'Aphrodite of the Foam', pp. 155–6.

57. Lawrence, 'The Ladybird', p. 44, and the missing two pages of manuscript reproduced by Brian H. Finney in *Review of English Studies*, XXIV (1973) pp. 191–2.

11

'Hibiscus and Salvia Flowers': the Puritan Imagination

TOM PAULIN

Lawrence wrote 'Hibiscus and Salvia Flowers' on the 31 January 1921. He was then staying at Fontana Vecchia, in Taormina, Sicily, a popular winter resort under Mount Etna. His poem may be regarded as a distinctively puritan response to the political situation in Italy – it is written 'to the moment' and represents a volatile complex engagement with Italian socialism. If we regard Lawrence as belonging to the libertarian, essentially right-wing strand within English non-conformism – as embodying an ethic of puritan individualism whose economic philosophy we now term 'monetarism' – it may be possible to argue that 'Hibiscus and Salvia Flowers' represents a movement of sympathy towards an ideological position hostile both to Lawrence's late-Romantic heroism and to individualism.

From 1918 to 1920 there was a growing conviction on the part of the Italian working class that a socialist revolution was inevitable. This conviction was shared by the mass of workers and socialists. However, in March 1919 Mussolini launched his Fascist movement and in the autumn of 1920 his Fascist squads began their punitive expeditions. When the Italian Communist Party was founded in January 1921 (the same month in which Lawrence wrote his poem), the revolutionary wave was on the ebb, the workers had been defeated and had lost their confidence in the possibility of revolution. In Britain, the July unemployment figures showed that 22.4 per cent of all insured workers were unemployed and it is likely that Lawrence's poem depends on an interplay between his sense of the condition of Britain and the developing political situation in Italy.

Lawrence's political statements are many and confusing, and his essay 'Democracy' can be seen as issuing from an essentially *laissez-faire* philosophy – that doctrine of 'doing as one likes' which Matthew Arnold criticises in *Culture and Anarchy* and which is hostile to his idea of the state. As a non-conformist and member of a faith and culture which Arnold despised, Lawrence detests the State – it is mechanical, not organic, and it reduces individual human beings to a statistical aggregate:

> What a loathsome little beast he is, this Average, this Unit, this Homunculus. Yet he has his purposes. He is useful to measure by. That's the purpose of all averages.[1]

For Lawrence, the law of averages 'holds good for the stomach', but in 'the free, spontaneous self, one man's meat is truly another man's poison' and it is therefore impossible to 'draw' any average. This brisk distinction between individual spiritual needs and average material necessities enables Lawrence to state confidently:

> Now we will settle for ever the Equality of Man, and the Rights of Man. Society means people living together. People *must* live together. And to live together, they must have some Standard, some *Material* Standard. This is where the Average comes in. And this is where Socialism and Modern Democracy come in. For Democracy and Socialism rest upon the Equality of Man, which is the Average. And this is sound enough, so long as the Average represents the real basic material needs of mankind: basic material needs: we insist and insist again. For Society, or Democracy, or any Political State or Community exists not for the sake of the individual, nor should ever exist for the sake of the individual, but simply to establish the Average, in order to make living together possible: that is, to make proper facilities for every man's clothing, feeding, housing himself, working, sleeping, mating, playing, according to his necessity as a common unit, an average. Everything beyond that common necessity depends on himself alone.[2]

Lawrence argues that the State exists merely for the 'proper adjustment of material means of existence' and for nothing else. The State, he argues, is a 'dead ideal' and Nation, Democracy and Socialism are similarly dead ideals:

They are just vast hotels, or hostels, where every guest does some scrap of the business of the day's routine – if it's only lounging gracefully to give the appearance of ease – and for this contribution gets his suitable accommodation.[3]

Lawrence's essay on democracy is part of his argument with Whitman and when he states that 'the Whitman One Identity, the *En Masse*, is a horrible nullification of true identity and being', Lawrence's puritanism, a puritanism which is necessarily based on the doctrine of the supremacy of the free individual conscience, rejects Whitman's concept of democracy as at best 'servile, serving the free soul', and at worst 'sheer self-destruction'. And like a preacher he rises to this declamatory conclusion:

Let us put them in their place. Let us get over our rage of social activity, public being, universal self-estimation, republicanism, bolshevism, socialism, empire – all these mad manifestations of *En Masse* and One Identity. They are all self-betrayed. Let our Democracy be in the singleness of the clear, clean self, and let our *En Masse* be no more than an arrangement for the liberty of this self. Let us drop looking after our neighbour. It only robs him of his chance of looking after himself. Which is robbing him of his freedom, with a vengeance.[4]

This is in fact a spiritual version of self-help, an ideology which expresses a peculiarly American – and therefore unBritish – hostility to social welfare, to the idea of community, compassion, the need to be responsible for and to other people. It is a naked monetarist ethic which is opposed nowadays by patrician conservatives, socialists, liberals and Marxists. Yet Lawrence belongs also to the opposition because of his hostility to private property, and in the conclusion to 'Democracy' he states:

If we are to keep our backs unbroken, we must deposit all property on the ground, and learn to walk without it. We must stand aside. And when many men stand aside, they stand in a new world; a new world of man has come to pass. This is the Democracy: the new order.[5]

Lawrence's letters for the period 1916–21 sometimes support the arguments of 'Democracy' and sometimes run counter to them.

Writing to Lady Cynthia Asquith he reacts to the news of Asquith's resignation and replacement by Lloyd George:

> I too expect a national disaster before very long. . . . It is no use adhering to that old 'advanced' crowd – Cambridge, Lowes Dickinson, Bertie Russell, young reformers, Fabians – they are our disease, not our hope. We want a clean sweep, and a new start. And we will have it. Wait only a little longer. Fusty, fuzzy peace-cranks and lovers of humanity are the devil. We must get on a new track altogether. Damn humanity, let us have a bit of inhuman, or non-human truth, that our fuzzy human emotions can't alter.[6]

This is characteristic rejection of the middle-ground, of compassion and of liberal humanism – it glints with that distinctive modernist cruelty and resembles an ideological, committed cast of mind.

Here, as so often in his work, Lawrence appears to occupy a position on the extreme right, and in March, 1920, he writes to Samuel Koteliansky: 'What remaining belief I had in Socialism dies out of me more and more as the time goes by.'[7] Nine months later, again writing from Sicily, Lawrence tells Eleanor Farjeon:

> If I knew how to, I'd really join myself to the revolutionary socialists now. I think the time has come for a real struggle. That's the only thing I care for: the death struggle. I don't care for politics. But I know there *must* and *should* be a deadly revolution very soon, and I would take part in it if I knew how.[8]

Ten days later, Lawrence wrote 'Hibiscus and Salvia Flowers', a poem which dramatises, like a personal letter or a quick, urgent piece of journalism, his feelings about revolutionary socialism.

The poem begins with a noisy refrain based on the traditional children's song which is also echoed in Ariel's first song in *The Tempest* – so the socialists disturb the peace, they are intruders like the mariners who land on Shakespeare's island. Dressed in the 'same unremarkable Sunday suit', the Sicilian socialists are young and loutish and stare with the 'gang-stare' and 'a half-threatening envy'. 'They' look at 'us', and by 'us' Lawrence means 'every *forestière*, / Every lordly tuppeny foreigner from the hotels, fattening on the exchange'.[9] It is clear from a letter Lawrence wrote two weeks earlier that he was uneasy at being identified with the rich foreigners in the hotels. Writing to Dr Anton Kippenberg, he gives detailed information about the differing prices of hotel rooms and adds: 'My wife and I are poor people. We live here and keep house for ourselves. So we know well enough what it is to be scared of hôtel prices.'[10]

The initial voice of the poem, however, is elegantly and confidently hostile towards the Socialists who are 'Sans any distinction at all except loutish commonness'. They are '-Ists! -Ists!', hissing ideologists –

> Bolshevists,
> Leninists,
> Communists,
> Socialists.

But in answer to the question which immediately precedes this litany – 'How do we know then, that they are they?' – Lawrence says 'Alas, salvia and hibiscus flowers' and he lovingly repeats the phrase, a phrase which both smooths out and preserves something of that hissing, spitting exclamation '-Ists! -Ists!'. There is a lovely combination of broad open vowels with a sticky fricative in the phrase 'Salvia and hibiscus flowers', and it is hard to avoid hearing a pun on 'saliva'.

It is at this point that we can begin to discern the form of Lawrence's poem – it is based on the technique of personal witness familiar to anyone who has listened to street preachers or attended evangelical church services. In a reprise of the opening refrain – and a reprise is one of the necessary techniques of extempore witness – Lawrence cries: 'Hark! Hark!/The dogs do bark! Salvia and hibiscus flowers'. He then introduces a standard puritan allusion to the Book of Exodus, asking 'Who smeared their doors with blood?' The socialists are like the Israelites in Egypt – the red flowers they wear are reminiscent of the Israelites' blood-smeared door-posts:

> And the blood shall be to you for a token upon the houses where ye are: and when I see the blood, I will pass over you, and the plague shall not be upon you to destroy you, when I smite the land of Egypt.[11]

Lawrence's allusion to this verse from Exodus isn't simply

personal – it springs naturally from his nonconformist, puritan inheritance. The Book of Exodus was central to the English puritan imagination and we may compare Lawrence's use of it with Richardson's *Pamela*:

> I think I was loth to leave the house. Can you believe it? – what could be the matter with me, I wonder? . . . Surely I cannot be like the old murmuring Israelites, to long after the onions and garlic of Egypt, when they had suffered there such heavy bondage?[12]

We may compare this with a statement by the contemporary puritan preacher, Dr Ian Paisley:

> Egypt – Moses forsook Egypt. Egypt offered leisure, pleasure (the pleasures of sin for a season) and it offered him treasure. Leisure, pleasure and treasure – they're all in the party interest. He laid them on the altar and instead he chose to be an heir of heaven. He chose the affliction of the people of God. *Moses* – his name is eternally linked with the lord of life and glory – what a reward compared with the beggarly elements of Egypt![13]

To Lawrence, therefore, these Sicilian socialists represent the chosen people about to break out of their Egyptian bondage, their enslavement by a tourist economy, by foreigners. And we remember that just two weeks earlier Lawrence had written that he and his wife were 'poor people' who knew what it was to be scared of hotel prices. Although he compares state socialism to a hotel in his essay 'Democracy', he here feels uncomfortable at being identified with the hotel dwellers, while the socialists appear as native free spirits outside hotel life. Wearing their bright red flowers, they are marked out, separated, chosen. They challenge the beggarly elements of Egypt and are beyond any nostalgic hankerings for its onions and garlic.

The flowers now 'Bloom along the Corso on the living, perambu-lating bush', but the poem's interrogative voice enacts the idea of presumption:

> Who said they might assume these blossoms?
> What god did they consult?

> Rose-red, princess hibiscus, rolling her pointed Chinese
>   petals!
> Azalea and camellia, single peony
> And pomegranate bloom and scarlet mallow-flower
> And all the eastern, exquisite royal plants
> That noble blood has brought us down the ages!
> Gently nurtured, frail and splendid
> Hibiscus flower –
> Alas, the Sunday coats of Sicilian bolshevists!

The flowers aren't simply natural and organic – they are the product of culture, training, breeding, tradition. They are royal plants, 'gently nurtured' and associated with 'noble blood'. It is as though the socialists have expropriated, suddenly and completely, both nature and aristocratic culture. Interestingly, Lawrence combines primitivism with high culture: 'Rose of the oldest races of princesses, Polynesian/Hibiscus'. Here, the allusion is clearly to Gauguin, whose work was a major influence on Lawrence's painting, and Lawrence had been reading Gauguin's *Noa-Noa* six months earlier. In a letter to Robert Mountsier, he refers to Gauguin, to Maugham's *The Moon and Sixpence* and to Melville's *Typee*, and exclaims: 'To think what has become of Melville's beautiful Typee! A million curses on European civilisation. It is collapsing, and it deserves to collapse. I spit on it.'[14] The socialists with their salvia and hibiscus flowers are outside hotels, outside European civilisation by their association through the flowers with an ancient Polynesian aristocracy.

The reference to Eve ('Eve, in her happy moments, / Put hibiscus in her hair') follows this primitivist theme and is consonant with the supreme image of English puritanism – Adam and Eve in the garden before the Fall. This aligns the prelapsarian Eve with a Polynesian princess, but it then forces Lawrence to confront the argument deep in his own imagination between the radical idea of human rights and a conservative idea of tradition, duty, hierarchy, art:

> The exquisite and ageless aristocracy
> Of a peerless soul,
> Blessed are the pure in heart and the fathomless in bright
>   pride;
> The loveliness that knows *noblesse oblige*;

> The native royalty of red hibiscus flowers;
> The exquisite assertion of new delicate life
> Risen from the roots:
> Is this how you'll have it, red-decked socialists,
> Hibiscus-breasted?

The socialists are interrogated as to whether they embody a Jeffersonian idea of natural aristocracy, but there is a confusing transition from this to the echo of the Sermon on the Mount ('Blessed are the pure in heart') and to the quietistic meekness of 'The loveliness that knows *noblesse oblige*'. There would appear to be an irreconcilable argument in Lawrence's imagination between what in 'Democracy' he terms 'the singleness of the clear, clean self'[15] and feudalism, hierarchy, aristocracy. Lawrence solves the problem by treating these irreconcilables as if they belong together and cries

> If it be so, I fly to join you,
> And if it be not so, brutes to pull down hibiscus flowers!

This is an echo of his letter of eleven days earlier to Eleanor Farjeon in which he expressed a wish to 'really join myself to the revolutionary socialists now'.

Turning to the blazing scarlet spikes of the salvia flower, he exclaims:

> Or salvia!
> Or dragon-mouthed salvia with gold throat of wrath!
> Flame-flushed, enraged, splendid salvia,
> Cock-crested, crowing your orange scarlet like a tocsin
> Along the Corso all this Sunday morning.

Clearly this is Lawrence's dated and sexist phallic consciousness, and it is meant to supplement or complement the figures of Eve and of the Polynesian princesses. It prompts a shift in tone – to a type of macho taunting which may be strategic:

> Is your wrath red as salvias,
> You socialists?
> You with your grudging, envious, furtive rage,
> In Sunday suits and yellow boots along the Corso.
> You look well with your salvia flowers, I must say.

Lawrence now moves to an identification with the 'dawn-cock's-comb flaring flower' which is a version of that wish to join the 'death struggle' which he had expressed two weeks earlier in his letter to Eleanor Farjeon. It is hard for us now to read these lines, because this is a romantic poetry of terrorism, of mass terror, of extermination:

> I long to be a bolshevist
> And set the stinking rubbish-heap of this foul world
> Afire at a myriad scarlet points,
> A bolshevist, a salvia-face
> To lick the world with flame that licks it clean
> I long to see its chock-full crowdedness
> And glutted squirming populousness on fire
> Like a field of filthy weeds
> Burnt back to ash,
> And then to see the new, real souls sprout up.

This is the climax of the poem and it issues, I believe, both from the historical currents of the age and from that intransigence and destructiveness which are so much a part of the protestant temperament. Six years later, Yeats was to end 'In Memory of Eva Gore-Booth and Con Markiewicz' with the lines:

> We the great gazebo built,
> They convicted us of guilt;
> Bid me strike a match and blow.[16]

Nourished as it is on the Book of Revelations, the protestant imagination reacts to extreme pressure by imagining apocalypse, purging fire, a new order.

Confronting the spectacle of a mass political movement, an ideology which denies the importance and primacy of the individual, and which in this specific case sends out party members with dandyish buttonholes, Lawrence becomes a kind of demonic gardener fighting the 'wicked, obstreperous weeds' and attacking 'a cabbage-idealistic level of equality'. His puritanism identifies with their puritanism, but he cannot follow them in believing in equality. It is at this point that Lawrence moves the conflict in the poem to that between his romantic conception of his supreme individuality and the threat posed to that individuality by 'the

louts along the Corso'. The vocal tone, it seems to me, is deliberately
hysterical, as if he is enacting a realisation that he must surrender
his personality to the socialists:

> What rot, to see the cabbage and hibiscus-tree
> As equals!
> What rot, to say the louts along the Corso
> In Sunday suits and yellow shoes
> Are my equals!
> I am their superior, saluting the hibiscus flower, not them.
> The same I say to the profiteers from the hotels, the money-
>   fat-ones,
> Profiteers here being called dog-fish, stinking dog-fish,
>   sharks.
> The same I say to the pale and elegant persons,
> Pale-face authorities loitering tepidly:
> *That I salute the red hibiscus flowers*
> *And send mankind to its inferior blazes.*
> Mankind's inferior blazes,
> And these along with it, all the inferior lot –
> These bolshevists,
> These dog-fish,
> These precious and ideal ones,
> All rubbish ready for fire.

By separating the hibiscus flowers from the socialists and then
lumping the socialists with the dog-fish, the profiteers, and 'all the
inferior lot', Lawrence begins to climb out of his uneasy, sometimes
hysterical querulousness, until he is able to angrily solve the
contradictions in his response by saying:

> And I salute hibiscus and the salvia flower
> Upon the breasts of loutish bolshevists,
> Damned loutish bolshevists,
> Who perhaps will do the business after all,
> In the long run, in spite of themselves.

In the calculated over-protestation here there seems to be a residual
admiration for the bolshevist louts. And echoing Milton's opening
paragraph to Book III of *Paradise Lost* ('but not to me returns / Day,

or the sweet approach of Ev'n or Morn'),[17] Lawrence moves into
stance of desperate puritan isolation:

> Meanwhile, alas
> For me no fellow-men,
> No salvia-frenzied comrades, antennae
> Of yellow-red, outreaching, living wrath
> Upon the smouldering air,
> And throat of brimstone-molten angry gold.
> Red, angry men are a race extinct, alas!
>
> Never
> To be a bolshevist
> With a hibiscus flower behind my ear
> In sign of life, of lovely, dangerous life
> And passionate disquality of men;
> In sign of dauntless, silent violets,
> And impudent nettles grabbing the under-earth,
> And cabbages born to be cut and eat,
> And salvia fierce to crow and shout for fight,
> And rosy-red hibiscus wincingly
> Unfolding all her coiled and lovely self
> In a doubtful world.

This is Samson as impotent aesthete, wishing to be part of the God
of Wrath, but helpless and powerless. And in a characteristic
puritan hoisting movement, Lawrence concludes:

> But yet
> If they pull all the world down,
> The process will amount to the same in the end.
> Instead of flame and flame-clean ash,
> Slow waters rotting back to level muck
> And final humus,
> Whence the re-start.
>
> And still I cannot bear it
> That they take hibiscus and the salvia flower.

It is a statement of loss and isolation, as if they have a power
and a beauty he does not have access to, as if he cannot finally

surrender his personality to comradeship and ideology and the dragonish dandyish beauty of the flowers. Like 'Snake', this poem is about wanting to lose self-conscious individuality and being unable to. If the desire for destruction seems with historical hindsight to be fascistic, it may in the context of Lawrence's culture and upbringing spring from the extremes of puritan subjectivity. In Joyce's terms, catholicism is a coherent absurdity and protestantism an incoherent absurdity. Here, in Lawrence's imagination the incoherent clashes with the coherent, and like Yeats's rose-poems 'Hibiscus and Salvia Flowers' is a study in the temptations, dangers and attractions of absolute commitment, of the surrender of personal subjectivity to a larger, a mass movement. And in the end, like Yeats, Lawrence feels that his freedom as an artist is not simply threatened by the ideological commitment. It may be that the Sicilian socialists incarnate an aesthetic freedom he thought he owned absolutely and which was his by right – perhaps by *noblesse oblige*. It is because of this subversive and disturbing challenge that he concludes:

> And still I cannot bear it
> That they take hibiscus and the salvia flower.

It is a poignantly self-critical conclusion to the poem and one which confronts Lawrence with the need to relinquish his own hysteria and self-conscious posturing – with the need to reject the very rant out of which this beautiful poem springs.

Notes

1. 'Democracy', *Phoenix*, p. 699.
2. Ibid., p. 701.
3. Ibid., p. 702.
4. Ibid., p. 709.
5. Ibid., p. 718.
6. 10 December 1916, *Letters*, III, p. 49.
7. 11 March 1920, ibid., p. 486.
8. 20 January 1921, ibid, p. 649.
9. 'Hibiscus and Salvia Flowers', *Complete Poems*, pp. 312–18.
10. 14 January 1921, *Letters*, III, p. 649.
11. *Exodus* XII, 13.

12. Samuel Richardson, *Pamela*, ed. Peter Sable (Harmondsworth, Middx: Penguin, 1980) p. 280.
13. See also 'Paisley's Progress' in Tom Paulin, *Ireland and the English Crisis* (Newcastle upon Tyne: Bloodaxe Books, 1984) pp. 155–73.
14. 12 July 1920, *Letters*, III, p. 566.
15. *Phoenix*, p. 709.
16. *Collected Poems of W. B. Yeats* (London: Macmillan, 1963) p. 264.
17. John Milton, *Paradise Lost*, Book III, lines 41–2; *The Poetical Works of John Milton*, ed. Helen Darbishire (London: Oxford University Press, 1960) p. 54.

12

Making the Classic Contemporary: Lawrence's Pilgrimage Novels and American Romance

L. D. CLARK

Lawrence's American literature studies stand high in current opinion, especially in America, where a flourishing school of mythic criticism is built on them.[1] A related question, equally significant but seldom addressed, is how his reading of Melville, Hawthorne and others affected form and substance in his own novels. An exception to the general silence on this question, Richard Swigg, has shown how much *Women in Love* owes to precepts Lawrence gleaned from 'classic' American literature.[2] But after that novel, Swigg declares, Lawrence's Old World intelligence resisted his New World irrationality, and after a season of 'spurious victories' culminating in 'the disaster of *The Plumed Serpent*', he recovered his balance, always exempt from the 'touch of mental bitterness, of black disorder' that plagued the American authors.[3] On the contrary, Lawrence's own 'mental bitterness' and 'black disorder' were the chief source of his affinity for these Americans. Nonetheless, judgements like Swigg's continue to be repeated, generally arriving at the conclusion that Lawrence's novels between *Women in Love* and *Lady Chatterley's Lover* are failures.[4]

Now this sets up a curious situation: an argument that while Lawrence was writing his worst novels, he produced criticism hailed as superlative in comprehending a national literature. Furthermore, late in this period, he turned out five essays on the art of the novel also admired as superb.[5] None of this knowledge, the accepted reasoning concludes, could he translate into his own work. Now to be sure, such a paradox is not impossible, but before we consider this one established, we owe it closer scrutiny in terms so far largely overlooked.

One obstacle to inquiry is the standard classification of Lawrence's novels. In an era when world politics dominated thought, *Aaron's Rod*, *Kangaroo* and *The Plumed Serpent* were set apart as 'leadership' novels.[6] Today, with much stress on the interaction between Lawrence's psychological make-up and his work,[7] a more rewarding procedure would be to group together all six novels between *Women in Love* and *Lady Chatterley's Lover*: *Aaron's Rod* – which I put first because Lawrence began it first – *The Lost Girl*, *Mr Noon*, *Kangaroo*, *The Boy in the Bush* and *The Plumed Serpent*. I will refer to these as 'pilgrimage' novels. All of them aim at rebirth of the human soul, through new access to the power of instinct, access gained only by pilgrimage from a wasteland to a land of regeneration: 'thought adventure' must be realised in geographical adventure.[8] In the new creation to come, human beings, especially males, must learn to be perfectly alone before becoming capable of fellowship, and a new equilibrium of gender would prevail. Politics would be religion, and religion politics, with males ascendant in this sphere, linking mankind with the gods and completing independent selfhood in sacred brotherhood.

The impetus for the pilgrimage novels was compounded of Lawrence's conviction that the Great War meant the end of Europe, and a self-revelation, around 1916 – *Sons and Lovers* notwithstanding – that his soul was still subject to Woman, and that he must deal with homoerotic impulses.[9] The new awareness of Woman went counter to his recent Hardy essay, where the Female as Law is the source of life, embodying the power of the Father. The Male is Love – Christ as Son: spiritual, abstract, dependent on the Female to connect him with the Father.[10] When Lawrence woke up to the implications of this line of thought, he must have realised that he was still reasoning like a mother-subjugated son – or now like a wife-dominated husband.[11] His thought took a radical change of direction, the symbology evolving from a duality of Law and Love to one of Power and Love. The fiction likewise veered, emerging into the distinctive territory of the pilgrimage novels. As Lawrence phrased the change in geographical terms in 1920, speaking of *The Lost Girl* and *Mr Noon*: 'somewhere they are the crumpled wings of my soul. They get me free before I get myself free . . . before I get my feet out of Europe.'[12]

In February 1916, a crucial time, Lawrence happened upon a copy of *Moby Dick*.[13] Soon he was engrossed in several early American authors, who authenticated concepts already germinating in his mind.[14] The essentials of these discoveries remained in suspense till he began to verbalise them in essay form in August 1917, and to apply them, in November, in *Aaron's Rod*.[15] The essays, which constitute among other things a metaphysic of fiction, find all American authors from Crevecoeur to Whitman compelled by the legacy of their Puritan forebears, who in a 'lust for anti-life' attempted by mental abstraction and spiritual idealism to annihilate 'the passional dark mystery' in the soul, and in the demonic landscape of America, a terrifying proximity. In appearance the Puritans had succeeded, establishing a 'perfect mechanical concord' which purported to unite Americans in democratic brotherhood but which came down to a 'negative, destructive form of oneness'.[16] They had failed because the dusky spirit of the continent would not be denied. Slowly it permeated the American soul, awaiting the moment to burgeon. All classic American literature Lawrence saw as prophetic of this process. Consciously, early American authors meant to create by stated American ideals, but the underlying power of place crept into their work beyond their knowing, from deep psychological sources, instilling 'a profound symbolic import', a 'hellish meaning' that foreshadows destruction of the white psyche and creation of a truly American race blended from native red man and immigrant white man, and occupying a Promised Land.[17]

In his own century, Lawrence did not see the fatal division between spirit and senses that haunted American authors as confined to their continent alone, but as ruling the entire white race.[18] The imperative was to seek rebirth in a pristine place, a recreated 'America' actual or imaginary. As a novelist ready to articulate this quest, Lawrence saw himself in direct succession from the classic Americans, rejecting the modernist experiments of his contemporaries and putting behind him the only tradition he had ever recognised: the English novel from George Eliot to Thomas Hardy.[19] His own discoveries in how actions spring from subliminal sources he could take with him to the form he now adopted and updated: the 'romance' of classic American fiction. During eight years of experiment with this form in the pilgrimage novels, Lawrence's essays on his American predecessors went through revision after revision.[20] Theory and practice converge and diverge in intricate ways. The present paper, whose purpose is to extract parallels between early American novels and Lawrence's own, can only touch upon a few of these complexities.

During a four-year process of composition, *Aaron's Rod* served as context for two other novels: *The Lost Girl* and the fragmentary *Mr Noon*. Unfortunately, all the earlier manuscripts of *Aaron's Rod* have vanished, so we cannot begin with discussion of the first novel Lawrence devoted wholly to pilgrimage as the alternative to defeat by the modern world. Still, through various links between this novel as published and the other two, some of the questions can be answered about Lawrence's initial efforts in shaping his own variety of romance. A survey of his comments on *The Scarlet Letter* is a good preliminary to observing elements of romance in the first published of the pilgrimage novels, *The Lost Girl*.

Hawthorne called his book a romance, Lawrence says, in order to cover a 'discrepancy between his conscious understanding and his passional understanding' – in other words, the split between mind and intuition characterising all early American literature.[21] But the term is inexact, according to Lawrence, and to show why, he sets up a historical scale starting with 'myth', which related man's self-discovery as a species. Next came 'legend', delineating the psyche of a particular race; and next 'romance', which created the individual as 'dynamic' though 'impersonal'.[22] This definition conforms perfectly, however, with the 'impersonal dynamic' of character Lawrence first proposed in 1914,[23] and so what he is really engaged in here is negotiating an artistic treaty with Hawthorne: to define a mutual interest under differing terminology. The term Lawrence settles on for *The Scarlet Letter* is 'legendary myth'. But then he assigns to its characters all the 'dynamic impersonality' he has just identified with 'romance'. Hester, Dimmesdale and Chillingworth are not realistic people but forces personifying the rupture between spirit and senses. In perverse reenactment of the Eve myth, 'purity' from the upper mind is vaunted above the 'sin' of the lower body. What truly ascends, against Puritan intention, is Hester's scarlet letter, the 'burning symbol of the sensual mystery'. The 'ultra-spiritual being', which in the New World resides in Dimmesdale, has utterly corrupted the male being. He secretly flagellates himself before the sensual mystery, which is worship by masturbation.[24] Hester, functioning by instinct in a world where the male has renounced his natural leadership, must become Dimmesdale's 'great nemesis', must destroy him, in alliance with a distorted survival of the ancient sensual sorcerer, Chillingworth.[25] The whole sequence, for Lawrence, dramatises the reduction preceding reconstitution of the human species. Whether we call this story 'legendary myth' or 'romance' – let it be 'romance', since that is the general term among critics – such narrative eschews realism for, in Hawthorne's words, 'a quality of strangeness and remoteness'; in Lawrence's words, 'utterances in defiance of reason' stemming from the 'primary or sensual psyche . . . in terms more or less monstrous'.[26]

Romance in the hands of Hawthorne and others had portrayed the disintegration of gender identity and interrelationship. Lawrence modified the form to relate further reaches of the crisis and potential recovery through pilgrimage. He began with male pilgrimage in *Aaron's Rod* but then shifted to the female pilgrimage of *The Lost Girl*. For one reason, also evident in *Mr Noon*, going back to early beginnings prepared Lawrence for the greater dilemma of Aaron Sisson and Rawdon Lilly. Another reason: place of composition, which became 'male' or 'female' to the post-war Lawrence, and which would figure prominently in the creation of all the pilgrimage novels. One reason why Lawrence discarded a partial draft of *The Lost Girl* done in Capri for a new start in Sicily was that here he could 'feel the *darkness* again. There is no darkness in Capri.'[27] From other writings of his we can surmise that in Sicily he acted under the dark female influence of witch-like Etna, a presence to supplement the remembered darkness of the Abruzzi mountains, where the Lawrences spent a few miserably cold but unforgettable days in December 1919, and from which he drew the final setting of *The Lost Girl*.[28]

This book makes bold use of the unreality of romance, taking its departure from Cooper and Hawthorne. The first third of the story, the caustic satire of Midlands life in Bennett-like realism, is there only for Alvina Houghton to 'lose' in sudden transition to the improbable, upon the arrival of the Natcha-Kee-Tawara 'tribe', some unlikely 'American Indians' concocted out of Europeans of various nationalities.[29] This shift into the obscure and fantastic is inconspicuously foreshadowed by such comments from the narrative voice as, 'What was wanted was a Dark Master from the underworld'.[30] Speech and action in later chapters reflect Cooper's theatrical Indians, and Lawrence knew the risk he was taking. But as he said of American romance, unrealistic narrative can appear childish if you overlook the symbolic meaning.[31]

In Alvina's escape from the degenerate everyday world through symbolic fantasy, complications on well-known Lawrence themes heighten the effectiveness of her passage. A victim of matriarchal rule and concomitant paternal failure, oppressed by restraints placed on women in provincial society, in the end rejecting a hulking but infantile lover, Alvina is confronted by another matriarchy in the Natcha-Kee-Tawara troupe. Madame Rochard – Indian name Kishwegin – is the domineering chieftainess over her troupe of young men, one of these being Ciccio, the dark, virile but half-savage Italian who is to transform Alvina's existence. Losing her virginity to him leads on to initiation as a Natcha-Kee-Tawara. But then rebellion by the lovers against the 'tribe' must come too – which Ciccio first shows signs of accomplishing by rejecting his customary role as slain warrior, leaping up during a performance and announcing that he is tired of playing dead.[32] The next level of action is now prepared for. After psychological advance to sexual maturity, Alvina must now experience what all protagonists of the pilgrimage novels go through: metamorphosis by geographical change. Accompanying Ciccio to his primitive mountain village, she must go 'out of the world, over the border, into some place of mystery', to live surrounded by 'the grand, pagan twilight of the valleys, savage, cold, with a sense of ancient gods who knew the right for human sacrifice'.[33] All of this, from the introduction of the 'Indian' masquerade, prefigures America. Alvina is 'over the border' from the mundane into the marvellous, as Ishmael is in his remote seas and Natty Bumppo in his forest. Or, to put it another way, the demonic past is under the surface of alpine Italy like an outreach of spirit of place from Hawthorne's wild America.

The last phase of Alvina's pilgrimage, and the new level of male–female interaction accompanying it, coincide with the war, the chaos dividing past and future. When Ciccio is called up for military service, he breaks down emotionally, abandons hope that he will survive, begs Alvina not to wait for his return. But her intuitive courage saves him from despair. Her repeated conviction that he *will* come back finally takes hold of him. His assurance grows, and that her own appears to lessen is an attitude she assumes to increase his determination, to give him strength to reassure her, to promise that when the war is over he will take her to America.[34] Alvina's soul has fortified itself greatly since her Woodhouse days, and as far as 'leadership' is in evidence, it awakens in her toward the next stage of life, not in Ciccio. What we note here is a feature of all the pilgrimage novels. Whatever Lawrence's insistence in the American essays that women submit to the control of men, sometimes in raging polemic, the women in the fiction possess a great deal of power and use it skilfully in steering the men in the direction they desire.

Alvina's destiny, of course, remains highly problematical, as she pauses suspended like all Lawrence's pilgrims between the past of mankind and the future. In any event, before moving on to the next phase of his own pilgrimage, Lawrence gave her his benediction in a letter: 'My Alvina, in whom the questing spirit is lodged, moves toward reunion with the dark half of humanity.'[35]

With *Aaron's Rod* over two years in abeyance, still, two days after finishing *The Lost Girl*, Lawrence undertook *Mr Noon*, a male equivalent of Alvina's quest: that is, Part I is a mocking satire from Gilbert Noon's point of view of life in Woodhouse, and Part II is the search for a transformed life on the Continent.[36] The two most apparent influences of American romance, at the outset, are Lawrence's use of a convention from earlier fiction that he had already revived in *The Lost Girl*: the intrusive narrative voice; and also a loose structure defended by disclaimers of any structure whatever. Lawrence's principal reliance for both of these is *Moby Dick*, with its notoriously digressive structure and constant commentary by a voluble narrator.[37] Lawrence's stance varies from Melville's in that *Mr Noon* is ostensibly a third-person tale. But as Gilbert Noon is a projection of Lawrence, and the clamouring persona of the narrator is on the scene as much as any character, the impression the story leaves is like that of *Moby Dick*: autobiography at a remove just sufficient to transform it into fiction. This self-consciousness is a generally recognised feature of American romance, allowing its authors to present, among other intentions, 'records of their own adventures in creating'.[38] Lawrence's attitude of throwing the story together just as he pleases – and to hell with book reviewers – is a pose to cover a dual purpose: open rebellion against conventional form reflecting the rebellion of his elopement with Frieda, and a bluff intention to instruct women: the 'gentle reader' he so often addresses being usually female. This may serve as 'male leadership' by persuasion, but then it is Johanna who releases Noon, and Noon's double, the narrative persona, from an imprisoning past – in so far as this dual personality *is* released.

In this revival of bygone experience, Lawrence restates all his old difficulties, and compounds them with those of the early 1920s. Johanna outspokenly blames mother-love for the damnation of modern males.[39] The unleashing of sexual desire is celebrated as a visitation from a thunder-god – celebrated under Johanna's influence, nevertheless, as a 'sacred, awful communion' worthy of flourishing between men and women without regard to fidelity or moral restraint.[40] But then in opposition to unrestricted sexual congress comes the struggle of man and woman to be free of one another: the male at least to seek a 'perfected aloneness' – which Gilbert glimpses at the summit of their climb over the Alps – and, beyond this, an 'eternal manly friendship' basic to a 'reckless manly life'.[41]

Gilbert's pilgrimage comes to a close in an unresolved complication of masculine/feminine intimacy. First, Johanna confesses that a hiking companion, an old acquaintance, has 'had' her along the route. Gilbert forgives her, but with an attitude that leaves her – she thinks – more in the wrong than ever, because, as both know, the jealousy will erupt again between them.[42] The problem is never settled. At Lake Garda, one night, Gilbert touches Johanna asleep, and some new energy springs alive in his soul. For the time being, this change maintains him as 'a new creature in a new world'. But it will not last. In summation of Gilbert's position, and in recommendation to both the 'gentle' female reader and the 'ungentle' male, the closing note is on a repeated injunction to fight against 'the old, enclosing mother of our days', with a reminder that always 'it needs a sort of cataclysm to get out of the old world into the new'.[43] Lawrence was dissatisfied with leaving Gilbert and the narrator at Lake Garda, and in a letter of December 1921 he reveals why: 'If I am to finish *Mr Noon* it shall be in the States.' In other words, Europe was not the place for creation of this work; but by the time Lawrence reached America, he had outgrown Gilbert Noon.[44]

For a while Lawrence worked now on *Mr Noon*, now on *Aaron's Rod*, until a change of place settled which he was to finish. About all we know of his long indecision on that novel is whether Aaron, on leaving England, would enter a monastery or run the whole gamut of experience.[45] Lawrence's first post-war visit to Germany brought the decision. Germany's 'great magnificent landscape' – male – where he felt like a Roman 'on the edge of the great Hercynian wood', freed him to dispatch Aaron on the road of experience and thus to flesh out his most masculine-oriented novel.[46]

Aaron's Rod shares numerous elements with *Moby Dick*. Like Ishmael, Aaron leaves home in sudden revulsion from his 'unspeakable familiar world', with Ishmael's generalised repugnance made specific: the women in Aaron's world 'destroy the man in a man'.[47] Ishmael is magnetised by Ahab into the quest to destroy the great white whale – which Lawrence interpreted as the mental being in man seeking to annihilate the 'deep, free sacral consciousness'.[48] Aaron, conversely, hopes for recovery of this consciousness, also by submitting to a more powerful man in Rawdon Lilly. Old Testament symbolism of paired males illuminates both novels: Aaron/Moses in *Aaron's Rod* and Ishmael/Ahab in *Moby Dick*. This leadership–brotherhood or unison of purpose, which Lawrence encountered, too, in Cooper's Natty Bumppo and Chingachgook as well as in Melville's Ishmael and Queequeg, is one of his greatest debts to American romance.[49] In *Aaron's Rod* he utilises it altogether for male salvation from women, of which Aaron needs a great deal. Not long after leaving his wife, he is seduced by Josephine – an American with Indian blood – then collapses, physically and psychically. He would have died had not Lilly found him and massaged all his lower body to rekindle the spark of life.[50] The transvaluation of homoeroticism seen in the discarded first chapter of *Women in Love* here takes another course, one which is well theorised in an unpublished essay on Whitman, in which Lawrence designates the source of response between males as 'cocygeal', that is, at the base of the spine: a centre that is not erotic except as wilfully perverted into homosexuality.[51]

Unfortunately, the comradeship achieved in *Aaron's Rod* ends abruptly over a difference of opinion. Aaron then departs for Italy to cross the obligatory dividing line in Europe between the old life and the new, the Alps, which then circle behind him like mythical beasts: 'sky-panthers' or great tigers, and make him feel that he is 'changing inside his skin'. The pilgrimage novels commonly bring in such creatures, which climax in the eagle-snake of *The Plumed Serpent* and which surely were first suggested as quest animals by Melville's leviathan.[52]

Still far from liberated, at least the next time Aaron falls victim to a woman he is able to extricate himself. The woman is another American, a Marchesa capable of killing her lovers like Cleopatra, and also a spiritual descendant of Hawthorne's Pearl, who, as Lawrence read *The Scarlet Letter*, grew up to marry an Italian aristocrat and become a predatory female like this Marchesa.[53]

So far, so good, but then Aaron's rod of power, the flute that guaranteed him an independent livelihood, is smashed in a terrorist bomb attack.[54] The only way ahead appears to be surrendering control of his life to Lilly, who is said to have reached self-sufficiency in 'life-centrality' – despite the powerful influence his wife Tannie exercises over him. In any event, he delivers a long discourse on the disastrous submission of man to woman in the dominion of Love, while under 'the great dynamic mode' of Power, woman submits to man. Any man, too, must bow to the greater man. But then Lilly declines to accept Aaron as disciple, advises him to go on seeking till his soul recognises its natural superior. Aaron's actual future course may already have come to him in a dream, which foresaw more trouble from woman, since he glimpsed an Astarte figure waiting for him beside a lake in America.[55]

In *Kangaroo*, rather than two males bordering on one identity, Richard Somers and his wife, Harriet, appear in such a guise. The male personal wrestles with ideas in the public sphere, while the female exercises her influence as a powerful presence. Somers is a not-so-common Lawrence male who truly does have 'a woman at the back of him', a woman without whom we cannot imagine his quest taking place.[56] The relative position of man and woman in Lawrence's ideal scheme, once again, is not, in the world of the novels, the hierarchy he propounds in theory in the essays.

As John Worthen establishes in *D. H. Lawrence and the Idea of the Novel*, *Kangaroo* is an adventure of ideas in which linear development gives way to the erratic course of Somers' encounters with beliefs that both attract and repel him, and with the believers, who offer him leadership through political action. More specifically, '*Kangaroo*'s break-through as a novel' is that it does not ultimately aim at promoting 'the organization of society, but the relationship of man to his universe'. This conclusion agrees precisely with the accepted distinction between English novel and American romance: that the novel engages issues of the individual in relation to community, and the romance sends the protagonist in search of individual values outside society, often through confrontation with universal or natural forces. According to these criteria, *Kangaroo* readily falls into the category of American romance.[57]

In this novel the issue between Love and Power, as Lawrence conceived them, is enacted as never before. The man Kangaroo exudes a devouring paternal love shutting out even the maternal, for what he offers his followers is a sort of pouch to enwomb all mankind. To control an Australia on the verge of political upheaval, he would impose a patriarchal fascistic order. This man, by the way, has been denied fictional credibility, yet in the 1970s he came to life so realistically in the Reverend Jim Jones that James B. Reston Jr made a passage from *Kangaroo* the epigraph for his book on Jones. Romance *does* sometimes come down to earth.[58]

The other kind of love in *Kangaroo*, based on mental and not blood sympathy, is the fraternal love Willie Struthers fosters through his socialist movement. Somers oscillates between Kangaroo and Struthers, with Harriet as corrective when male excess threatens. She does not represent possessive love, as one might expect, but simply the stabilising power of strong feminine attachment, in which she is not a hindrance but rather a support to Somers' attainment of true isolate selfhood. Not that their union is by any means smooth sailing. Lawrence 'got stuck' in the middle of the novel trying to incorporate the stresses of marriage, and he called on Melville for symbols to extricate him.[59] In the chapter 'Harriet and Lovat at Sea in Marriage', the good ship *Harriet and Lovat* is the *Pequod* all over again, which has sailed far off to the 'lone and wasteful waters of the sea of perfect love', where 'fierce, full-blooded lusty bull-whales rushed at her and all but burst her timbers'. Harriet's attitude is in clear contrast to that of Ahab's sailors: she has resisted the 'mystic man and male' in Somers, while of course the crew of the *Pequod* fall under their captain's spell.[60] The pilgrim couple also pursue a 'sacral consciousness' in the form of the dark gods, not to destroy but to embrace. By implication they encounter a sort of leviathan, too: the man Kangaroo, who must die before the pilgrims can proceed. The anticipated destiny of the Somers' *Pequod* is not that of the original; they have distant oceans yet to sail. Within the complexity of marriage Somers sees the inconsequence of aspirations to leadership, and of political action for the attainment of more ample being. The outcome is rejection of both fatherly and brotherly love, and a fresh view of Power as the divine energy emanating from the dark gods into the integral soul – it is in *Kangaroo* that these are first given a specific identity. In quest of them the two pilgrims set out for America at the close of the book. One of Harriet's final impressions of Australia is that it coils about her like a serpent, seeking to pull down her bird-like soul. Lawrence was to discover the full potency of this image in America, where in fact he wrote the definitive last chapter of *Kangaroo*.[61]

Again Lawrence takes his cue from Melville for narrative tone and form. Somers and Lawrence's narrator persona are complementary halves, as Melville and Ishmael are: making fiction resemble autobiography, setting up a dialectic between narrator and protagonist. Point of view for both Lawrence and Melville is dictated by the necessity of the moment, not by aesthetic theory. Also like Melville, Lawrence wrote in whatever style he thought expedient, from journalese to philosophical discourse, each author quoting from any stray source that might contribute to larger purpose. In *Kangaroo* as in *Moby Dick*, the casual sequence of narration goes with insistence that form is tentative and exploratory. The following quotations from *Moby Dick* would be perfectly at home in *Kangaroo*: 'Out of the trunk, the branches grow; out of them, the twigs. So, in productive subjects, grow the chapters'; or 'This whole book is but a draught – nay, but a draught of a draught. Oh, Time, Strength, Cash, and Patience.'[62] Besides these stylistic and structural elements to demonstrate the proximity of Lawrence's methods to Melville's, such remarks as the following about Melville show how clear-sighted Lawrence was and how much he was willing to risk in emulation of his classic American forerunner in search of a romance-like form for the novels of the pilgrimage period, for analogous things have often been said about Lawrence: 'Nobody can be more clownish, more clumsy and sententiously in bad taste, than Herman Melville, even in a great book like *Moby Dick*. He preaches and holds forth because he's not sure of himself. And he holds forth, often, so amateurishly.'[63]

In the earliest version of *Studies in Classic American Literature*, Lawrence had lauded Cooper to the skies, and whatever his reservations in the final version, he still saw the Leatherstocking novels as 'true "romance"', with a 'myth meaning', and this 'true myth', as he goes on to say, 'concerns itself centrally with the onward adventure of the integral soul'.[64] Even so, up to now he had been for the most part wary of the high-flown story-telling that makes Cooper the most romantic of the American romancers, and yet Cooper was surely at the back of his mind when he spoke in Australia of doing an American novel 'with Indians in it'.[65] In the event, however, his treatment of Indian themes in his American fiction had little to do with Cooper. Another anticipation of an American novel – that it be on the order of *Kangaroo* – suggests for one thing that a white male is to encounter a wild continent.[66] For reasons too far to seek at the moment, female characters were always in the forefront of Lawrence's New World fiction,[67] and one result of this was that the reach ahead from *Kangaroo* meant a turning back to Australia as the source for his most Cooperesque tale, *The Boy in the Bush* – back to what may even have been a premonition of such a tale. For early in 1922 Lawrence had convinced Mollie Skinner to undertake a novel about the pioneers of her native Australia.[68] At the beginning of September 1923, in Los Angeles, he first turned his attention to the manuscript she had sent him. He had little more than finished correcting the proofs of his first Australian novel when the second, so to speak, caught up with him.[69] At once he wrote to Mollie Skinner suggesting a collaboration, his part to be a 'recasting' of her story.[70] She agreed – though Lawrence did not wait for her approval before starting to rewrite. From the raw material that she had supplied, as first shown by Harry T. Moore and then more extensively by Charles Rossman, Lawrence made *The Boy in the Bush* his own.[71] In the process it became a work with many characteristics of American romance as that genre expanded into the popular regions of the American western novel and the western movie.

While in Los Angeles, Lawrence was anxiously awaiting word from his American publisher on the first version of *The Plumed Serpent*, already sure that he must 'go all over it again', but before returning to this 'much more important' Quetzalcoatl novel, he would attempt, he said, to make a 'popular' novel out of the Skinner manuscript.[72] By 'popular', as the product affirms, Lawrence meant an adventure story in emulation of Cooper, and of course he might hope to match Cooper's achievement – the dream of every novelist – to write a best-seller with nuances for the wiser sort of reader. Lawrence's contacts with the popular frontier literature that Cooper fathered went back a long way. He knew the works of Mayne Reid and Gustave Aimée, for instance, and had read some of Zane Grey, perhaps in Australia.[73] In the fall of 1922 he may already have been familiar with the pulp magazine *Adventure*, although the first record of his avid interest in it dates from six months later.[74] And since he rewrote a sizeable 'first part' of *The Boy in the Bush* in Los Angeles, a Hollywood influence is not out of the question.[75]

Any contemporary student of American literature knows that the hero of a Clint Eastwood movie is a direct descendant of Cooper's Natty Bumppo. Jack of *The Boy in the Bush* is just that sort of cowboy hero, without the cows but very much with the horse, and with a few Lawrence extremes laid on. Starting out as an angelic–demonic boy, Jack becomes a man apart who scorns respectability for allegiance to a code from dark sources of power. He can ride an outlaw stallion with ease. He can wrestle a kangaroo and slug it out with an enemy beyond him in muscle and years. When the time comes for the showdown with that enemy – Easu/Esau in conflict with Jack/Jacob for a typical Lawrence biblical parallel – the event takes place in the spirit of a shootout on a cowtown street: Easu comes at Jack with an axe, Jack shoots him not between the eyes but in the forehead: the 'mystic place', the text reports.[76] Like the death-oriented Natty Bumppo and the superhuman gunfighter in a western movie – but also like Count Dionys of *The Ladybird* – Jack Grant is a Lord of Death, inscrutable, invincible. He is also ultimately isolate and whole within his male citadel. Often enough he prefers the company of horses to women. All the same he reclaims the woman Easu has taken away from him, demanding that she submit to his dark god. He repudiates the faithful Tom – indeed all men, and any remaining trace of Lawrence's Rananim ideal with them. In the last chapter, 'The Rider on The Red Horse', Jack rides away into the bush to be alone in his own element, though carrying the promise of a girl that when he returns she will be a second wife to him. His patriarchal scheme is to start a new aristocratic world in the far bush of Australia.[77] Lawrence had learned his lesson from Cooper to perfection: beyond his time, in fact, since the many connections between *The Boy in the Bush* and American romance in the western movie/western novel form as we know it today could hardly have been observed clearly at the time, as they can now from the vantage point of more than half a century later.

During his first months in America, on completing the final version of the American studies, and shortly before starting the first version of *The Plumed Serpent*, Lawrence had written 'The Future of the Novel', his first essay on the art of fiction, denouncing most of his contemporaries for concentrating too much on personality, too little on putting together fiction and 'philosophy', too little on exploring the unconscious.[78] Later on, in the summer of 1925, during final revisions of *The Plumed Serpent*, he wrote the essay on art and morality and at least two of his other four essays on the novel, and then the other two that autumn – so that years of thought came into focus with the creation of that novel.[79] These essays generalise the chief conviction of *Studies* – first implied, in fact, in the Hardy essay – that the true meaning of all great novels belies the stated meaning of the novelist. Since Lawrence also asserts that the novel is the greatest expression of human psychology ever conceived, a strange conclusion must follow: the greatest practitioners of the highest art wrought in ignorance of what they were doing. So the novel truly is the instrument of the unconscious, with a life of its own, and the novelist cannot deceive it. But what about the problem this poses for Lawrence or any other novelist: how can one be a conscious practitioner of a necessarily unconscious art? If Lawrence was aware of this contradiction as he went consciously about delving into the unconscious, he never admits to it. But precisely herein lay the attraction of American romance. Even if shaped by conscious artifice, its unrestricted point of view and licence in choice of material, most of all its interworking of realism and unlikely invention, made a perfect form for surface narrative with an underlying 'unconscious' or 'myth-meaning'.

All the pilgrimage novels up to now had foreshadowed America and regeneration through the myth inherent to American literature. Lawrence had seen 'the Aztec principle' at work in Hester Prynne undermining abstract spirituality; he knew the prophecy of *The Last of the Mohicans*: 'The time of the red-men has not yet come again'.[80] But it was one thing to perceive the dark gods as fulfilment of such prescience, and quite another to dramatise their existence. Here he could again call upon the aid of American romance, for, as Michael Bell writes, it takes naturally to 'experimenting with the possibility of making imaginary or irrational subjective states the objects of literary mimesis'.[81] Reaching America as destination also meant attempting to establish finally the goals motivating the quest from the beginning: the yearning for aloneness in touch with universal potency; the need for a new conception of male and female and of all human relationships; and in the end a reconstitution of community.

Lawrence's dependence on American romance to create *The Plumed Serpent* is thus the outgrowth of years of absorption by the genre. A great many parallels are deducible from analyses of romance by several present-day critics. A. N. Kaul discusses 'heroic withdrawal' from society as a common theme in romance – precisely the action of all Lawrence pilgrims. And whenever an American romancer evinces a 'preoccupation with the theme of human community' restored, he deals in 'symbolic constructs and ideal relationships', often on far-fetched principles – exactly the community of *The Plumed Serpent*, with its ritual brotherhood, ritual marriage and the bond of apotheosis among the chief characters.[82] Even more significant comments, for the present purpose, are those on the core of romance, ranging from Hawthorne to current critics. Romance, Hawthorne wrote, provides 'a theatre . . . where the creatures of [the author's] brain may play their phantasmagorical antics'. He imposes one important limitation, however: a 'neutral territory' must be maintained between 'the Actual and the Imaginary' where each can 'imbue itself with the nature of the other'. However, as Hawthorne cautions elsewhere, the modernisation of romance, by bringing it 'into positive contact with the realities of the moment', may endanger credibility.[83] What happens to the 'neutral territory' then, as Michael Bell has observed, is that it becomes 'a moral or psychological battlefield'.[84] In this narrow zone, as Bell defines it, the main thrust of *The Plumed Serpent* is concentrated: on one side the realism of Kate's life as a foreign resident of Mexico, on the other the costumery, the chanting, the myth-making of the Quetzalcoatl movement. What operates in the meeting-ground between this actual and this imaginary, to borrow a phrase from Bell, is a 'sacrifice of relation' between actual and imaginary which in all romance must be compensated for by making the strangeness of character and action acceptable to the reader. In Hawthorne's metaphor, this acceptance is conveyed by atmosphere, as though moonlight, not sunlight, shone on the scene.[85] Lawrence's hope of making his strange atmosphere convincing is contained in this assertion: 'In every great novel, who is the hero all the time? Not any of the characters, but some unnamed and nameless flame behind them all.'[86] Maintaining a bond across the dividing line between momentary person and eternal source had been Lawrence's central concern in fiction since he conceived the idea before the war, but his greatest test in making the connection came with *The Plumed Serpent*, and with that connection he proposed resolutions to other vital questions of identity raised at the start of the pilgrimage cycle and his romance fiction.

Isolate male selfhood and the blood-brotherhood to complete it find a ready solution in *The Plumed Serpent*. The difficulties are eased by the framework and atmosphere Lawrence creates for the book, which support a realistic enough personal identity for Ramón and Cipriano, and at the same time place them at the distance of fable or romance. Ramón's defeat of the all-possessive spiritual female in his first wife, Carlota, is incorporated in all respects with the emergence of his god-self through the ritual destruction of the Christian images and other rites. The marriage with Teresa confirms his triumph in a victorious new identity.[87] Cipriano is also well characterised by the standards of romance. He is the 'dark half of humanity' that Lawrence's Europeans have long sought. Cipriano's Pan-like potency stands out vividly, but Lawrence does not overlook his fierceness and what may be atavism in its worst form – his revival of human sacrifice, for example, which Ramón allows, or which, perhaps, he is powerless to prevent.[88] Beyond their individuality, these two men unite in the sacred fraternal bond envisaged since *Aaron's Rod*. This too is altogether credible within the assumptions of the narrative, by which their relationship can be ceremonialised. In all matters pertaining to these heroes, though their solution might raise doubts within the conventions of a novel, none fail to yield to the resources of romance.

The case of the heroine is more involved. We may as well begin with her foil, Ramón's new wife, Teresa, who enters late in the book. She is also due particular notice for being the submissive woman invoked in version after version of the American essays – and Lawrence is not content with her when she at last appears. It is Kate who demands his attention, who speaks for Woman at the close of the pilgrimage cycle, and not only for Woman but also for an ineradicable force in the character of the white race: the all-questioning intellect which is yet capable of commitment. Lawrence's determination to shape her character right led him through several revisions in the last chapter of the book, all of which point to strengthening Kate both in herself and in relation to the two men; and, more problematically, to universalising her in the bridging of the gap between humanity and dark divinity.[89]

If we were to view Kate's situation in purely novelistic terms, common motivation would suffice. She has given herself in marriage to Cipriano and accepted Ramón as leader. Yet she still has the option of independence: she can sail away from this exotic country and return to her native land. To what this alternative can offer an aging woman, however, she prefers what her husband and her leader can give her in Mexico. By an indirection typical of women in novels, she first accuses these men of confining her –

then, when they tell her she is free to go, she protests they do not want her. When Ramón then offers her advice, she uses it as a wedge between leader and husband, prompting the husband to demand that she ignore the leader's counsel. The brotherhood is momentarily weakened, and Ramón walks away. Kate now wheedles Cipriano into saying, 'I love you' – in Lawrence a sure sign of male concession. Kate now maintains that although she would like to leave Cipriano, his love imprisons her, will not let her go. In these circumstances, Kate is obviously far from submissive. We leave her more in control of herself and the men in her life than they imagine, and more than the majority of readers have recognised.

For the other face of Kate's fortunes, only the outlook of romance will do. We find her planted squarely in the disputed ground between the actual and the imaginary. One force here, easy for Lawrence to deal with, is the antithesis in spirit of place. His inimitable description strikes a balance between America's 'terrifying grandeur and cruel power' – in Joel Porte's phrase – and the paradise-regained setting at the novel's end, which fulfils the prophecy Lawrence saw in the Leatherstocking Tales.[90] To cement the bond between temporal and eternal in Kate, however, is another matter. The deification she shares with the two men reaches across what is assuredly not 'neutral territory', but that space as a region of intense psychological struggle. In this realm the choices open to Kate can be understood if translated into the mythic terms of romance. A way ahead for her – that is, ongoing pilgrimage – is out of the question, and so is progress into the future by humanitarian principles like those of democracy. She must choose between a regression to the old world or a leap into the perilous, God-permeated future. The alternatives come down to complacent residence in the City of Destruction or acceptance of apocalypse. This most crucial of Kate's decisions can be easily obscured by demands that the book account for itself on realistic grounds. Realism is characterised by order, which is what Kate would regain by returning to Europe, but a decadent order bound to end in the damnation of mankind. Apocalypse is surrender to disorder, for her to the unpredictable chaos of the future in a fantastic Mexico which may or may not attain a new creation, but certainly the deceptive order of Europe can never lead to new creation. On this premise Kate submits to apocalypse, a 'sacrifice of relation' beyond logic. This turn of affairs may well leave

The Plumed Serpent the most inconclusive of Lawrence's novels. Nevertheless, the ending is a perfectly realised dramatisation of what Lawrence had long seen as the twentieth-century impasse of human history. Society does not evolve. The only way out is to leap across the chasm, to traverse the territory between the actual and the scarcely-to-be-imagined imaginary. The crossing is phantasmagoria; the theatre is Lawrence's mind. Nightmare hovers at the edge of the narrative and at the bounds of consciousness, but also a fantastic hope. The quest for a new consciousness cannot come to pass except outside the pale of realism, of any rational motivation. These are the terms Lawrence sets down, basing them ultimately on the dark prophecies he heard in the words of his American predecessors. To approach *The Plumed Serpent* on any other grounds is to ask for a novel while staring at a romance.

Notes

1. Praise for Lawrence's views on American literature began when his reputation as a novelist was still at a low ebb: see Edmund Wilson, *The Shock of Recognition* (New York: Doubleday, Doran, 1943), and the growing swell in such works as Leslie Fiedler's *Love and Death in the American Novel* (New York: Criterion Books, 1960). For a summary of attitudes on the subject, see a review article by Michael Colacurcio, 'The Symbolic and the Symptomatic: D. H. Lawrence in Recent American Criticism', *American Quarterly*, XXVII, 4 (1975) pp. 486–501. For an illuminating discussion of how Lawrence's criticism deals with national distinctions between English and American novels, see Richard L. White, 'D. H. Lawrence the Critic: Theories of English and American Fiction', *DHL Review*, XI, 2 (1978) pp. 156–74.
2. Richard Swigg, *Lawrence, Hardy, and American Literature* (New York: Oxford University Press, 1972) pp. 309–44. Swigg's claim that *The Rainbow* was significantly influenced by *The Scarlet Letter* is questionable, depending as it does on inconclusive internal evidence. No record has been located to show that Lawrence read Hawthorne's novel before January 1917 (see *Letters*, III, p. 66).
3. Swigg, *Lawrence, Hardy, and American Literature*, pp. 360–1.
4. A list of works in this vein would be a long one, beginning during the revival of interest in Lawrence's work with F. R. Leavis's *D. H. Lawrence: Novelist* (London: Chatto and Windus, 1955) and including most of the major Lawrence critics. When not dismissed as 'pure corn' [Eliseo Vivas, *D. H. Lawrence: The Failure and the Triumph of Art* (Evanston, Ill.: Northwestern University Press, 1960) p. 69], Lawrence's fictional creations of the period are often judged in terms

like those of Julian Moynahan in *The Deed of Life* (Princeton, NJ: Princeton University Press, 1963): that Lawrence wrote on the verge of desperation which in spite of flashes of insight brought him always to 'a fundamental self-betrayal' (p. 112). For exceptions to the general dissatisfaction, see Keith Sagar on *The Plumed Serpent* in *The Art of D. H. Lawrence* (Cambridge: Cambridge University Press, 1966), Alastair Niven on *Kangaroo* in *D. H. Lawrence: The Novels* (Cambridge: Cambridge University Press, 1978) and John Worthen's estimate of *Kangaroo* in *D. H. Lawrence and the Idea of the Novel* (London: Macmillan, 1979). Leavis revises his views to recognise that *The Plumed Serpent* is important, though still not successful, in *Thought, Words and Creativity: Art and Thought in Lawrence* (London: Chatto and Windus, 1976). Brian Lee makes a beginning at analysing Lawrence's long fiction of the middle years through his discoveries in American literature, but Lee's conclusions are also adverse: 'Doubts about the validity of human society' and 'extreme symbolic situations' do not add up to novels: 'America, My America', in *Renaissance and Modern Essays Presented to Vivian de Sola Pinto*, ed. G. R. Hibbard (London: Routledge and Kegan Paul, 1966) p. 188. Lee recognises no distinction between novel and romance.

5. Separately collected in the two *Phoenix* volumes, these essays are now available in D. H. Lawrence, *Study of Thomas Hardy and Other Essays*, ed. Bruce Steele (Cambridge: Cambridge University Press, 1985) pp. 149–55, 169–205. The last four of these were introduced by a preliminary essay on the 'living interrelatedness' of all things in painting, entitled 'Art and Morality'. Lawrence felt that 'the point was easier to see in painting, to start with' (*Thomas Hardy and other Essays*, pp. xlviii, 163–8).

6. The origin of the term is traceable to Lawrence's well-known letter to Witter Bynner in March 1928 (see Moore, II, pp. 1045–6).

7. Recent outstanding works in this area are Daniel Dervin, *'A Strange Sapience': The Creative Imagination of D. H. Lawrence* (Amherst, Mass.: University of Massachusetts Press, 1984); Judith Ruderman, *D. H. Lawrence and the Devouring Mother* (Durham, N.C.: Duke University Press, 1984); Daniel J. Schneider, *The Artist as Psychologist* (Lawrence, Kan.: University Press of Kansas, 1984).

8. D. H. Lawrence, *Kangaroo* (New York, 1923) p. 327; L. D. Clark, *The Minoan Distance: The Symbolism of Travel in D. H. Lawrence* (Tucson: University of Arizona Press, 1980).

9. *Letters*, II, p. 90. An extended treatment of this stressful period can be found in Paul Delany, *D. H. Lawrence's Nightmare: The Writer and His Circle in the Years of the Great War* (New York: Basic Books, 1978). In the fiction, see the rejected 'Prologue to *Women in Love*', *Phoenix* II, pp. 92–108.

10. Lawrence, *Thomas Hardy and other Essays*, pp. 7–128. Lawrence's phoenix, in the shift from Law/Love to Power/Love, underwent a change of gender. It is female in 'The Crown', *Phoenix* II, p. 382, and male in *Kangaroo*, p. 201.

11. *Letters*, III, pp. 301–3.

12. Ibid., p. 522.
13. Ibid., II, pp. 526–9.
14. Lawrence first began to conceptualise the need to escape woman's possessiveness in revising earlier Italian essays and writing new ones for *Twilight in Italy*, finished in October 1915 and published in 1916. One compelling reason the Italian men have for migrating to America is to free themselves from female domination at home.
15. *Letters*, III, p. 156; *The Quest for Rananim: D. H. Lawrence's Letters to S. S. Koteliansky*, ed. George Y. Zytaruk (Montreal: McGill–Queen's University Press, 1970) p. 219.
16. D. H. Lawrence, *The Symbolic Meaning: Uncollected Versions of 'Studies in Classic American Literature'*, ed. Armin Arnold (Fontwell, Arundel: Centaur Press, 1962) pp. 25, 27, 39, 57.
17. Lawrence, *Symbolic Meaning*, p. 19; *Studies in Classic American Literature* (London: Secker, 1924) p. 24.
18. Richard Swigg calls the period of writing *Women in Love* 'that point in Lawrence's life when the disaster of the War, the sense of civilization's imminent collapse, were interpreted through his vision of the American precedent in downfall' (*Lawrence, Hardy, and American Literature*, p. 332).
19. Some of the affinities Lawrence found between his work and that of the Italian Futurists enter into the symbolism of the Hardy essay (*Thomas Hardy and other Essays*, pp. 75–6). He felt, moreover, that the early American authors were direct ancestors of the Futurists, saying of Melville, for instance: 'He was a futurist long before futurism found paint' (*Studies in Classic American Literature*, p. 146). For Lawrence's negative comments on contemporaries writing in English, see 'The Future of the Novel', *Thomas Hardy and other Essays*, pp. 149–55; *Letters*, III, pp. 166–7.
20. The full story of Lawrence's writing and rewriting of his American 'studies' may not be deciphered for some time, though the forthcoming Cambridge Edition of these essays (being prepared by Harold Shapiro) is expected to assist considerably in solving the problem, since the Smith papers that came to light in 1979 can be taken into account in this edition: Warren Roberts, *A Bibliography of D. H. Lawrence*, 2nd edn (Cambridge: Cambridge University Press, 1982) pp. 526–8. From August 1917 until at least September 1920, Lawrence reshaped these essays several times: *Letters*, III, *passim*. A great deal more might be known about the links between the symbology of the American essays and that of such earlier works as the Hardy study and 'The Crown' if the lost 'At the Gates' and 'Goats and Compasses' were ever located. 'At the Gates' may have been returned to Lawrence by J. B. Pinker, the literary agent, in early 1920, but if so it has since disappeared [see E. W. Tedlock, *The Frieda Lawrence Collection of D. H. Lawrence Manuscripts* (Albuquerque, N.M.: University of New Mexico Press, 1948) p. 89].
21. Lawrence, *Symbolic Meaning*, p. 126.
22. Ibid., p. 124.
23. *Letters*, II, pp. 182–3.

24. Lawrence, *Symbolic Meaning*, pp. 127–8.
25. Ibid., pp. 130, 137–8.
26. Ibid., pp. 124–5; Nathaniel Hawthorne, *Novels* (New York: Library of America, 1983) p. 149.
27. *Letters*, III, p. 481; cf. pp. 479–80.
28. Ibid., pp. 431–7, 488, 498; Frieda Lawrence, 'Not I, But the Wind . . .' (New York, 1934; reprint Carbondale and Edwardsville, Ill.: Southern Illinois University Press, 1974) p. 107; cf. the opening pages of D. H. Lawrence, *Sea and Sardinia*.
29. D. H. Lawrence, *The Lost Girl*, ed. John Worthen (Cambridge: Cambridge University Press, 1981) ch. 7. The style of the 'Indian' passages in this novel is often closely patterned on Cooper's, especially that of *The Last of the Mohicans*.
30. Lawrence, *The Lost Girl*, p. 48.
31. Lawrence, *Studies in Classic American Literature*, p. 7.
32. Lawrence, *The Lost Girl*, p. 162.
33. Ibid., pp. 306, 315.
34. Ibid., pp. 335–9.
35. *Letters*, III, p. 521.
36. Tedlock, *The Frieda Lawrence Collection*, p. 90; *Letters*, III, pp. 513–22.
37. It is commonly taken for granted that Lawrence is imitating a narrative voice from earlier English fiction. By far the most likely source is the classic Americans. He had not read any of the English classics for quite a while, the classic Americans absorbed his analytic attention at the time, and they were the only writers he considered worthy of serving as models in fiction.
38. Richard H. Brodhead, *Hawthorne, Melville and the Novel* (Chicago: Chicago University Press, 1976) p. 23.
39. D. H. Lawrence, *Mr Noon*, ed. Lindeth Vasey (Cambridge: Cambridge University Press, 1984) pp. 124–5.
40. Ibid., p. 226.
41. Ibid., pp. 208–9, 221, 227–8, 267.
42. Ibid., pp. 276–7.
43. Ibid., pp. 290–2; cf. 'New Heaven and Earth', *Complete Poems*, pp. 256–61.
44. Lawrence, *Mr Noon*, pp. xxxii–xxxiii.
45. Earl and Achsah Brewster, *D. H. Lawrence: Reminiscences and Correspondence* (London: Secker, 1934) p. 243.
46. *Letters*, III, pp. 726, 728, 732; D. H. Lawrence, *Letters to Thomas and Adele Seltzer*, ed. Gerald Lacy (Santa Barbara, Calif.: Black Sparrow Press, 1976) p. 35.
47. D. H. Lawrence, *Aaron's Rod* (New York, 1922) p. 29; Herman Melville, *Moby Dick* (New York: Library of America, 1983) p. 795.
48. Lawrence, *Symbolic Meaning*, p. 213.
49. Ibid., pp. 85–6, 88, 95, 97, 102, 216–17.
50. Lawrence, *Aaron's Rod*, pp. 86–7, 107–12.
51. Unpublished manuscript entitled 'Studies in Classic American Literature (XIII)' on one line and 'Whitman' on the line below as sub-title. This manuscript is among the Smith papers (see Roberts, *Bibliography*,

2nd edn, Item E382.b). This may be the version of Lawrence's Whitman essay that he sent in a complete manuscript of *Studies in Classic American Literature* to Benjamin Huebsch, shortly after 10 October 1919. The overt references to homosexuality were perhaps the reason for Lawrence writing 'The essay on Whitman you may find it politic not to publish. . . . The rest are unexceptionable' (*Letters*, III, pp. 400, 405).

52. Lawrence, *Aaron's Rod*, p. 174. See also Robert Hogan, 'The Amorous Whale: a Study of the Symbolism of D. H. Lawrence', *Modern Fiction Studies*, V, 1 (1959) pp. 39–46: one of the few published attempts to relate the fiction of Lawrence's middle years to early American fiction.
53. Lawrence, *Aaron's Rod*, chs 18 and 19; *Symbolic Meaning*, pp. 136–7. Hawthorne does not give the nationality of Pearl's rumoured husband, reporting only that letters from her reaching the New World came 'with armorial seals upon them, though of bearings unknown to English heraldry' (Hawthorne, *Novels*, p. 343).
54. Lawrence, *Aaron's Rod*, ch. 20.
55. Ibid., ch. 21.
56. *Letters*, I, p. 503.
57. Worthen, *D. H. Lawrence and the Idea of the Novel*, ch. 8.
58. James B. Reston Jr, *Our Father Who Art in Hell* (New York: Times Books, 1981).
59. Mabel Dodge Luhan, *Lorenzo in Taos* (New York: Alfred A. Knopf, 1932) p. 25. Compare Lawrence's 'getting stuck' in two other pilgrimage novels, *Aaron's Rod* and *Mr Noon* (Lawrence, *Letters to Thomas and Adele Seltzer*, p. 39). At least in *Aaron's Rod* and *Mr Noon*, the obstacle to composition arose just where the male protagonist feels frustrated in efforts to live beyond woman.
60. Lawrence, *Kangaroo*, pp. 199–200, 202.
61. Lawrence, *Letters to Thomas and Adele Seltzer*, p. 44. Textual differences exist between the English and American editions (see Roberts, *Bibliography*, 2nd edn, pp. 70–1).
62. Melville, *Moby Dick*, pp. 946, 1102.
63. Lawrence, *Studies in Classic American Literature* (New York, 1923) p. 215.
64. Ibid., p. 92; Lawrence, *Symbolic Meaning*, pp. 90, 98; *Letters*, III, p. 41.
65. Unpublished letters to Robert Mountsier, 7 July and 17 July 1922.
66. Lawrence, *Letters to Thomas and Adele Seltzer*, p. 35.
67. Clark, *The Minoan Distance*, ch. 11.
68. Edward Nehls, *D. H. Lawrence: A Composite Biography*, vol. II (Madison, Wisconsin: University of Wisconsin Press, 1958) pp. 136–9.
69. Keith Sagar, *D. H. Lawrence: A Calendar of His Works* (Manchester: Manchester University Press, 1979) pp. 130–1.
70. Letter to Mollie Skinner, *Letters*, IV, pp. 495–6; Nehls, *A Composite Biography*, vol. II, pp. 217–74.
71. Harry T. Moore, 'Preface', *The Boy in the Bush* by D. H. Lawrence and M. L. Skinner (Carbondale and Edwardsville, Ill.: Southern Illinois University Press, 1971) pp. vii–xviii; Charles Rossman, '*The Boy in the Bush* in the D. H. Lawrence Canon', in *D. H. Lawrence: The Man Who*

Lived, ed. Robert J. Partlow, Jr and Harry T. Moore (Carbondale and Edwardsville, Ill.: Southern Illinois University Press, 1980) pp. 185–94.

72. Lawrence, *Letters to Thomas and Adele Seltzer*, p. 115.
73. Nehls, *A Composite Biography*, vol. iii, p. 109; Lawrence, *Kangaroo*, ch. 10. In 'The Fox' Henry is familiar with the American frontier novels of Thomas Mayne Reid.
74. Dorothy Brett, *Lawrence and Brett: A Friendship* (Philadelphia, Penn.: Lippincott, 1933) pp. 81, 253–4; Nehls, *A Composite Biography*, vol. ii, p. 416.
75. Lawrence, *Letters to Thomas and Adele Seltzer*, p. 111.
76. Lawrence, *The Boy in the Bush*, chs 5, iv; 7, ii; 11, i; 20, iii.
77. Ibid., chs 19; 22, iii; 23, ii, iii; 26.
78. Lawrence, *Thomas Hardy and other Essays*, pp. 151–5.
79. Ibid., pp. 169–209.
80. Lawrence, *Symbolic Meaning*, p. 134; James Fenimore Cooper, *The Leatherstocking Tales*, vol. i (New York: Library of America, 1985) p. 877.
81. Michael Davitt Bell, *The Development of American Romance: The Sacrifice of Relation* (Chicago, Ill.: University of Chicago Press, 1980) p. 148.
82. A. N. Kaul, *The American Vision* (New Haven, Conn.: Yale University Press, 1963) pp. 308, 321.
83. Hawthorne, *Novels*, pp. 149, 352, 633.
84. Bell, *Development of American Romance*, p. 16.
85. Hawthorne, *Novels*, pp. 149, 150.
86. Lawrence, *Thomas Hardy and other Essays*, p. 182.
87. D. H. Lawrence, *The Plumed Serpent* (London: Secker, 1926) chs 18, 21, 25.
88. Ibid., ch. 23.
89. Ibid., ch. 27.
90. Joel Porte, *The Romance in America* (Middletown, Conn.: Wesleyan University Press, 1969) p. 3; Lawrence, *Symbolic Meaning*, pp. 102–3.

Index